STATE CONSTITUTIONAL LAW

IN A NUTSHELL

SECOND EDITION

By

THOMAS C. MARKS, Jr.
Professor of Law
Stetson University

and

JOHN F. COOPER
Professor of Law
Stetson University

Mat #16805661

West Group has created this publication to provide you with accurate
and authoritative information concerning the subject matter covered.
However, this publication was not necessarily prepared by persons
licensed to practice law in a particular jurisdiction. West Group is not
engaged in rendering legal or other professional advice, and this
publication is not a substitute for the advice of an attorney. If you
require legal or other expert advice, you should seek the services of
a competent attorney or other professional.

Nutshell Series, In a Nutshell, the Nutshell Logo and West Group are
registered trademarks used herein under license.

TEXT IS PRINTED ON 10% POST
CONSUMER RECYCLED PAPER

To Jan Eric Cartwright and Harold L. Sebring,
our teachers;
and Nancy Marks and Denise Cooper,
our wives.

*

PREFACE

The same thoughts and sentiments we expressed in the Preface to the First Edition to this text continue to apply. However, we would like to thank our able research assistants Andrei Antohi, Kathleen Ashcroft, Joe Kurek, and Wendi M. Weiner, who gave so freely of their talents and time in the preparation of the Second Edition. We would also like to express our appreciation for the unparalleled and exceptional faculty support staff available at Stetson University College of Law. We would specifically like to thank the director of this department Connie Evans, Shannon Mullins, Sharon Gisclair, Louise Petren, Sue Stinson, Marge Masters and Linda Bell.

Finally, we would like to thank our spouses, Nancy Marks and Denise Cooper, and our children, Christy Marks Ossi, her husband, Peter Ossi, Hadley Cooper and Adam Cooper, without whom none of this would have any meaning.

THOMAS C. MARKS, Jr.
JOHN F. COOPER

St. Petersburg, FL
March 2003

*

V

ACKNOWLEDGMENTS

Appreciation is given for permission to reproduce the Model State Constitution. We gratefully acknowledge the Legislative Drafting Research Fund, Columbia University, Frank P. Grad, Editor, *Constitutions of the United States: National and State*, looseleaf service (Oceana Publications, 1978), Vol. 1.

Appreciation is also expressed to Professor Thomas R. Dye whose book, *Politics in States and Communities*, published by Prentice Hall, Inc. in 1969, suggested a reason for what we have called Reaffirmations of Existing Power on page 6 of the text.

*

OUTLINE

Chapter 1. Introduction

Section

Chapter 2. Rule of Construction

Chapter 3.   State Declarations of Rights

Chapter 6. The Judicial Branch

Chapter 7. Separation of Powers

Chapter 8. Local Government

OUTLINE

TABLE OF CASES

References are to Pages

***

A

B

C

D

E

F

G

I

J

K

L

M

N

O

P

Q

R

S

T

U

V

W

Y

Z

STATE
CONSTITUTIONAL
LAW

IN A NUTSHELL

SECOND EDITION

*

CHAPTER 1

INTRODUCTION

Section 1. The Purpose of the State Constitution

Political scientists and constitutional lawyers alike have noted that under American federalism the federal government is a government of limited enumerated powers possessing only those powers delegated to it by the people, while state governments possess all inherent power necessary to govern. Like most general rules, the alluring simplicity of this rule conceals a complexity which at times renders the general rule meaningless. Nonetheless, when this general principle is blended with a modicum of political theory, and tempered with the practical realities of Twentieth Century American federalism, the basic principle can still serve as a useful analytical tool in understanding, interpreting and applying state constitutions.

The distinction between delegated and inherent powers arguably arises as a result of the operation of the philosophical theory of political power which philosophers have labeled the "Social Contract." Under this view of political power man is perceived to have originally lived in an absolute state of freedom commonly referred to as license. While

1

freedom was complete, security of person and property was virtually non-existent. The Eighteenth Century British philosopher, Thomas Hobbes, described life at this stage of political development as "solitary, poor, nasty, brutish, and short." Hobbes, *The Leviathan,* D.P. Sutton 1950, Part I, p. 104.

When man perceived the need to establish a method to protect both individuals and property, he entered into an understanding with government which has been referred to as the "Social Contract." Under this theory man surrendered some of his unbridled freedoms in exchange for the protection of himself and his property. This surrendered power is generally described as all of the necessary power to govern. Therefore, when we say that state governments are governments of inherent power, we are really saying that the people have vested the totality of power necessary to govern in the state, subject to only those restrictions which the federal constitution might impose. The idea that since the states have inherent powers, a state constitution cannot grant that which is already there should be crystal clear. Yet, state courts frequently describe the state constitution as granting a certain power to one branch or another of state government. Consider the following from the Supreme Court of Arizona.

Just because the State Constitution expressly *authorizes* the legislature to enlarge the jurisdiction of a court or entity does not mean that such power is unlimited ... [t]here are, of necessity, implied limitations on the *grant* of express power.

. . .

> [However], the legislature need not look to an
> express *grant* of authority to justify an enactment
> but . . . any exercise of legislature power is sub-
> ject to limitations imposed by the Constitution
> . . . *Citizens Clean Elections Commission v. Myers*
> (2000) (emphasis supplied.)

One is tempted to ask the Court, "Well which way
is it, grant or inherent power?"

The correct view was expressed by the Court of
Appeals of Oregon.

> that [the plenary power of the legislature subject
> only to constitutional limitation] is because the
> state constitution does not grant the legislature
> authority but, rather, only limits it. *Sherwood
> School District 88J v. Washington County Edu-
> cational Service District* (2000).

Carrying this analysis to its logical conclusion
raises the issue as to what actual purpose state
constitutions serve. If the state can function as a
government without any written document, what is
the real value of a written instrument?

Section 2.   Limiting the Exercise of State Power

The first and paramount purpose of a state constitution is to impose limitations and restrictions on
the exercise of state government's inherent power.
Americans have historically been distrustful of the
concentration of power government. Fueled by this
sentiment, detailed state constitutions denying cer-

tain power to state governments have been the norm rather than the exception in our system. A good illustration is the provision currently found in most constitutions, which prohibits the imprisonment of an individual for nonpayment of debt. *See, e.g.*, New Jersey Constitution, Article I, Paragraph 13. In the absence of this type of an explicit provision, and subject to any limitations imposed by federal constitution, federal law or federal treaty under the Supremacy Clause of the federal constitution, any state would clearly have the power to imprison an individual for nonpayment of indebtedness.

Section 3. Regulating the Exercise of Power

The second purpose of a state constitution is to prescribe the manner in which the state is required to exercise its inherent power. While such provisions are technically limitations on the exercise of power rather than complete prohibitions, they do serve to prohibit the state from exercising its power in a manner which is inconsistent with the constitution. The thrust of a provision of this type is akin to the interpretive doctrine of *expressio unius est exclusio alterius*. Under this doctrine, which serves as an aid in interpreting constitutions and statutes, where a document prescribes one method of accomplishing a specific act, that will be viewed as the exclusive method under which that act can legally be accomplished.

An illustration of a provision of this type is the impeachment power. Few would dispute the assertion that a government possesses the power to remove public officers who violate their public trust. Thus, this power would clearly fall within the realm of inherent power. Nonetheless, most state constitutions contain provisions for either the impeachment or removal of officers guilty of misconduct or illegal acts. Generally, because these provisions are present, certain state officers may only be removed by exercise of the impeachment power. Although not uniform, such a clause would require *inter alia* a vote of impeachment by a two thirds majority of the House of Representatives, followed by a trial before the Senate with a two thirds vote required in that body for conviction and removal. *See, e.g.,* Virginia Constitution, Article IV, Section 17. For subordinate officers, less complicated procedures are generally available. *See, e.g.,* Michigan Constitution, Article V, Section 10. Such provisions clearly do not create the right to remove defalcating officers, they merely circumscribe the manner in which this power can be exercised.

Section 4.   Reaffirmation of Existing Power

The third purpose of a state constitution is to affirm the continuing existence in state government of certain powers. These provisions merely reaffirm that state government possesses a power that it inherently possessed to begin with. This entire concept may sound duplicative since no new power is created, nor is any governmental action restricted by such provisions. Provisions of this type are included to clearly establish the existence of the power or to emphasize a strong state policy. For those seeking to interpret a state constitution, such provisions interject a considerable amount of confusion, because they invariably contain language which appears facially to confer power rather than restricting its exercise.

An example of such a provision is a clause found in a number of state constitutions which permits the legislature, in its discretion, to appropriate state funds to school districts, counties and cities. *See, e.g.,* Florida Constitution, Article VII, Section 8. Facially, such a clause seems to empower such appropriations. However, in the absence of an express prohibition elsewhere in the constitution, the legislature would be free to enact such appropriations.

One might properly inquire as to the rationale behind cluttering a fundamental governing document with such redundancies. The only articulated justifications for the existence of such provisions, are to act as a safeguard to prevent a court from interpreting the constitution to deny the existence of such power and to act as an encouragement to the legislature to utilize its power. As has been explained by the Florida Supreme Court:

This section [of the 1885 Florida Constitution] was not a grant of power to the Legislature, nor was it a limitation upon the power of the Legislature. It is simply an expressed recognition of a power existing in the legislature department of the state government. [Citation omitted.] The

Legislature had inherent authority to create and empower a Public Utilities Commission. *In re Advisory Opinion of the Governor* (1969).

Section 5. Allocation of Power Between Branches of the State Government & the State and Its Subdivisions

One of the primary functions of a state constitution is to establish the structure of state and local government. Toward that end, state constitutions contain detailed provisions allocating power between the various branches of state government and between the state and its local governments. As to the former, consider the various systems of state courts generally discussed in Chapter 6. The state constitution, when it assigns jurisdiction to the various courts, does not *grant* that jurisdiction but merely *allocates* that part of inherent judicial power known as jurisdiction. Thus, where one court is given a certain type of jurisdiction *exclusively*, no other court may exercise it and the power of those courts is thus *limited* by the state constitution.

As to the latter, the state being the repository of *all inherent power,* the people can actually grant, through constitutional provision, some portion of that inherent power, the power to tax for example, to its local governments.

In that way, since local governments have no inherent power, the state constitution can actually grant power to them and to the extent that the grant is exclusive, say a certain type of tax, that grant to the local government is a limit on the state's ability to levy the type of tax the people through their constitution having given it exclusively to local government. Consider Article VII of the 1968 Florida Constitution. Section 1 in pertinent part provides that "no state ad valorem taxes shall be levied upon real estate or tangible personal property." This is supplemented by Section 9 which in pertinent part reads, "Counties, school districts, and municipalities shall, . . . be authorized by law to levy ad valorem taxes."

Section 6. Federal v. State Constitutional Power

By way of contrast, the federal government, with the exception of what the Supreme Court has described as the "powers of external sovereignty," is a government of delegated power. *United States v. Curtiss–Wright Export Corporation* (1936). As a result, the federal government only possesses those powers which are expressly conferred upon it by the federal constitution or are necessarily implied from such express powers. In determining whether the federal government may constitutionally act in a given area it is necessary to isolate an explicit grant of power in the federal constitution as it has been interpreted by the federal courts. To the extent that the people of the United States have delegated power exclusively to the federal government, that power is denied to the states, even though otherwise such power would be inherent in the state.

Therefore, in determining whether state government possesses the requisite power to act in a given area, the following analysis is proper. It must first be determined whether the power at issue has been exclusively delegated to the federal government or denied to the state by federal constitution, federal law or federal treaty. Assuming this has not occurred, it must then be presumed that the state government possesses the inherent power to act in the area involved. This presumption of inherent power can only be overcome by an express prohibition in a state constitution on the exercise of the power at issue, or a provision regulating the manner in which it must be exercised.

By proper utilization of this analytical framework, it is possible to draw into cohesive focus an otherwise confusing array of interpretative case law. The readers are advised to bear these basic rules in mind as the substantive provisions of the state constitutions are discussed.

CHAPTER 2

RULE OF CONSTRUCTION

Section 7. The Basis for Rules of Constitutional Interpretation

A state constitution is the supreme law of the state and must be interpreted and given effect as the paramount law of the state. *State ex rel. Stephan v. Parrish* (1994). The purpose of constitutional interpretation is to effectuate the intent of those individuals who drafted the constitution and the electorate which ratified it. *Sneed v. Greensboro City Board of Education* (1980). In determining the meaning of a constitutional provision, a court will first look at the language of the provision itself. Where its meaning is clear on its face, a court will not look beyond the language to divine drafter or voter intent. *State ex rel. Taft v. Franklin County Court of Common Pleas* (1998). The rationale for this rule is obvious. The language chosen by the drafters is generally the best indication of what they intended the meaning to be and also of what the voters thought they were approving. *Cardiff v. Bismarck Public School District* (1978). In most instances, it would be absurd to argue that a constitutional provision meant something other than what it clearly stated. Moreover, the adoption of such a position would logically assume that the

10

electorate was aware of and approved an interpretation of a constitutional provision which was not clearly present on the face of the provision.

Occasionally, a court will be presented with a dilemma if it believes a literal interpretation of a constitutional provision would not accurately implement the intent of either the drafters of the constitutional provision or the electorate which approved it.

Generally, such instances will occur where unusual fact patterns are present, or where changed circumstances create a situation that could not reasonably be contemplated by the drafters of the provision.

In response to these situations, the rules of constitutional interpretation or construction evolved. The rules of construction were born out of a desire to fully implement the intent of the original drafters of the constitution. However, to many observers this argument is fatally flawed and internally inconsistent. To these critics it is a conundrum that a court would attempt to effectuate the purpose of a constitutional provision by ignoring what the provision literally states. To these observers, it would be more logical if the Court literally applied the provision, forcing the legislature and the electorate to address changing circumstances through the amendment process. This argument ignores the reality that courts, for policy reasons that may or may not have to do with the actual intended meaning, find it invaluable to possess an arsenal of flexible rules that will assist them in interpreting constitutional provisions in a non-literal fashion. From the electorate's perspective, this policy argument provides minimal comfort. Frequently, the electorate is placed in a position of voting for a constitutional provision without a clear knowledge of how the provision will ultimately be construed by the courts. Nevertheless, courts continue to rely heavily on the rules of construction, even at the expense of the literal meaning of constitutional provisions.

Section 8.   Literal Meaning, Intent, and Absurd Results

In construing a constitutional provision, it is presumed the words utilized have been employed in their usual, normal or customary meaning. *Buckeye Community Hope Foundation v. Cuyahoga Falls* (1998). If this language is clear, the Court "need not look elsewhere." *Rand v. Rand* (1977). Absent "confusion" or "ambiguity," courts are not justified in applying the rules of construction to reach a result different from the literal meaning of the provision. *In re Interrogatory of House of Representatives* (1972). However, where the literal application of a provision will give rise to an absurd result, the courts have frequently found the existence of the requisite ambiguity that justifies the utilization of the canons of construction. *Sherman v. Holiday Construction Company* (1967).

An illustration of this principle may be seen by reference to a Florida Supreme Court decision. Arti-

cle VIII, Section 1(h) of the Florida Constitution
provides that counties cannot levy taxes on city
residents for services provided "exclusively" to
county residents who live outside the boundaries of
these cities. The intent of this provision was to
preclude county taxation of city residents where city
residents received no tangible benefit from the taxation. A literal application of the constitutional provision would have defeated this purpose. The existence of *any* benefit to the city residents, no matter
how slight, would lead to the conclusion that the
referenced activity did not "exclusively" benefit the
non-municipal county residents. To effectuate what
it perceived to be the true intent of the constitutional provision, the Court ignored the literal exclu-
sivity requirement of the provision, and interpreted
the provision to require a "substantial" benefit to
city dwellers before such county taxation would be
proper under Article VIII, Section 1(h). Finding the
expenditures at issue provided a real and substantial benefit to the city residents, the Court upheld
the county tax. *City of St. Petersburg v. Briley, Wild
& Associates, Inc.* (1970). For similar reasons, it has
been held that the word "employee" in Article XI,
Section 10(b) of the California Constitution includes
an applicant for employment. In the view of the
California Court of Appeal, a contrary conclusion
would be inconsistent with the intent of the framers
of the Constitution and the people who voted for it.
In addition, it would promote an absurd result.
*Cooperrider v. San Francisco Civil Service Commis-
sion* (1979). According to another California case,

Stanton v. Panish (1980) this type of problem can best be described as a "latent ambiguity." In *City of St. Petersburg v. Briley, Wild & Associates, Inc.* (1970), the latent ambiguity was in the meaning of the word "exclusively." It was simply not foreseen that the choice of that word would lead to a result different from that intended.

While this "latent ambiguity" approach may represent a majority rule, it is certainly not a universally accepted approach. Some courts express indifference to any absurd consequences that may result from a literal application of a constitutional provision. In *Gallagher v. State* (1985), the Texas Court of Criminal Appeals found that patently unambiguous words which have but one meaning "must be given their full effect without regard to the consequences." The application of this principle resulted in the reversal of conviction and dismissal of a criminal information in a case involving allegedly shocking behavior by a public official. The Texas Constitution provided that jurisdiction in cases of "official misconduct" was vested in the district court and not the county criminal court. *See* Texas Constitution, Article V, Section 8. Although the defendant was charged with the distinct statutory crime of "official oppression" rather than "official misconduct" (which was also a statutory crime), the Court found both statutory crimes included in the clear, literal, constitutional meaning of "official misconduct." As a result, the state's attempt to prosecute the matter in county court was invalid. *Gallagher v. State* (1985).

Although an argument can be made that the latent ambiguity argument may be more persuasive in *Cooperrider* than in *Gallagher*, one is left with the distinct impression that some courts are simply more reluctant than others to alter by interpretation the literal meaning of a constitutional provision. Taken at its word, the Texas Court of Criminal Appeals would have reached a result different from the Florida or California courts had it been confronted with the *Briley, Wild & Associates, Inc.* or *Cooperrider* fact situations. This type of approach is generally justified through the expression of the fear that when a court departs from the clear meaning of a constitutional provision, it subjects itself to the charge that it is making or amending law rather than interpreting it. *City of Bristow ex rel. Hedges v. Groom* (1944). In spite of this, the Texas cases are not all in accord with the *Gallagher* Court's apparent nonchalance about the outcome to which the literal meaning rule might lead. Although the Texas Supreme Court's decision in *Director of Department of Agriculture and Environment v. Printing Industries Association of Texas* (1980) appears consistent with *Gallagher* where the Court stated that "the consequences of constitutional interpretation do not control," an analysis of that case reveals more judicial flexibility than one might assume from the language. In supporting its argument, the Court cited its previous decision in *Koy v. Schneider* (1920), which, while paying lip service to this principle, does recognize limited exceptions.

No matter how far-reaching and disastrous would be the consequences ... we would not decline to make the declaration if such was believed to be the true intent of the language of the Constitution. It is a proper inquiry, however, in ascertaining whether a certain interpretation should be given to the language of the Constitution, to consider whether its framers and the voters by whom it was adopted intended the consequences which must follow such interpretation.

Thus, even in Texas, the "latent ambiguity" doctrine appears to have limited applicability.

Section 9. Intrinsic Evidence of Meaning: *Expressio Unius Est Exclusio Alterius*

The rule of interpretation *expressio unius est exclusio alterius*, which literally means that the mention of one thing implies the exclusion of another, has at times been applied to state constitutions. Generally speaking, this doctrine primarily applies to documents that grant power such as the United States Constitution and statutes. In the instance of the United States Constitution, the granting of legislative power to a congress composed of a senate and a house of representatives, precludes, under the doctrine of *expressio unius est exclusio alterius*, attempts to create a one-house federal congress. Because the people granted the power to two legislative houses, it is presumed that the people did not desire any other type of legislature. In other words, the doctrine states that when something is granted, it is under the terms of the grant and no other. The same holds true of statutes or other types of legislative enactment that grant certain prerogatives. When a legislative body creates the privilege, for example, of holding a liquor license, it is presumed that the terms of obtaining and retaining the license are the only ones under which such a license can be procured. Such is not the case with state constitutions which are limitations on power. As discussed in the introduction, states, especially state legislatures, have plenary governmental power except as limited by state or the federal constitution. Therefore, when a state constitution limits state power in a certain way, it is not generally asserted that the constitutional method is exclusive. This has led many courts to state that the doctrine of *expressio unius est exclusio alterius* has no applicability in interpreting state constitutions. *Eberle v. Nielson* (1957).

Perhaps because many state constitutions are drafted in granting language, or are designed to merely reaffirm inherent power, many courts consider applying the doctrine *expressio unius est exclusio alterius* in constitutional settings.

Realistically speaking, the issue is really one of intent. If a state constitution appears to "grant" legislative power to a senate and house of representatives it is properly read as stating that the legislative power can only be exercised by a bicameral legislature. The constitution could as easily have stated, "The legislative power of this state shall only be exercised by a legislature composed of a senate and house of representatives." In such instances, the application of the doctrine of *expressio unius est exclusio alterius* merely treats granting terminology as if it were a limitation on state power. As a result, it is erroneous to assert that the doctrine has no application to state constitutions. Instead, the doctrine should properly be viewed as applicable in those instances when its use would clearly effectuate the intent of the provision.

The doctrine should not be employed by the courts, however, in interpreting provisions which reaffirm inherent power. Were the doctrine applied in such instances, original intent would be ignored with potentially disastrous consequences. If the doctrine were applied to reaffirmations of existing power, an unnecessary provision restating the existence of a specified power would be turned into a limitation on the exercise of that very power. To avoid this problem courts have simply stated that the doctrine of *expressio unius est exclusio alterius* is not applicable in constitutional interpretation. *Eberle v. Nielson* (1957). As suggested above, the proper approach requires more flexibility. The Florida Supreme Court has said that "*expressio unius est exclusio alterius* should be applied with great caution." *State ex rel. Moodie v. Bryan* (1905). Applying this caution, the Court found that a constitutional provision mandating that the legislature exclude from public office individuals guilty of certain types of conduct, did not preclude the legislature from adding other types of conduct that would also bar one from public office. *State ex rel. Moodie v.*

Bryan (1905). However, the rule enunciated by the Florida Supreme Court is sufficiently flexible to permit application of the doctrine in those instances when it is necessary to effectuate the intent of the provision. *Interlachen Lake Estates, Inc. v. Snyder* (1973).

Section 10. Intrinsic Evidence of Meaning: Inconsistencies Within Constitutions

Seeming inconsistencies in constitutional provisions should be resolved by harmonizing them so as to, if possible, avoid conflict and give effect to each one. *In re Great Outdoors Colorado Trust Fund*, (1996). In *Burnsed v. Seaboard Coastline Railroad Company* (1974) the Florida Supreme Court, consistent with this principle, succeeded in harmonizing two seemingly inconsistent constitutional provisions. In *Burnsed, supra*, the Court held that a section of the Florida Constitution which provided that certain *orders* of lower courts were appealable as of right to the Supreme Court was intended to be limited to *final orders*. This finding was necessary to harmonize that provision with another constitutional provision which made review of interlocutory orders discretionary. If it is impossible to harmonize two conflicting provisions, a court should inquire into the specificity of each competing provision as well as determining which provision was more recently adopted. *Serrano v. Priest* (1971). In *Jackson v. Dravo Corporation* (1979) the Court held that where there was apparent conflict between a constitutional provision that gave a right to recover in tort for injury or death sustained in mine accidents and another provision which substituted a worker's compensation remedy for a tort remedy in mine accidents, the compensation remedy prevailed. The Court reached this result because the compensation provision was adopted after the tort remedy, and was thus the latest expression of the will of the people.

In *Kadan v. Board of Supervisors of Elections* (1974), the Court held that a specific provision in the Maryland Constitution pertaining to orphan's courts prevailed over more general provisions regarding courts. In that case, the general provisions required judges to be members of the Maryland Bar. However, the section pertaining to the orphan's court imposed no such requirement. Finding the specific orphan's court provision to be applicable, the Court concluded that orphan court judges did not have to be members of the Bar.

Unlike many of the other rules of interpretation, this rule is relatively straightforward. A court must avoid an interpretation which renders a provision of a state constitution meaningless, and must favor an interpretation which will render every provision meaningful. *Havens v. Board of County Commissioners of County of Archuleta* (1996). This is necessary so that every provision of a constitution may be applied to the fullest extent possible. In *Burnsed*, it was possible to harmonize conflicting provisions. However, in *Jackson* and *Kadan* it was not, so the rule of more recent adoption (*Jackson*) and the rule of "specific over general" (*Kadan*) were used. At times, harmony between seemingly conflicting provisions may be difficult, but it can be achieved.

The Michigan Constitution provides for voter approval of certain statutes proposed by popular initiative and the legislature. Referendum is mandatory in the former and optional in the latter. A conflict between the two constitutional provisions arose when a legislative proposal was placed on the ballot along with an initiative proposal relating to the same subject. The two proposals conflicted and could not be harmonized. However, both were approved by the voters. The Michigan Supreme Court harmonized the two constitutional provisions by interpreting them to be read to allow both proposals on the ballot with the one receiving the highest number of votes prevailing. *In re Proposals D & H* (1983).

Section 11.   Extrinsic Evidence of Meaning: Consideration of the Circumstances Surrounding the Adoption of the Constitution

When in doubt concerning the intent of a particular constitutional provision, courts frequently examine the circumstances surrounding the adoption of the constitutional provision. This examination occurs to assist the Court in accurately determining the meaning of the particular provision. Courts occasionally even resort to legislative history in instances where the meaning of a provision is clear on its face. For example, a statement in a constitution explicitly recognizing taxpayers standing to sue hardly necessitates a judicial examination of the circumstances that caused its adoption. Nevertheless, in *Waterford School District v. State Board of Education* (1980) the Court explained the plain meaning of the constitutional provision by reference to taxpayer revolt, popular control of state spending and "litigation to force compliance with constitutional provisions."

In other instances an examination of the circumstances surrounding the adoption of the constitutional provision at issue is critical to a proper interpretation of the provision. For example, in *State ex rel. Vogel v. Garaas* (1978), recent changes to the North Dakota Constitution allowed the governor to fill vacancies in certain judicial offices by appointment from a list of persons provided to him by a judicial nominating committee or by calling a special election. Since the legislature had not complied with the constitutional mandate to create the nominating committee, the governor filled the vacancy by appointment. This was done without the advice of the committee. The Court determined that the circumstances surrounding the constitutional amendment indicated that the will of the people would be better served by allowing appointment without the nominating committee rather than by restricting the vacancy filling process to a specially-called election.

Surrounding circumstances can also be used as a basis for departing from what is arguably the clear meaning of constitutional language. Thus the principle can be used to avoid what the Court considers an undesirable result. *In Director of Department of Agriculture and Environment v. Printing Industries Association of Texas* (1980), reference was made to Article XVI, Section 21 of the Texas Constitution. It provided in part as follows:

> All stationery, printing, ... and printing and binding of laws, journals, and department reports, and all other printing and binding ... shall be performed under contract, to be given to the lowest responsible bidder.

If this language had been read literally to mean that the Texas government could not do its own printing, the state would have had to discontinue its extensive printing operation. This would have resulted in forced disuse of considerable equipment and increased difficulty in meeting the state's printing needs. The Court, however, examined the extensive corruption that had surrounded the awarding of government printing contracts prior to the constitutional provision. It concluded that the provision was intended to insure that contracts be awarded based on competitive bidding. As a result, the Court concluded that the state was constitutionally free to operate its printing business.

Section 12.   Extrinsic Evidence of Meaning: Legislative Interpretation of Constitutions

Although courts have the ultimate authority to interpret constitutions, legislative bodies also interpret constitutions. This legislative interpretation occurs every time a legislature enacts a law, and sometimes when it fails to enact one. While the legislature obviously does not have the benefit of the adversary process to illuminate constitutional meaning, it does have its own counsel. Further, the entire legislative process in which proponents and opponents of proposed legislation play prominent roles aids the legislature in performing its function in constitutional interpretation. In this area, the critical inquiry is frequently to what extent the courts should defer to a legislative reading of the constitution when it enacts a law?

When a legislature enacts a statutory provision in close proximity of time to the adoption of a constitutional provision dealing with the subject matter of the statute, the courts generally view this contemporaneous legislative activity as evidence of the meaning of the constitutional provision. Thus, the legislative history of the statute is also considered contemporaneous evidence of the meaning of the constitutional provision. *Austin, Nichols & Company, Inc. v. Oklahoma County Board of Tax–Roll Corrections* (1978). Some courts construe this requirement very broadly. As a result, some courts consider recent legislative enactments as relevant evidence of the meaning of an existing constitutional provision. *Humana of New Mexico, Inc. v. Board of County Commissioners* (1978). A classic illustration of the use of contemporaneous legislative enactment to judicially interpret a constitutional provision is found in *Greater Loretta Improvement Association v. State ex rel. Boone* (1970). In that case, the Florida Supreme Court was confronted with the issue of whether bingo was prohibited as a result of a constitutional ban on lotteries. In reviewing the history of the provision, the Court noted that the same legislature that had placed before the electorate a new constitution which included a ban on lotteries, had also enacted a law, in that same session, that authorized bingo. Obviously, the legislature did not believe that the lottery ban applied to bingo. Finding this contemporaneous legislative interpretation persuasive, the Court held that the constitutional ban was not applicable to bingo.

While contemporaneous legislative interpretation is particularly compelling to courts, the courts will not totally ignore non-contemporaneous legislative and administrative interpretation in construing constitutional provisions. While generally not as persuasive as contemporaneous interpretation, non-contemporaneous interpretation is predicated on the thought that a well-settled interpretation of a constitutional provision should be accorded great weight. In *Greater Loretta Improvement Association v. State ex rel. Boone* (1970), the Court, in addition to the contemporaneous legislative interpretation, also justified the result by reference to a long and unbroken history of legislative authorization of both bingo and keno at times in which lotteries were constitutionally prohibited.

Non-contemporaneous interpretation is not always persuasive. In *State v. Nelson* (1972) the Kansas Supreme Court struck down a statute which authorized bingo as violative of an anti-lottery provision in the state constitution. The bingo statute apparently did not have a long history and the Court refused to accede to a subsequent legislative definition of lottery as excluding bingo. Non-contemporaneous interpretation also played a role in *Director of Department of Agriculture and Environment v. Printing Industries Association of Texas* (1980). There, the Texas Supreme Court found it persuasive, in determining whether the constitution allowed the state to do its own printing or required that it be contracted to the lowest bidder, that Texas had been engaged in meeting its own printing needs for a considerable length of time. However, an earlier Texas decision referenced by the Court succinctly summarizes the weaknesses of non-contemporaneous doctrine. In *Terrill v. Middleton* (1916), the Court stated: "A wrong cannot be sanctioned by age and acquiescence and transformed into a virtue ... The will of a sovereign people as expressed through their organic law is supreme, and necessity, legislative construction, and legislative act cannot weaken, impair or destroy it."

Many courts view these doctrines as particularly compelling. As a result, some courts have stated that if a constitutional provision is reasonably subject to more than one meaning, the legislature's choice is "conclusive." *Vinales v. State* (1981). *Mears v. Hall* (1978). Alternatively, it has been held that even a long pattern of non-contemporaneous legislative interpretation is not binding. *Colo v. Treasurer and Receiver General* (1979). The rules of contemporaneous and non-contemporaneous legislative interpretation serve as useful tools to the courts. Nevertheless, they should only be applied when the meaning of a constitutional provision is ambiguous or doubtful. Even then they should not be viewed as binding the courts.

Section 13.   Extrinsic Evidence: Ballot Summary and Similar Matters

Although the language utilized in a ballot title submitting a proposed change in a constitution to the electorate is clearly subordinate to the language of the provision itself, courts will frequently refer to the ballot title to determine the voters' understanding of the amendment. *City of Sacramento v. State* (1984). As the California Court was careful to explain in the above cited case, the ballot summary may actually differ substantially from the literal meaning of the words in the constitution. Although the plain meaning of words used must prevail over the ballot summary, such a rule may promote injustice.

Many cases refer to such extrinsic evidence as ballot pamphlets, statements by the drafters, reports of the drafters, ballot arguments, existing statutory definitions of terms used, debates in constitutional conventions, existing law and the circumstances surrounding the adoption of the provision in construing constitutional provisions. All are described as useful, but may only be resorted to when the meaning of the constitutional provision is not clear on its face.

Section 14.   Choice of Rule of Interpretation

Assuming that a court has determined that the wording of a constitutional provision will not allow the application of the literal meaning rule, the choice of a particular rule of interpretation can easily dictate the outcome. For example, Article IX, Section 2 of the Arizona Constitution provides as follows:

Stocks of raw or finished materials, unassembled parts, work in progress or finished products constituting the inventory of a retailer or wholesaler located within the State and principally engaged in the resale of such materials, parts or products, whether or not for resale to the ultimate consumer, shall be exempt from taxation.

In *McElhaney Cattle Company v. Smith* (1981) the issue presented to the Arizona courts was whether operators of cattle feedlots were wholesalers as to the cattle which they fattened and then sent to market. The Arizona Court of Appeals recognized that the word *wholesaler* as applied to the feedlot operators was not entirely clear. In seeking to interpret the constitutional provision, the Court referred to the definition of wholesaler in the state tax statutes. The Court decided that the statutory definition covered, although it did not specifically refer to, feedlot operators. *Id.* On appeal, the Arizona Supreme Court turned to a different extrinsic source, the public debates and discussion concerning the constitutional provision at the time of its adoption. In the view of the Court, the debates established that the provision was never intended to extend the wholesaler exemption to feedlot owners. As a result, the Court held that the Arizona constitution did not exempt feedlot operators from taxation. *McElhaney Cattle Company v. Smith* (1982). The choice of extrinsic rules by each court obviously dictated the outcome in each instance. In reaching its decision, the Arizona Supreme Court departed from what appears to be a well-recognized rule that constitutional terms are usually given the statutory definition in existence at the time the constitutional provision was adopted. *County of Fresno v. Malmstrom* (1979). If the Court had selected that rule of interpretation, it would, have reached the same result as the Court of Appeals. As a result, the mere selection of the appropriate rule of construction is often outcome determinative of the result.

Section 15.   The Effect of Mandatory Provisions

As a general rule, where a state constitution mandates legislative action, this imposes a moral duty on the legislature which the judiciary cannot enforce. *State ex rel. Vogel v. Garaas* (1978). In *Garaas, supra*, the Supreme Court of North Dakota held that the failure of the legislature to establish a judicial nominating commission in violation of a command of the state constitution that "a judicial nominating commission shall be established by law" violated the constitution. However, despite this, the Court held that "for non-action there would be no remedy." The Court, however, was able to protect the governor's judicial appointment power by holding that residual appointive power was retained from the earlier constitutional provision until such time as the legislature breathed life into the new provision, by enacting legislation requiring the governor to select his or her appointee from a list submitted by a nominating commission. Another illustration of the same principle with a different result is *Dade County Classroom Teachers Association v. Legislature* (1972). In that case, the Florida Supreme Court responded to the legislature's failure to enact legislation mandated by the constitution to ensure public employees could effectively engage in collective bargaining. The Court conceded that it could not force the legislature to enact the mandated legislation. It did not, however, concede as did the North Dakota Supreme Court in *Garaas, supra*, that no remedy existed. The Court advised the legislature that if, within a reasonable time, the legislature had not followed the constitutional mandate, the Court "would have no choice but to fashion such guidelines by judicial decree in such manner as may seem to the Court best adapted to meet the requirements of the constitution." *Dade County Classroom Teachers Association*. This threat was sufficient. The legislature thereafter speedily complied with its constitutional mandate.

Section 16. Use of Rules of Statutory Construction

Although it has been said that "the technical rules of *statutory* construction do not apply when construing a constitution," *People v. Nash* (1983), most courts seem willing to use them as a tool to determine the meaning of constitutional language when the literal meaning rule cannot be used. Sometimes the use of the rules of statutory construction is tempered by the notion that since a constitution is a "living" document and more permanent than a statute, it should be given a "broader construction," *Florida Society of Ophthalmology v. Florida Optometric Association* (1986). This apparently means that the interpretation of constitutions should be more flexible and dynamic than statutes. However, resorting to rules of statutory construction may be misleading if they are to be applied differently in a constitutional setting. Recently, in attempting to interpret the meaning of the word "bill" in Article IV, Section 22 of the New Mexico Constitution, pertaining to the governor's veto power, the New Mexico Supreme Court found that resort to the normal rules of statutory construction was appropriate. However, the rule the Court utilized was the maxim that a provision should be interpreted to effectuate the purpose for which it was enacted. *State ex rel. Wood v. King* (1979). Generally, rules of constitutional construction are the same as rules of statutory construction. Nonetheless, courts occasionally persist in distinguishing the rules of statutory construction from rules of constitutional interpretation. *See, e.g., Coalition for Political Honesty v. State Board of Elections* (1976). The better view is that the rules for interpreting the two types of documents are similar.

Occasionally, courts do at times seem to fully utilize statutory rules of construction in constitutional decision making. The Florida Supreme Court in *State ex rel. Winton v. Town of Davie* (1961) was faced with interpreting the following language from the 1885 Florida Constitution:

> The Supreme Court may issue writs of mandamus and quo warranto when a state officer, board, commission or other agency authorized to represent the public generally, or a member of such board, commission or other agency, is named as respondent, ...

Since the case involved a quo warranto proceeding against a municipal corporation, the Court applied the rule of statutory construction called *ejusdem generis* to conclude that the word *state* modified not only the word *officer* but also "other agency authorized to represent the public generally." It is interesting to note that the Court bolstered its use of *ejusdem generis* by reference to the intent of the provision. As the constitutional original jurisdiction of the Supreme Court was designed to resolve statewide problems, the Court concluded it was not likely that the provision was intended to vest this type of problem in the Court.

CHAPTER 3

STATE DECLARATIONS
OF RIGHTS

Section 17. The Purpose of State Declarations of Rights

Every state constitution contains detailed guarantees of individual liberties. Many of these constitutionally guaranteed rights are similar or identical to rights assured by the Federal Constitution. By way of illustration, virtually all state constitutions contain a clause which represents that a person will not be deprived of life, liberty or property without "due process of law." *See, e.g.*, Nevada Constitution, Article I, Section 8. Likewise, many state constitutions have Bill of Attainder proscriptions identical to their Federal counterpart. *See, e.g.*, South Carolina Constitution, Article I, Section 4. Predictably, this duplication has raised an issue as to whether state Declarations of Rights serve any legitimate purpose or whether they are just surplusage. In actuality state Declarations of Rights perform a vital role in the Federal makeup of the American political system. This vital role has both historical and contemporaneous roots.

Section 18.   The Historical Role of State Declarations of Rights

Under our original constitutional structure, the Federal Bill of Rights was intended, and was judicially construed, as only protecting the enumerated rights from Federal interference. *See, Barron v. Mayor and City Council of Baltimore* (1833). Thus, throughout most of early American legal history, state constitutions and state courts served as the exclusive judicial guardians of American civil liberties, including such fundamental guarantees as the right to be free from unreasonable search and seizures.

Moreover, the Federal courts did not aggressively pursue their subsequent role as defenders of the Bill of Rights, even in the exclusively Federal sphere. Federal judicial hesitancy is perhaps best illustrated by the simple statement that one of the earliest decisions of the United States Supreme Court, utilizing a provision of the Bill of Rights to declare a Federal law unconstitutional, was the infamous Dred Scott decision in 1857. *See, Dred Scott v. Sandford* (1857). However, even the reasoning in that case was approved only by a plurality of the court. The combined factors of a limited applicability of the Bill of Rights and the passivity of the Federal courts in enforcing these guarantees terminated with the adoption of the Fourteenth Amendment to the United States Constitution in 1868.

Gradually, the United States Supreme Court, through the process that ultimately became known as "selective incorporation," extended the protective reach of the Federal Bill of Rights against state interference. Although this process has not extended every Federal guarantee, most provisions of the Federal Bill of Rights have been held by the Supreme Court to bind the several states. In addition to federalizing this aspect of the federal-state relationship, the Supreme Court has expansively and liberally interpreted these provisions and has impressed this national perspective on the states through "selective incorporation."

These two developments clearly turned the original federalist judicial structure on its theoretical head. As a result, the Federal courts to a large extent supplanted the state courts as the ultimate guardians of civil liberties. This growth caused many to question whether state constitutional Declarations of Rights had outlived their usefulness. These concerns were unjustified.

Section 19.   State Guarantees of Rights Differing From the Federal

While many state constitutional guarantees are identical to or substantially similar to federally protected constitutional rights, this is not universally true. To the extent that a state constitution confers constitutional protection to rights not recognized at the Federal level, the state constitutional provisions will operate independently of any Federal intervention in protecting the conduct subject to the applicable provision. By way of illustration, it is generally accepted that the Federal Constitution does not confer a specific right of privacy on citizens. Thus, the existence of any such right must arise from judicial construction. In recent decisions, the United States Supreme Court has expressed reluctance to expand a Federal right of privacy through judicial construction. *See, e.g., Bowers v. Hardwick* (1986).

Many state constitutions do establish a constitutional right to privacy. For example, Article I, Section 22 of the Alaska Constitution expressly guarantees a right of privacy to Alaska citizens. In interpreting the scope of this provision the Alaska Supreme Court has referred to such local factors as the pioneer spirit and concepts of individualism which are reputed to have motivated those settling America's last frontier. In one highly publicized opinion of this nature, the Alaska Supreme Court struck down the application of state drug laws that prohibited possession of small quantities of marijuana in the home. *See, Ravin v. State* (1975).

Another provision commonly found in state constitutions without a Federal counterpart is the so-called access to courts clause. For example, Article I, Section 21 of the Florida Constitution guarantees that the courts of that state "shall be open to every person for redress of any injury, and justice shall be administered without sale, denial or delay." In interpreting this provision, the Florida Supreme Court has held that where a citizen had a right of access to the state courts by common or statutory law at the time of the adoption of the Declaration of Rights of the Florida Constitution, the legislature is without power to abolish that right without providing a reasonable alternative, unless there is an overpowering public necessity. Based on this provision, the court struck down as violative of the state Declaration of Rights a provision of a Florida "no-fault" statute which abrogated in certain instances an action for property damage without provision of an alternative remedy. *See, Kluger v. White* (1973).

In yet other instances, state constitutional provisions will confer specific constitutional protection on its citizens which have no Federal counterpart. By way of illustration, Article I, Section 14 of the Florida Constitution specifically guarantees, subject to certain restrictions, all citizens a right to bail "unless charged with a capital offense or an offense punishable by life imprisonment and the proof of guilt is evident or the presumption great." In such instances, the plain specific protection will operate to fill a void which can only be filled at the Federal level by a statute or judicial interpretation.

Section 20.   An Adequate and Independent State Ground

Federal judicial activism appears to have peaked, at least temporarily, in the late 1960's. Throughout the 1970's and 1980's, this activism has appeared to have waned in favor of a more restrained judicial approach. One side effect of this perceptible change in judicial philosophical outlook has been the tendency of the United States Supreme Court to limit, or at least not further expand, judicial interpretation of Federal constitutional rights. One commentator views this retreat as so substantial that he has described the Supreme Court as abdicating its role as the "Keeper of the Nation's Conscience." *See*, Wilkes, *The New Federalism in Criminal Procedure: State Court Evasion of the Burger Court*, 62 Ky. L.J. 421, 421 (1974).

Whether one views this new found judicial restraint derisively or as a salutary development in American federalism, the fact of this change appears inescapable. Nonetheless, these developments have also nurtured a re-emergent federalist function for both the state courts and state Declarations of Rights. This growth spurt is predicated upon a legal theory which has been implicit in our legal system almost from the adoption of the Constitution. This theory is commonly referred to as the adequate and independent state ground doctrine. This well settled principle of Federal appellate jurisdiction provides that the Federal courts will not disturb a state court judgment which is based on an "adequate and independent" state ground, so long as the result does not violate the Federal Constitution. Phrased slightly differently, this doctrine means that the Federal Constitution serves as a floor, or in current parlance, a safety net, which assures a minimum level of civil liberties. Once this minimal level of rights has been provided, the Federal Constitution has been satisfied. However, should the state courts in interpreting their own constitutions determine that their state provisions guarantee a higher level of protection than the Federal minimum, their actions in this regard are not subject to Federal review if the state constitutional ground is adequate and independent. Thus, the state courts are perfectly free to interpret their local constitutions to be more protective of civil liberties than the Federal Constitution. This process has continued apace since the 1970's.

Section 21. The Development of the Adequate and Independent State Ground Doctrine

The adequate and independent state ground doctrine was formally enunciated by the United States Supreme Court in *Murdock v. City of Memphis* (1874). In *Murdock, supra*, the court concluded that where a state court interpreted Federal law against the existence of a Federal right, the Supreme Court had jurisdiction to entertain an appeal. If the court determined that the state court had properly construed Federal law, then the court would affirm the state judgment. However, if the state court improperly interpreted Federal law, but the state court's judgment was also based on state law, and these state grounds were "sufficiently broad to maintain the judgment," the court would also affirm the judgment. This policy was predicated on practical as well as comity concerns. Clearly, if the Supreme Court reversed the state court for an erroneous interpretation of Federal law, the result on remand would be identical because the state court would merely rehear the matter solely on the state ground which was otherwise sufficient to sustain the original state decision.

In *Eustis v. Bolles* (1893) the Supreme Court logically extended this doctrine. In *Eustis,* the court concluded that where a state court clearly misinterpreted Federal law, if the judgment was otherwise substantiated by adequate state grounds, the Supreme Court could dismiss the appeal, because even if the appeal was heard it could not affect the outcome.

Some argue that the adequate and independent state ground doctrine is constitutionally compelled by our federalist system. *See, Fay v. Noia* (1963) (Harlan, J., dissenting). However, the *Murdock* case was exclusively an interpretation of Federal appellate law. For this reason, it is generally accepted that the rule is statutory rather than constitutional in origin. Nonetheless, the doctrine has been described as "so deeply imbedded in our law that it may fairly be deemed a part of our working constitution." *See*, Sandalow, *Henry v. Mississippi and the Adequate State Ground: Proposals for a Revised Doctrine*, 1965 Sup. Ct. Rev. 187, 189 (1965).

The most clearly articulated rationale for the existence of the doctrine is found in an extremely succinct statement of Justice Jackson in *Herb v. Pitcairn* (1945).

This court from the time of its foundation has adhered to the principle that it will not review judgments of state courts that rest on adequate and independent state grounds. The reason is so obvious that it has rarely been thought to warrant statement. It is found in the partitioning of power between the state and federal judicial systems and in the limitations of our own jurisdiction. Our only power over state judgments is to correct them to the extent that they incorrectly adjudge federal rights. And our power is to correct wrong judgments not to revise opinions. We are not permitted to render an advisory opinion, and if the same judgment would be rendered by the state court after we corrected its view of federal law, our review could amount to nothing more than an advisory opinion.

While Justice Jackson's admonition concerning advisory opinions is persuasive, the Supreme Court, and in particular individual justices, has found it difficult to affirm or dismiss an appeal where a state court has misinterpreted Federal law. Thus, instances abound where the court will frankly concede the existence of an adequate and independent state ground, but somehow manage to advise the state court of its erroneous interpretation of Federal law, *i.e.*, in effect render an advisory opinion. *See, Colorado v. Nunez* (1984) (White, J., concurring).

While the adequate and independent state ground doctrine sounds simple in theory, it has proven itself extremely complex to apply. Consequently, in 1983 the Supreme Court enunciated a new test for determining the existence of valid state grounds in a state court judgment. *See, Michigan v. Long* (1983). This standard is colloquially referred to as the "Plain Statement" rule.

Section 22.   The Plain Statement Rule

The main difficulty the Supreme Court encountered in applying the adequate and independent state ground doctrine was defining the content of adequate and independent. This judicial inquiry was further obfuscated by a tendency of state courts to cite both state and federal precedent in support of a proposition of law. In the vast majority of cases, where only state law was cited by the state court, the adequacy or inadequacy of a state ground was relatively simple to determine. However, in those instances where the state court mixed federal and state authority, the court had to probe whether the state ground was adequate and independent. *See, e.g., Abie State Bank v. Weaver* (1931).

When faced with this judicial task and uncertainty, the Supreme Court utilized three separate approaches in testing the adequacy of the state ground. First, it could vacate, continue or remand the case to the state court to afford the state court an opportunity to clarify the basis of its decision. *See, e.g., Montana v. Jackson* (1983). Although this device facially appeared deferential to state sovereignty, it was criticized as cumbersome, time consuming and a waste of both state and federal judicial resources.

Second, the Supreme Court could assume that the state ground was adequate and independent and dismiss the appeal. This was the traditional approach to the problem. *See, e.g., Lynch v. People of New York* (1934). While this approach combined ease of administration with extreme deference to state decisions, it was routinely criticized as promoting lack of uniformity in Federal law, particularly where a state opinion mixed aspects of federal and state law.

Third, the Supreme Court could examine the applicable state law and determine on its own whether the state ground was adequate and independent. This approach consumed the most extensive use of judicial resources of all three alternatives and also was the most intrusive into state sovereignty. By way of illustration, in *Oregon v. Kennedy* (1982), the Supreme Court was uncertain as to whether an adequate and independent state ground was present. Nonetheless the Court heard the appeal because "(e)ven if the case admitted of more doubt as to whether federal and state grounds for decision were intermixed, the fact that the state court relied to the extent it did on federal grounds requires us to reach the merits." *Id*.

Finding all three of these alternatives unsatisfactory, the Supreme Court speaking through Justice O'Connor reformulated the test for determining the existence or absence of an adequate and independent state ground. This new rule has become known as the "Plain Statement" rule. In *Michigan v. Long* (1983) the rule was enunciated as follows:

Accordingly, when as in this case, a state court decision fairly appears to rest primarily on federal law, or to be interwoven with the federal law, and when the adequacy and independence of any possible state law ground is not clear from the face of the opinion, we will accept as the most reasonable explanation that the state court decided the case the way it did because it believed that federal law required it to do so. If a state court chooses merely to rely on federal precedents as it would on the precedents of all other jurisdictions, then it need only make clear by a plain statement in its judgment or opinion that the federal cases are being used only for the purpose of guidance, and do not themselves compel the result that the court has reached.

In short, the court will presume that where a state court cites both state and federal authority, that the decision was based on federal law unless the opinion contains a plain statement indicating to the contrary. As an administrative device, this new rule has much to commend it. The rule minimizes the Supreme Court's judicial task by obviating the need of the court to make a case by case individual inquiry into the adequacy of state law grounds. Further it appears to encourage the states to actively develop their own law without intimidation from the shadow of the Supreme Court. It further minimizes judicial effort by eliminating the need of time consuming remands to clarify state issues. Finally, it is anticipated that the new rule should have some impact on the Supreme Court caseload. In many recent decisions pertaining to the adequacy of a state ground, these issues were simply not raised until briefs were filed or in oral argument. The new rules should cause these issues to be identified at an earlier stage of the proceedings or be waived.

Despite these positive attributes, the new rule has faced extensive criticism. In a vigorous dissent in *Michigan v. Long* (1983), Justice Stevens viewed the rule as damaging to federalism by encouraging federal review of matters that could be settled by local law.

Section 23.   Identical or Similar Constitutional Provisions

As suggested above, a state court is on its strongest foundation in interpreting its state constitution more protectively than the federal constitution, where the state constitutional provision at issue has no federal counterpart. Clearly, if the right at issue is independently guaranteed by the state constitution, there would appear to be minimal interference or overlap with a federal provision. However, this is not to say that the adequate and independent state ground doctrine has no applicability where the state provision at issue is similar or identical to a federal provision.

This principle can be illustrated by reference to *People v. Anderson* (1972). In that case, the California death penalty was attacked as violating the Eighth Amendment to the United States Constitution and Article 1 Section 6 of the California Constitution. While the federal provision at issue proscribed "cruel *and* unusual punishment," the state provision prohibited "cruel *or* unusual punishment." In deflecting any possible federal review, the

state court based its decision solely on the state
constitutional provision. In declaring the death penalty violative of this provision, the court noted that
the federal provision required punishment to be
both cruel and unusual. The California provision,
however, was in the disjunctive. Thus, punishment
being either cruel or unusual would violate this
provision. Finding this distinction to be intentional,
the court struck down the death penalty. This case
is also illustrative of a new type of federalism because the California electorate responded to the
court's decision by amending the constitution to
specifically permit the death penalty. *See*, California
Constitution, Article 1, Section 27.

However, even if the state and federal provisions
at issue are identical, a state court can still interpret its provision to have a different content than
the federal provision. For example, in *People v.
Brisendine* (1975), the California Supreme Court
conceded that the search and seizure provisions of
the state constitution were textually indistinguish-
able from the provisions of the Fourth Amendment
to the United States Constitution. Despite this con-
cession, the court went on to conclude that the
Supreme Court's opinion in *United States v. Robinson* (1973) was an inaccurate interpretation of the
identical state provision. As a result, the state constitutional provision was determined to afford more
protection than the federal counterpart.

This seemingly incongruous approach has drawn
strict examination. A chief critic of this approach
was former Chief Justice Burger, who asserted that

this type of approach was injurious to the uniform national application of the law. In a concurring opinion to a dismissal of a writ of certiorari where the court found a state opinion based on an adequate state ground, Burger referred to the Florida history in this area. Specifically, the Florida Supreme Court interpreted the search and seizure provision of the Florida Constitution to be more protective than the federal constitution. As a backlash to opinions of this type, the Florida electorate amended its constitution so that its search and seizure provisions would have an identical content to the Fourth Amendment as construed by the United States Supreme Court. Burger praised the actions of the Florida electorate.

> With our dual system of state and federal laws, administered by state and federal courts, different standards may arise in various areas. But when state courts interpret state law to require *more* than the Federal Constitution requires, the citizens of the state must be aware that they have the power to amend state law to ensure rational law enforcement.

Florida v. Casal (1983) (Burger J., concurring). (emphasis in original)

Section 24.   The Future of State Declarations of Rights

Recently many state courts have rediscovered and applied long dormant provisions of their state constitutions in a manner that is more protective of its citizens than the federal constitution would require.

While much of this renewed vitality has occurred in the area of criminal law, this phenomenon is not exclusive to that arena. In the civil area, state constitutions have provisions protecting the following rights which previously had been determined to have less protection under the federal constitution. *See, e.g., Right to Choose v. Byrne* (1982) (public funding of abortion); *State v. Coe* (1984) (freedom of expression); *Robinson v. Cahill* (1973) (method of funding public education); *Southern Burlington County N.A.A.C.P. v. Township of Mt. Laurel* (1975) (exclusionary zoning).

With each passing year, the number of reported cases in which state courts construe their constitutions more protectively than the federal constitution increases. As this proliferation continues, and the federal courts continue to pursue judicial restraint, the Declarations of Rights in state constitutions are undergoing a renaissance. In anticipation of a more pervasive role for state Declarations of Rights, Justice Hans Linde of the Oregon Supreme Court has recommended a new methodology where mixed state and federal issues are involved. Under Linde's approach, a state court should defer all federal issues until all state issues are resolved. This approach is recommended because the resolution of the state claims may be outcome determinative of the federal issues. *See*, Linde, *First Things First: Rediscovering the State's Bill of Rights*, 9 U. Balt. L. Rev. 379 (1980). According to its proponents, this approach would minimize the waste of federal judicial resources and spur the healthy growth of state court systems. Linde's approach has found limited recognition by the state courts. *See, State v. Ball* (1983). However, the Florida Supreme Court seemingly adopted this approach in *Traylor v. State* (1992).

While most observers view the impact of state Declarations of Rights as too limited to warrant this restructuring of traditional orthodoxies, its mere enunciation is demonstrative of the growth spurt that the state Declarations of Rights are currently undergoing. Only the passage of time will determine whether this growth will continue.

Section 25. Recent Applications of State Constitutions with a Resultant Expansion of Protection Afforded by State Constitutions

State courts have found many instances of state constitutional protections where the federal courts have declined to see a federal constitutional interest. For example, both the Hawaii and Vermont Supreme Courts have determined that state statutory prohibitions on same sex marriage violate the provisions of the respective state Constitutions. *See, Baehr v. Miike* (1997) (affirming a circuit court opinion to that effect) and *Baker v. State* (1999). The Arkansas Supreme Court recently invalidated a state statute criminalizing sodomy on the basis that the statute violates the Arkansas Constitution. *Jegley v. Picado* (2002).

State constitutions have also been found to prohibit the application of certain antiquated statutory rape statutes, *see J.A.S. v. State* (1998); parental consent abortion statutes for minors, *see In re T.W.* (1989); and restrictions on an individual's right to refuse medical treatment, *In re Guardianship of Browning* (1990).

Although the United States Supreme Court has ruled that use of school vouchers at parochial schools does not violate the principles of Separation of Church and State, under the First Amendment of the United States Constitution, *see Zelman v. Simmons–Harris* (2002), the question still exists whether such programs violate the provisions of state constitutions with most restrictive provisions. Although such a case has not yet reached a state supreme court, a Florida Circuit Court recently held that the provisions of its state constitution prohibited the use of vouchers in parochial schools in that state. *Holmes v. Bush* (2002).

CHAPTER 4

THE EXECUTIVE BRANCH

Section 26. The Governor

The function of the executive branch is to honestly and efficiently administer and enforce the laws as written and as interpreted by the courts. 16 C.J.S *Constitutional Law* § 215. Most state constitutions allocate the executive power of the state to the governor. The governor has been held to bear the same relationship to a state that the President bears to the United States. C.J.S. *Constitutional Law* § 215. Others, apparently in order to clarify that other officers in the executive branch of government exercise some executive power, describe the governor as possessing the supreme executive power. *See*, Article IV, Section 1 of the New York Constitution. Article VI, Sections 1 and 2 of the Oklahoma Constitution. Such provisions are usually combined with a constitutional provision requiring that the governor insure that the laws are faithfully executed. *See*, Article V, Section 4 of the Arizona Constitution. Together these allocations of executive power to the governor are, absent a clear contrary intent in the constitution, exclusively the governor's. *Tucker v. State* (1941). Absent a specific constitutional allocation of executive power to the governor, a provision charging the governor with the obligation to insure the faithful execution of the laws should be sufficient to clarify that executive power is the governor's alone. Without a contrary provision in the constitution, other holders of office in the executive branch possess only administrative or ministerial power. In other words, they may assist the governor but only the governor carries out executive functions.

Some state constitutions specifically assign a number of executive functions to the governor rather than relying on a general definition of executive power. These functions, which are discussed in subsequent sections, include the power to appoint and remove officers, control over state's armed forces, and exercise of the clemency power. Provisions dealing with gubernatorial interaction with the legislature will be discussed in Section 28 and Chapter 5 of this work.

Section 27.   The Governor's Election, Qualifications for and Term of Office

All state governors are directly elected by the people. This statement must be qualified by the unlikely event that a lieutenant governor, having entered that office by appointment, may subsequently fill a vacancy in the governorship. (*See* Section 32 *infra*.) A number of state constitutions express great concern about the election of the governor and other principal officers of the executive branch. They frequently spell out detailed procedures for holding and contesting elections. It is common practice for the time and places for the elections to be specified and a procedure established for the returns to be verified by the legislature in joint session or by the lower house. Questions involving the number and legality of the ballots for each candidate and the breaking of ties are determined by the legislature thus assembled. Sometimes the legislature or the lower house, as the case may be, is assisted by a board appointed to verify the winner's election. If the legislature cannot break the tie, the winner is sometimes determined by lot. Contested elections are decided by both houses of the legislature as established by law. *See, e.g.*, Article VII, Sections 2 and 3 of the West Virginia Constitution, and Article II, Sections 2, 3 and 4 of the Maryland Constitution.

The vast majority of state constitutions establish the qualifications for the office of governor in terms of age, United States citizenship and state residency. Most set the determinative date as the time of the election, of filing for office, or qualifying as a candidate or the inauguration. *See, e.g.*, Article V, Section 22 of the Michigan Constitution; Article III, Section 2 of the Alaska Constitution; and Article V, Part First, Section 4 of the Maine Constitution. The most common age is thirty. However, a number of states set the age at twenty-five, and one, Oklahoma, requires that the governor be thirty-one on the day of his election. Virtually all states require United states citizenship either directly or indirectly by requiring that the person elected must be a registered voter in that state. *See, e.g.*, Article III, Section 6 of the Delaware Constitution, and Article

V, Section I of the Hawaii Constitution. Some states require U.S. citizenship for a particular length of time. For example, Section 117 of the Alabama Constitution imposes a ten year citizenship requirement.

The length of residency within the state varies with the most common being either five or seven years. *See, e.g.*, Article V, Section 4 of the North Dakota Constitution; and Article VI, Section 5 of the Arkansas Constitution. Some states exclude absences from the state from consideration if the individual was on the public business of the United States or the state. *See, e.g.*, Article V, Section I Paragraph 2 of the New Jersey Constitution. In Kansas, the constitution authorizes the legislature to determine the qualifications for the governor. *See, e.g.*, Article I, Section 1 of the Kansas Constitution.

The age and United States citizenship limitations on the office of governor pose no serious question of violation of the United States Constitution. *Massachusetts Board of Retirement v. Murgia* (1976) (age classifications trigger minimal rationality test of federal equal protection) and *Foley v. Connelie* (1978) (classifications based on citizenship trigger minimal rationality test of federal equal protection when applied to policy-making positions in state government). The state residency requirement, at least to the extent it does not extend beyond seven years (ten years might be the outer limit), appears to pass United States constitutional muster. *See, e.g., Chimento v. Stark* (1973), sum affirmed, *cited with approval, Clements v. Fashing* (1982).

Most state constitutions establish a four year term of office for the governor. A number of these states arrange the governor's term so that gubernatorial elections are held in those even numbered years when there is no election for President of the United States. It is reputed that at least some of such constitutional provisions were designed to insure that a Republican candidate for governor could not ride into office on the coattails of a popular and successful Republican presidential candidate.

Many state constitutions limit the number of terms that a governor may serve. The most common variety of this type of limitation provides that after two terms a governor cannot succeed him or herself in office. The intent is to make the governor "sit out" every third four-year period. The wording of this limitation varies. One of the most unique is found in Article V, Section 1 of the Oregon Constitution: "No person shall be eligible to such office for more than Eight [years] in any period of twelve years." A number of others provide that a governor cannot succeed him or herself in office. *See, e.g.,* Article V, Section 116 of the Mississippi Constitution. Other constitutions limit the governor to a specific number of terms. For example, in Delaware a governor is limited to two terms. Article III, Section 5 of the Delaware Constitution provides: "[The Governor] shall not be elected a third time to said office." Other constitutions place no limit on the number of terms a governor can serve.

The rationale for limiting the number of terms that the governor can serve, either in succession or *en toto*, is rooted in the political history of the United States. Due to poor communications and rampant political patronage, it was feared that without such limits, a governor could become entrenched in office. Vigorous competition for the office was thought to further political pluralism. *State ex rel. Maloney v. McCartney* (1976).

Limitations of one or two terms with a hiatus of one term before again being eligible to serve are not violative of the United States Constitution. *Maddox v. Fortson* (1970). *En toto* limitations are probably constitutional but no case precisely on point has been located. The fact that the limit only applies to the office of governor and lieutenant governor (if applicable) and to no other statewide office does not, considering the importance of the office, make the classification unconstitutional. For example, only the governor is authorized to veto legislation. *See, Maddox, supra*.

Many state constitutions contain incompatibility clauses that place total or partial limits on the governor holding any other office during his term or terms as governor. *See, e.g.*, Article V, Section 2 of the California Constitution (no other public office), Article III, Section 6 of the Alaska Constitution (no other federal, state or local office or position of profit). There is little chance of a federal constitutional problem given there are somewhat similar provisions in the United States Constitution: Article I, Section 6, Clause 2 (members of Congress) and

Article II, Section 1, Clause 2 (members of the electoral college).

Section 28. The Governor and the Legislature

It has long been recognized that despite the principle of separation of powers, each of the three branches of government overlaps to some extent. *Springer v. Philippine Islands* (1928) (Holmes, J. dissenting). Frequently, these overlaps are labeled checks and balances. One of the most well-recognized of these checks and balances is the power of the governor to veto legislation. Generally, the governor's veto is subject to being overridden by a specified super-majority of the legislature. The super-majority can work in a number of different ways. It can be, for example, two-thirds of those members "present and voting in each house." *See*, Article IV, Section 22 of the New Mexico Constitution. Or, it can be two-thirds of the members "elected to that House." *See, e.g.*, Article IV, Section 7 of the New York Constitution. While the New Mexico Constitution requires only a simple majority of those members present in each house to enact legislation initially, the New York Constitution requires a simple majority of the members elected to each house to enact legislation. *See*, Article IV, Section 17 of the New Mexico Constitution and Article III, Section 14 of the New York Constitution. New York simply requires the requisite majority to be of the whole potential membership both for initial passage and for veto override. Alabama appears to have a different rule in that a simple majority of a quorum in each house is necessary for initial passage of a bill, while a simple majority of all of the members elected to each house is necessary to override a veto. *See*, Sections 52, 63 and 125 of the Alabama Constitution. Strangely enough, in several states, Indiana being an example, the governor's veto can be overridden by the same majority in the legislature that was necessary to enact the bill in the first instance. *See*, Article V, Section 14; and Article IV, Section 25 of the Indiana Constitution. Because the governor's veto is an executive exercise of legislative power, it is occasionally found in the executive article of state constitutions and at other times in the legislative article. *Compare*, Article III, Section 18 of the Tennessee Constitution (in the executive article) with Article IV, Part Third, Section 2 of the Maine Constitution (in the legislative article).

The standard practice is for the legislature to submit any bill enacted by it to the governor. The governor must then act by either signing the bill or vetoing it within a specified number of days, usually five to seven working days. If the governor elects to veto the bill, the governor must return it to the legislature, or sometimes to a specific house thereof, with the reasons for the veto. If the governor fails to return it within the allotted time, the bill generally becomes law without the governor's signature. Upon receipt of the veto and the governor's message stating his or her reasons for it, each house must in turn spread the Governor's veto message on the pages of its journal and, after debate, again vote on the bill. As previously indicated, the usual standard is to require a super-majority, usually two-thirds of the membership of each house of that body to override the governor's veto.

In addition to the governor's power to veto a piece of legislation in its entirety, many constitutions provide that the governor has the power to veto individual items in an appropriation act. This is the so-called line item veto. *See*, Article VI, Section 10 of the Montana Constitution. This power of line item veto also justifies the exclusion of appropriation acts from the otherwise general rule that a piece of legislation must have a single subject. *See* Chapter 5, *infra*. As indicated in Chapter 5, *infra*, the purpose of the single subject requirement is to prevent logrolling. Appropriation acts must have as their subject appropriation of money, no other subject can be included therein, but appropriation of money for a myriad of subjects is permissible. Therefore, it is possible to engage in the practice of logrolling within the appropriation act itself. One item of appropriation may be included as a trade-off for another or an item may be included that is essential to the welfare of the state or that the governor may greatly desire. Without the line item veto, the governor would be faced with the difficult choice of approving the whole bill, including appropriations the governor considered unwise, or vetoing the whole bill with the attendant difficulties that would cause. *Green v. Rawls* (1960). The governor, therefore, is given the line item veto as a weapon to deal with logrolling in appropriation acts.

A split of authority exists as to what is subject to a line item veto. Some state constitutions have been interpreted to define an "item" as an appropriation for a set purpose. As a result, an appropriation for the department of legal affairs would constitute an item. Any provision or condition on that appropriation, for example, a set figure for the salary of the attorney general, would not be a separate item, but would be considered part of the item appropriated for the legal department. *See, Commonwealth v. Dodson* (1940). Other states define an "item" as any specified sum of money for a particular purpose. *See, Green v. Rawls* (1960).

Most state constitutions allow the governor what has become known as a "pocket veto." If the legislature adjourns prior to the expiration of the number of days which the constitution sets aside for the governor to consider whether to veto the bill or allow it to become law, the governor can effectively veto the bill by refusing to sign it. Some states have denied the governor the "pocket veto" by providing that a bill will become law within a fixed number of days, if it is not affirmatively vetoed, regardless of whether the legislature adjourns in the interim. *See*, Article III, Section 8 of the Florida Constitution. Although it has been suggested that the pocket veto is inappropriate, the legislature can prevent its application by timely submission of the legislation to the governor. *See, Green v. Rawls* (1960).

Most state constitutions also allocate to the governor some power to call and adjourn legislative sessions. Frequently, the governor is allowed to call the legislature into special session, usually for a single purpose. *See, e.g.*, Article IV, Section 9 of the Colorado Constitution. Some constitutions allow the governor to designate more than one purpose for the special session. Others allow the governor, combined with a super-majority vote of the legislature, to permit the consideration of additional subjects. *See*, Article V, Section II, Paragraph 7 of the Georgia Constitution. Frequently, the governor is allowed to adjourn the legislature when the two houses cannot agree on the time of adjournment. *See, e.g.*, Section 80 of the Kentucky Constitution.

In most states, the governor is required to address the legislature once each session on the condition of the state. Normally, this occurs at the beginning of the session. The governor is frequently authorized to address the legislature at other times as well. The governor may also be required to present the legislature with a budget prepared by the governor's office. *See, e.g.*, Article IV, Section 8 of the Idaho Constitution.

Section 29.   The Governor's Appointment and Removal Power

Although the text of the governor's appointment power varies considerably from state-to-state, most constitutions allocate to the governor the power, in whole or in part, to appoint state officers. The Nebraska Constitution is illustrative of the process by which most state constitutions allocate the appointment power to the governor. *See*, Nebraska Constitution, Article IV, Sections 10, 11 and 12.

Under Article IV, Section 12 of the Nebraska Constitution, the governor, with the approval of the legislature, may fill by appointment all offices established either by the constitution or by law unless the constitution or statutes makes them elective or establishes another method of appointment. Other constitutions require approval only of the state senate. *See, e.g.*, Article V, Section 5 of the New Mexico Constitution. Under the Nebraska provision, one merely has to look to see if the constitution or statutes provide for election or another method of appointment of the affected office. If not, the general language controls and the office may be filled by the governor. Different procedures apply to judicial vacancies. For example, under the Nebraska Constitution a different procedure is established for the appointment of judges. The governor still appoints the judge, but the governor must select a candidate recommended by the judicial nominating commission. *See*, Nebraska Constitution, Article V, Section 21. In some states, the legislature can expand the governor's appointment power by removing the requirement for approval by the senate. *See, e.g.*, *Snider v. Shapp* (1979), interpreting a provision of the Pennsylvania Constitution that is similar but not identical to the Nebraska Constitution.

There is a split of authority regarding the extent of legislative control over the appointment process. Article XV, Section 1 of the Indiana Constitution provides that: "All officers, whose appointment is not otherwise provided for in this constitution shall be chosen in such manner as now is, or hereinafter may be, prescribed by law." In spite of this language, the Indiana Supreme Court has concluded that the appointment power is exclusively the governor's unless the exercise of that power is clearly incident to the duties of the legislature, the courts or other executive or administrative officers. *Tucker v. State* (1941).

In Kansas, a contrary conclusion has been reached. In *Leek v. Theis* (1975) the Kansas Supreme Court held that the appointment power is not an exclusively executive one, and that the legislature can determine the method of appointment to an office, including who does the appointing, unless that power is otherwise limited by the constitution. Note, however, that *Leek, supra,* involved the power of the legislature to reject a governor's appointment to a state agency, a power not specified in the Kansas Constitution. This power has been distinguished from the appointment power itself. *See, e.g., Biggs v. State, Department of Retirement Systems* (1981). Moreover, the Kansas Constitution did not contain an explicit requirement for separation of powers, while the Indiana Constitution did.

The Illinois Constitution, as do a number of others, clarifies that the legislature's power to establish other methods of appointment, or to make an office elective, does not authorize the legislature to assume the appointment power. Illinois Constitution, Article V, Section 9(a). In *Walker v. State Board of Elections* (1976), the Illinois Supreme Court interpreted that section of the Illinois Constitution. In that case, the court ruled that an arrangement, whereby the Speaker of the House and the House Minority Leader each nominated two persons for membership on the state Board of Elections with the governor appointing one of the two selections of each legislative officer, was unconstitutional. In so holding, the Court rejected the argument that the two legislative officers, rather than the legislature itself, were involved, and that the governor actually did the appointing. The Court also held that the scheme was not saved by constitutional authorization to the legislature to "determine the size, manner of selection, and compensation of the Board." *Id.* The ban on legislative involvement limited the types of selection open to the legislature. Finally the Court ruled that even though the Board was to some extent quasi-legislative or quasi-judicial, its principal function was executive. *Walker v. State Board of Elections* (1976). While this part of the Illinois Constitution only precludes legislative selection of executive officers, Nebraska precludes legislative selection of all officers whose office is established by constitution or by law.

In regards to the filling of elective offices by appointment where vacancies arise, the Nebraska Constitution provides that, with the exception of judicial officers and the lieutenant governor, the governor shall fill an elective office "until his successor shall be elected and qualified in such a manner as may be provided by law." Nebraska Constitution, Article IV, Section 11. This insures that the legislature cannot veto a governor's appointment to a vacancy but also allows the legislature to determine when a successor must seek election.

In the case of a vacancy in appointed office, excluding judicial officers, the governor appoints subject to legislative approval unless the legislature is not in session, then the appointment, generally known as a recess appointment, is subject to approval at the next legislative session, be it a regular session or special session. Nebraska Constitution, Article IV, Section 12.

State constitutional provisions relating to the power of the governor to remove public officials vary dramatically from state-to-state. All of these provisions must be considered against the rule announced by the Supreme Court of Pennsylvania in *Watson v. Pennsylvania Turnpike Commission* (1956). Under the rationale of that case, unless the office at issue has express limits on its terms or duration, the governor can remove the office holder at his or her pleasure unless his or her power is constitutionally limited in other ways. In the case of an office with a set term it is presumed that the creators of the office intended the occupant to serve out the term unless good cause could be shown as to why he or she should be removed. Constitutions and statutes must be examined to determine the exact arrangement in any given state as to when and whom the governor can remove at will. As to removal for cause, one must also look to the state constitution and statutes to determine what constitutes cause and what procedures are to be used to remove an official. This rule effectively shields elected officials from the governor's power to remove at will because every elective office is for a set term. However, some constitutions do provide for the governor to play a more specific role in the removal of some elected officers. Article VI, Section 7 of the Pennsylvania Constitution authorizes the governor to remove all elected civil officers except the governor, lieutenant governor, members of the legislature and judges of courts of record. In removing an official, the governor must have reasonable cause. Prior to removal, the officer is entitled to a hearing and removal is final only when two-thirds of the state senate concurs in the removal.

The great variety of approaches to the governor's removal power contained in state constitutions provides a myriad of potential variations. Again, the Nebraska Constitution is fairly representative of the general pattern. Article IV, Section 10 of the Nebraska Constitution establishes the power of the governor to remove a person appointed by him or her for a term. However, he or she may do so only for cause and after a public hearing. Other appointed officials may be removed at will or as the constitution describes it, "at any time and for any reason." This is consistent with the general framework because it is the legislature that sets the term for the office to which the governor has made an appointment. It can be assumed that by not establishing a term for the office the legislature recognized that those officers could be removed at the governor's will. This issue is further complicated because a distinction must be drawn between office holders within the ambit of the governor's removal power and officers and employees who may be protected by civil service, or as it is sometimes known, merit retention. *See, e.g.*, Article XV, Section 2 of the Kansas Constitution. It is impossible to generalize on this point other than to recognize that officers subject to removal at will cannot be within the ambit of any ordinary civil service or merit retention system.

The power of the governor to remove an officer from office is an integral part of the entire constitutional scheme of the removal of public officials from office. This scheme may include one of a number of methods of removal. State constitutions provide for impeachment, conviction and consequent removal from office of various officers. *See* Chapter 11, *infra*. Many state constitutions authorize recall of certain elected public officials by the voters. *See* Chapter 11, *infra*. Some state constitutions also provide for removal of judicial officers by procedure confined to the judicial branch. *See* Chapter 6, *infra*. The power of the governor to remove an official from office for cause may partially overlap one or more of these other removal provisions. For example, Article IV, Section 7 of the Florida Constitution allows the governor to suspend from office (the actual removal from office is carried out by the state senate), among others, "any state officer not subject to impeachment." This obviously precludes any interaction with the impeachment method of removal from office. However, it does allow the governor to remove certain judges who also may be ousted from office under the Florida judicial qualification procedure. *See, e.g., Kirk v. Baker* (1969). Other constitutional provisions are also worded to preclude confusion. For example, Article VI, Section 9 of the South Carolina Constitution provides: "Officers shall be removed for incapacity, misconduct, or neglect of duty, in such manner as may be provided by law when no other mode of trial or removal is provided by this Constitution."

Once it has been established that the particular officer can be removed for cause and that the governor is the one to do so, procedures for removal vary. However, the provisions of the New Mexico Constitution are representative. Under Article V, Section 5 of the New Mexico Constitution, the governor is empowered to remove from office anyone he or she appoints on the basis of incompetency, neglect of duty or malfeasance in office. Thus, only officers appointed by the Governor can be removed by the governor, and even then, only for cause. In a state that does not provide in its constitution for the governor's removal power, the legislature can, unless otherwise precluded, limit gubernatorial removal power by establishing terms for some officers and not for others. In addition, the legislature can further circumscribe the gubernatorial removal power by establishing a definition of cause. However, to the extent that the constitution provides other means of removal, this legislative prerogative would be limited.

Florida has one of the more complex provisions. The governor can suspend state and county officers for a variety of reasons, but municipal officers may only be suspended if they are indicted. The state senate, however, under statutorily established procedure must either actually remove the officer or restore him or her to office. *See*, Article IV, Section 7 of the Florida Constitution.

Section 30. Clemency

Clemency is an inherent power found in the sovereign state subject to regulation or limitation by the state constitution. Through the state constitution, the clemency power can be allocated in full or in part to one or more of the branches of government, or it can be denied to the state altogether. *Jamison v. Flanner* (1924). This power, which usually includes full pardons, partial pardons, conditional pardons, commutation of sentence, reprieves, and sometimes amnesty and parole, is normally relegated by the state constitution in one form or another to the executive branch of government.

A full pardon frees the recipient who accepts it of each and every consequence of his criminal conviction. A partial pardon relieves the recipient of part but not all of the consequences of conviction. A conditional pardon is, as the name suggests, predicated on conditions which the potential recipient must accept for the pardon to be effective and which, if violated, can terminate the pardon. Reprieves suspend, usually for a set time, the execution of a sentence. Commutation changes punishment from a more to a less severe form. *State ex rel. Gordon v. Zangerle* (1940). Amnesty has been described as a general or collective pardon without any legal distinction from any other full pardon. *Way v. Superior Court* (1977). Parole frees a person from physical confinement prior to completion of his sentence, but the remainder of that sentence is served in lesser forms of custody, such as supervision by state officers appointed for that purpose and subject to conditions that if not complied with can lead to a termination of the parole. *Mileham v. Arizona Board of Pardons and Paroles* (1974).

Frequently the state constitution assigns all or some of this clemency power to the governor alone subject to limitations on the offenses for which pardon can be granted and also subject to legislative regulation of the procedure for seeking clemency. An illustration is found in Article III, Section 21 of the Alaska Constitution which provides in pertinent part, "Subject to procedure prescribed by law, the governor may grant pardons, commutations and reprieves, and may suspend and remit fines and forfeitures. This power shall not extend to impeachment." This type of provision is usually interpreted to place no limitation on the governor other than those expressly set out. *People ex rel. Symonds v. Gualano* (1970). In addition to legislative regulation of procedure and the prohibition on the use of executive clemency in cases of impeachment, - a number of constitutions also preclude clemency in cases of treason and allow clemency to be granted only after conviction. *See, e.g.*, Arizona Constitution, Article V, Section 5.

Other state constitutions allocate the clemency power to the governor but allow the legislature to regulate not just the procedure for seeking it, but also its exercise. The Arizona Constitution is an example of this type. It subjects the power to "such conditions and with such restrictions and limitations as may be provided by law." *See*, Arizona Constitution, Article V, Section 5. Thus the governor is limited in his or her exercise of the clemency power by the recommendation of a legislatively created board of pardons and paroles. *Laird v. Sims* (1915).

In a number of states the clemency power is exercised by a board of which the governor may or may not be required by the constitution to be a member. Such constitutional provisions usually provide that the governor acting alone is empowered to grant reprieves involving any offense cognizable by the board until the board's next session. *See, e.g.*, Article VII, Section 12 of the Utah Constitution and Article IV, Section 7 of the Idaho Constitution.

Apart from the constitutionally allocated legislative power to regulate the executive clemency power, the role of the legislature in the granting of clemency is usually considered to be very limited or nonexistent. When the constitution requires that the operation of executive clemency be post conviction, it has been suggested that the legislature may be free to exercise clemency at other times. *See, e.g., Ex parte Miers* (1933). This rule would appear to be applicable to the concept of amnesty to the extent that it is thought to be principally exercised prior to conviction. *See, Hutton v. McCleskey* (1918). A general amnesty can be granted by the legislature and indeed a constitutional allocation of this power to the executive branch does not preclude the legislature from also exercising the clemency power. *State v. Morris* (1978). The largest area of uncertainty appears to be attempted retroactive legislative application of lesser criminal penalties. In *State v. Morris, supra*, a divided Ohio Supreme Court upheld the power of the legislature to retroactively apply legislation that reduced criminal penalties. The dissent argued that such legislation impermissibly infringed on the governor's constitutional commutation power.

In a related area, under a constitutional provision that allows the executive branch of government to exercise the clemency power after conviction, it has been held that the legislature may, by statute, provide immunity from prosecution for the purpose of obtaining testimony. It was suggested that had the clemency power not been so limited, the legislation would have been an unconstitutional infringement upon it. *Ex parte Miers* (1933). In spite of this opinion, the importance of immunity statutes today seems to have eclipsed any thought that they infringe on executive clemency power. *See*, Article VI, Section 12 of the Montana Constitution and Section 46–15–331 M.C.A.

Although it has been suggested that the clemency power includes parole power, the better view appears to be that since parole is not really a form of clemency, the legislature can vest the power in an executive board or commission even if the constitution assigns the clemency power to the governor. *Pinana v. State* (1960).

Section 31.   The Governor's Military Power

Most state constitutions allocate to the governor the leadership of the state's armed forces. Usually the governor is granted the title of commander-in-chief. In some New England states, the governor is described as the captain general, terminology which is presumably a holdover from that state's colonial charter. In Vermont, the governor is described as both. *See*, Chapter II, Section 20 of the Vermont Constitution. These provisions involve the governor in the organization, equipping, training, and use of state armed forces. Since public monies are necessarily involved, the legislature also has a role. *See, e.g.*, Article 8, Section 2 of the Kansas Constitution. Most constitutions, where they speak to the issue at all, express an understandable reluctance to have the governor command the state's forces in the field. Section 75 of the Kentucky Constitution allows the governor to do this only by legislative resolution. Because state armed forces, although frequently referred to as state militia are usually the National Guard component of the military reserves of the United States, the governor's power ceases when the state forces are called into federal service. Further, the governor's power is limited by the practical necessity of having the National Guard conform to federal standards of organization, equipment and training.

Constitutions frequently state that the governor may use the armed forces to execute the laws, suppress insurrection and resist invasion. *See, e.g.*, Article IV, Section 4 of the Idaho Constitution. This power is to be in support of the existing civil authority and is not to be confused with martial law which supplants civil authority with military authority. *State ex rel. O'Connor v. District Court In and For Shelby County* (1935). The imposition of martial law is an attribute of state sovereignty invoked by the governor, usually on the authority of the legislature under that body's inherent power. The general legislative practice, to the extent that there is one, is to allow the governor to declare martial law in areas of the state where the military has been called out. Under some constitutions the power is allocated directly to the governor, subject to some legislative oversight. *See, e.g.*, Article III, Section 20 of the Alaska Constitution.

To the extent that the governor is acting under constitutional authority, the power to utilize the state military forces in enforcing the law, including suppressing insurrection and similar evils, cannot be usurped by the legislature. The governor's exercise of the power is usually a matter of executive discretion and as such is not subject to interpretation by the judiciary. *State ex rel. Branigin v. Morgan Superior Court* (1967). However, the governor's exercise of this power can be checked when it violates constitutional rights, especially if the governor uses it as a substitute for martial law. *Wilson & Company v. Freeman* (1959). Constitutions place

several specific limits on the governor's military
power. (1) The military is to be subordinated to civil
power. (2) Troops cannot in peacetime be quartered
in any dwelling without the consent of the owner,
and in wartime only as set out by law. (3) Habeas
corpus shall not be suspended only in dire emergencies. *See*, Article I, Sections 8, 17 and 18 of the
Nebraska Constitution.

Section 32. Lieutenant Governor and Succession to the Office of Governor

The majority of state constitutions provide for the
office of lieutenant governor. Generally, the lieutenant governor is required to have the same qualifications as the governor. The major purpose of the
office of lieutenant governor is to provide a successor in the event the office of governor becomes
vacant. State constitutions frequently control the
allocation of other duties to the lieutenant governor. Absent constitutional authorization, the legislature cannot assign duties to the Lieutenant governor without violating the concept of separation of
powers. However, if the constitution so provides,
and perhaps even if it does not, the governor can
assign additional duties to the lieutenant governor
as long as they do not include those that the constitution specifically assigns to the governor. *State ex
rel. Peterson v. Olson* (1981). Some state constitutions specify assignment of duties to the lieutenant
governor by the governor alone or by both the
governor and the legislature. *See, e.g.*, Article V,

Section 7 of the North Dakota Constitution and Article III, Section 7 of the Alaska Constitution.

The lieutenant governor is almost always designated by the constitution as president of the state senate. Generally, the lieutenant governor can vote only to break a tie. One court has held that absent specific constitutional authorization, the lieutenant governor as president of the senate could vote to break ties only on procedural matters because the lieutenant governor's vote on substantive issues would interfere with the governor's veto power. *State ex rel. Sanstead v. Freed* (1977). The North Dakota Constitution was amended subsequent to *Freed* to allow the lieutenant governor/senate president to exercise a tie-breaking vote on substantive matters as well.

Where a state constitution provides for the office of lieutenant governor, it usually assigns to the lieutenant governor the duties of acting governor, whether or not so designated, during the governor's temporary inability to perform the duties of governor. Such temporary inability might include physical or mental impairment, extended absence from the state, or during impeachment proceedings against the governor. The temporary disability may be announced by the governor or determined by a neutral third party, most commonly the highest state court. The constitution usually provides who has standing to raise the issue of the physical or mental disability of the governor. The governor can, subject to procedure for challenge, announce the end of the disability or the body charged with determining the existence of the disability can decide whether it is at an end. Apparently, the above types of temporary disability do not, without more, make the office of governor permanently vacant although they can obviously play a role in the office becoming permanently vacant, *i.e.*, death, conviction upon charges of impeachment, resignation, refusal to serve, or sometimes, failure to qualify for the office, or conviction of a felony. Most constitutions which recognize the office of lieutenant governor provide that upon assuming the office of governor, in the event of a permanent vacancy, the lieutenant governor shall hold that office until the end of the current term. Others provide for an election of governor prior to the expiration of the current term, usually the next general election. *See, e.g.*, Article V, Section I, Paragraph V of the Georgia Constitution. In the event of the lieutenant governor succeeding to the office of governor, some constitutions will allow the lieutenant governor to nominate a successor. The successor must then be approved or elected by majorities of both houses of the state legislature. *See, e.g.*, Article IV, Section 15 of the Louisiana Constitution. Another procedure is for the constitutional officer next in line of succession to assume the office of lieutenant governor as he or she would if that office became vacant in any other way. *See, e.g.*, Article IV, Section 19 of the Connecticut Constitution. He or she would hold that office either until the end of the term or the next general election. Other constitutions allow the office of lieutenant governor to remain vacant with succession to the office of governor continuing down the line of succession. *See*, *e.g.*, Article I, Section 11 of the Kansas Constitution.

Where the state constitution does not provide for a lieutenant governor, the line of succession to the office of governor is either specified by the constitution or is to be determined by legislative enactment. Where the constitution establishes the line of succession, it usually begins with the chief officers of the two houses of the state legislature, or with the other elected members of the executive branch, with the Secretary of State or the Attorney General normally being first on the list. *See, e.g.*, Article III, Section 12 of the Tennessee Constitution; and Article V, Section 6 of the Arizona Constitution.

Section 33. Executive Officers and Departments

In addition to the governor, and frequently the lieutenant governor, state constitutions usually name various principal officers of the executive branch of state government and contain provisions pertaining to the structure and organization of that branch. Although the list of officers varies from state-to-state, it usually includes Attorney General, Secretary of State, Treasurer and Controller (Comptroller) or Auditor. The list also frequently includes Insurance Commissioner, Commissioner of Agriculture and Superintendent of Public Instruction. Some constitutions make no mention of principal officers. However, such constitutions frequently require the legislature to create a number of executive departments. *See, e.g.*, Article V, Section 6 of the Hawaii Constitution. Sometimes officers or executive departments are described in a section of the constitution apart from the one that discusses the governor. Presumably this is done to emphasize that their role is different from that of the chief executive officer of the state. *See, e.g.*, Article VI of the Oregon Constitution. Some states merge the duties of the various principal officers. For example, in Oregon, the Secretary of State is also the Auditor. *See, e.g.*, Article VI, Section 2 of the Oregon Constitution. In Colorado, the Superintendent of Public Instruction is also, ex officio, the State Librarian. See, Article IV, Section 20 of the Colorado Constitution.

The general rule is for these officers to be elected at the same election and for the same terms as the governor and lieutenant governor. *See, e.g.*, Article V, Sections 1 and 4 of the Minnesota Constitution. The rule requiring the governor and lieutenant governor to sit out one term of office after one or two four-year terms usually does not apply to other elected officers. Apparently the concern discussed in *State ex rel. Maloney v. McCartney* (1976), about the power of entrenched office holders in "foreclosing access to the political process," did not include officers other than the governor and lieutenant governor. As a result, it has been possible for officers other than the governor and lieutenant governor to become very powerful by virtue of long tenure in office. *See generally*, Article IV of the Florida Constitution. Sometimes one or more of these officers is not elected but is appointed either by the legislature or by the governor with the consent of the legislature. In Colorado, the State Auditor is selected by a majority of both houses of the legislature. *See*, Article V, Section 49 of the Colorado Constitution. Also in Colorado, the Insurance Commissioner is appointed by the governor with the advice and consent of the state senate. *See*, Colorado Constitution, Article IV, Section 23. In Maine, the Secretary of State is chosen by the legislature. *See*, Article V, Part 2, Section 1 of the Maine Constitution.

The qualifications and terms of such offices are frequently the same as those for governor and lieutenant governor. However, it is a somewhat common practice for the minimum age for these officers to be set at twenty-five rather than thirty, the latter being quite common for the governor and lieutenant governor. *See, e.g.*, Article IV, Section 4 of the Colorado Constitution. Normally, the successive term of office limitation does not apply to them. However, Arizona places a two consecutive term limitation on its Treasurer. See, Article V, Section 1, Version 2 of the Arizona Constitution. Usually, in addition to the other qualifications, the Attorney General is required to be a member of the state bar. *See, e.g.*, Article IV, Section 5 of the Pennsylvania Constitution. Sometimes, the membership must have been held for a specified length of time. *See*, Article V, Section III, Paragraph II(b) of the Georgia Constitution. Occasionally, other professional qualifications for holding office are required. For example, in Colorado, the State Auditor must be a certified public accountant. *See*, Article V, Section 49 of the Colorado Constitution. In New Mexico, the Superintendent of Public Instruction must be "a trained and experienced educator." *See*, Article V, Section 3 of the New Mexico Constitution.

In some states, the constitution provides that the duties of the principal executive officers are to be determined by the legislature. *See, e.g.*, Article III, Section 7(2) of the North Carolina Constitution. In others, the constitution specifically prescribes the duties. Their constitutionally prescribed duties are not surprising. In Connecticut, for example, the Treasurer receives and disburses state money as directed by law; the Secretary of State has the care and custody of public records and documents, and keeps the great seal of the state; the Comptroller adjusts and settles all public accounts. *See*, Article IV, Sections 22, 23 and 24 of the Connecticut Constitution. The constitutional listing of duties may be simple or it may be detailed. In Florida, the Attorney General is simply described as being the chief legal officer of the state; the Commissioner of Agriculture as having supervision over agricultural matters and Commissioner of Education as supervising the education system. *See*, Article IV, Sections 4(c)(f) and (g) of the Florida Constitution. At other times, the duties may be set out in extreme detail. The Maryland Constitution contains a two-page listing of the duties of Attorney General all of which could arguably be covered by describing the Attorney General as the state's chief legal officer. *See*,

Maryland Constitution, Article V, Section 3. Many states qualify the specified duties as subject to legislative limitation or additional duties as specified by the legislature. *See, e.g.*, Article IV, Section 4(f) and (g) of the Florida Constitution. Even if such a qualifier is not found, an argument can be made that the legislature can add to or control the duties set out, so long as the major functions of the office are not changed.

The organization of the executive branch is a legislative function. *VanSickle v. Shanahan* (1973). State constitutions, however, contain many types of restrictions on this legislative power. As has already been suggested, most constitutions limit legislative discretion over the executive branch by naming a number of the principal officers of the executive branch. These, of necessity, must fit somewhere into the organization of the executive branch. For instance, in Minnesota the constitution basically confines itself to naming three principal officers in addition to the governor and lieutenant governor: Secretary of State, Auditor, and Attorney General. *See*, Article V, Section 1 of the Minnesota Constitution. Presumably the intent was to allow the legislature carte blanche to organize the executive department any way it chose, taking into consideration these four officers and the governor and any constitutionally prescribed duties.

At other times, limitations on this legislative power arise from the constitutional creation of executive departments. For example, the Arizona Constitution designates four principal officers of the executive branch in addition to the governor. These are Secretary of State, State Treasurer, Attorney General and Superintendent of Public Instruction and specifies that their duties be prescribed by law. *See*, Article V, Sections 1 and 9 of the Arizona Constitution. In addition, the Arizona Constitution creates: a commission on judicial appointments. (*See* Arizona Constitution, Article VI, Section 36); a state board of education, regents of the state university system, and an elected superintendent of public instruction. (*See*, Arizona Constitution Article XI, Sections 3, 4 and 5); and the Corporation Commission (*See*, Arizona Constitution, Article XV). Some state constitutions do not consider commissions and boards similar to those set out above to be within the basic organization of the executive branch. *See*, Hawaii Constitution, Article V, Section 6 (temporary commissions and agencies for special purposes not included); North Carolina Constitution, Article III, Section 11 (regulatory and quasijudicial agencies not included); and Michigan Constitution, Article V, Section 2 (the governing bodies of institutions of higher education not included).

Other state constitutions circumvent the legislature by requiring that in the organization of the executive branch, there be no more than a set number of departments, the usual figure being twenty, with a few states setting the limit of twenty-five. *See, e.g.*, Michigan Constitution, Article V, Section 2; and Florida Constitution, Article IV, Section 6. The usual practice is to exclude certain types of executive activity from the departmental numerical requirement.

A number of state constitutions, in order to give the governor more control over the governmental branch of which he or she is the head, allow him or her to reorganize the executive branch within certain limits and subject to legislative veto. Representative of this type of provision is Article I, Section 6 of the Kansas Constitution. In order to further the goal of "transferring, abolishing, consolidating or coordinating" all or part of a state agency and its functions should the governor consider it "necessary for efficient administration," the governor may issue one or more numbered "executive reorganization orders" which are sent to the legislature during the first thirty days of a regular session with explanation of the reasons for the order. The executive reorganization orders will take effect with the force of a general law unless within a time certain one house of the legislature exercises its right of veto. The order may not apply to agencies of the legislative or judicial branch or to any function that is provided for in the constitution. The Supreme Court of Kansas has stated that the purpose of this provision is to recognize that "reorganization of the executive department is first and foremost a responsibility of the governor which should be sustained on a continuing basis . . ." and that its "clear intent is to facilitate executive reorganization issued by the Chief Executive." *VanSickle v. Shanahan* (1973). While it creates, in effect, a legislative veto of the executive branch, it does not violate any federal constitutional limit on state power. *Id.* Rather, it is an innovative approach to executive reorganization. *See*, Eley, *The Executive Reorganization Plan: A Survey of State Experience*, Institute of Governmental Studies, University of California, Berkeley (1967).

As the holder of executive power, the governor is authorized to seek advice, information and reports from the principal officers and departments of the executive branch. *See, e.g.*, Florida Constitution, Article IV, Section 1(a). In spite of the relatively clear distinction between the governor as holder of executive power and subordinate officers, such provisions are necessary to insure against improper displays of independence on the part of the other officers and departments.

CHAPTER 5

THE LEGISLATIVE BRANCH

Section 34. Introduction

All state constitutions contain provisions that allocate legislative power to the legislative branch of government. For example, Article II, Section 1 of the Florida Constitution provides as follows "The legislative power of the state shall be vested in a legislature of the State of Florida consisting of a Senate and a House of Representatives."

Such provisions appear in virtually all state constitutions. There is probably no more definitive statement of the purpose of this legislative power than that of Oliver Wendell Holmes, Jr., when sitting as Circuit Justice in *Johnson v. United States* (1908) he said, "The legislature has the power to decide what the policy of the law shall be." The courts of the several states recognize the same concept. In construing Article III, Section 1 of the Florida Constitution, the Florida Supreme Court adopted Holmes' view. "The Constitutional provision vesting legislative power requires, of course, that only the legislature shall establish the legislative policies and standards of the state." *Florida Welding & Erection Service, Inc. v. American Mutual Insurance Company* (1973).

Courts have generally concluded that these law-making functions cannot be delegated away. Recently, the New York Court of Appeals recognized this in *Levine v. Whalen* (1976) when it stated:

Because of the constitutional provision that "[t]he legislative power of this State shall be vested in the Senate and Assembly" (N.Y. Const., Art. III, Section1), the legislature cannot pass on its lawmaking functions to other bodies.

The delegation problem is further considered in Chapter 7.

In addition to allocating legislative power to the legislature and insuring that such power will only be exercised by it, such provisions operate as limitations in that, with the exception of Nebraska, all state constitutions mandate a bicameral legislature. *See* Article III, Section 1 of the Nebraska Constitution.

It has been held that "[C]onstitutional restrictions on the Legislature's power to act are strictly construed and doubts are resolved in favor of the Legislature's action." *Sutter's Place, Inc. v. Kennedy* (1999).

Section 35. Legislative Sessions

Most state constitutions require that the legislature meet in annual regular session usually beginning in January. Article III, Section 2 of the Iowa Constitution is typical. "The General Assembly shall meet in session on the second Monday of January of each year." A few state legislatures have regular sessions only every other year. Article V, Section 5 of the Arkansas Constitution provides that, "The General Assembly shall meet at the seat of government every two years on the first Tuesday after the second Monday in November until said time shall be altered by law." Some state legislatures have organizational sessions prior to the convening of regular legislative sessions; *see, e.g.*, Article IV, Section 7 of the North Dakota Constitution which provides for such sessions.

In a few instances, state constitutions discuss the consequences of the failure of the legislature to organize within the constitutionally prescribed period. Such penalties include non-payment of legislators. Article IV, Section 12 of the Oregon Constitution illustrates this principle:

Two-thirds of each house shall constitute a quorum to do business, but a smaller number may meet; adjourn from day to day, and compel the attendance of absent members. A quorum being in attendance, if either house fail to effect an organization within the first five days thereafter, the members of the house so failing shall be entitled to no compensation from the end of the said five days until an organization shall have been effected.

As illustrated by Article V, Section 5 of the Arkansas Constitution, *supra*, legislatures are generally required to meet at the seat of government, which is commonly the state capital. However, occasionally provision is made for an alternative meeting place. Article III, Section 9 of the South Carolina Constitution is an example. In pertinent part it provides that, "[s]hould the casualties of war or contagious disease render it unsafe to meet at the seat of government, then the governor may, by proclamation, appoint a more secure and convenient place of meeting."

The most frequent quorum requirement found in state constitutions is a majority of each house of the legislature. One example is Article IV, Section 13 of the Minnesota Constitution which provides: "A majority of each house constitutes a quorum to transact business, but a smaller number may adjourn from day to day and compel the attendance of absent members in the manner and under the penalties it may provide." In some states, a quorum is two-thirds of each house in the legislature. *See, e.g.*, Article IV, Section 12 of the Oregon Constitution. In others, a super-majority may be necessary to enact certain types of legislation. Chapter II, Section 14 of the Vermont Constitution provides in pertinent part that "[A] majority [of the House of Representatives] shall constitute a quorum for transacting any other business than raising a state tax, for which two-thirds of the members elected shall be present...." As has been illustrated by some of the provisions already alluded to, it is not uncommon to allow a contingent smaller than a quorum to meet and then adjourn from day to day while attempting to establish a quorum. Efforts to establish a quorum may be assisted by provisions authorizing penalties for absentee members.

The length of the regular session of the legislature is usually set by the state constitution and varies from state-to-state. Consider Article III, Section 15 of the Maryland Constitution which is quite detailed.

> The General Assembly may continue its session so long as in its judgment the public interest may require, for a period not longer than ninety days in each year. The ninety days shall be consecutive unless otherwise provided by law. The General Assembly may extend its session beyond ninety days, but not exceeding an additional thirty days, by resolution concurred in by a three-fifths vote of the membership in each House. When the General Assembly is convened by Proclamation of the Governor, the session shall not continue longer than thirty days, but no additional compensation other then mileage and other allowances provided by law shall be paid members of the General Assembly for special session.

Article III, Section 6 of the South Dakota Constitution provides for different lengths depending on whether the legislature is meeting in an even or odd numbered year.

> A regular session of the Legislature shall be held in each odd-numbered year and shall not exceed forty legislative days, excluding Sundays, holidays and legislative recess, except in cases of impeachment, ...

> A regular session of the Legislature shall be held in each even-numbered year beginning with the

year 1964 and shall not exceed thirty-five legislative days, excluding Sundays, holidays and legislative recess, except in cases of impeachment, ...

The time of adjournment must be agreed upon by both houses of the legislature and neither can temporarily adjourn or recess for more than a short time without the consent of the other house. Failing agreement, state constitutions frequently allow the governor to adjourn the legislature. For example, Article II, Section 10 of the Alaska Constitution provides, "Neither house may adjourn or recess for longer than three days unless the other concurs. If the two houses cannot agree on the time of adjournment and either house certifies the disagreement to the governor, he may adjourn the legislature."

In addition to regular legislative sessions, state constitutions provide in varying ways for additional sessions usually called "special sessions." Frequently the legislature can call itself into special session as can the governor. An example is Article III, Section 2 of the Connecticut Constitution which, after establishing times for regular sessions, provides for the convening of special sessions "at such other times as the general assembly shall judge necessary; but the person administering the office of governor may, on special emergencies, convene the general assembly at any other time." Delaware requires a special session to be called jointly by the presiding officers of both houses of the legislature or by the governor. Article II, Section 4 of that state's constitution reads, "The General Assembly shall convene on the second Tuesday of January of

each calendar year unless otherwise convened by
the governor or by mutual call of the presiding
offices of both Houses." In Virginia, the legislature
can call itself into special session only by petition by
super-majority of each house. Article IV, Section 6
of the Virginia Constitution provides, "The Governor may convene a special session of the General
Assembly when, in his opinion, the interest of the
Commonwealth may require and shall convene a
special session upon the application of two-thirds of
the members elected to each house." In some states,
only the governor can call a special session of the
legislature. Illustrative of this type of provision is
Article V, Section 9 of the Nevada Constitution.

> The Governor may on extraordinary occasions,
> convene the Legislature by Proclamation and
> shall state to both houses when organized, the
> purpose for which they have been convened, and
> the Legislature shall transact no legislative busi-
> ness, except that for which they were specially
> convened, or such other legislative business as
> the Governor may call to the attention of the
> Legislature while in session.

Article IV, Section 2 of the Nevada Constitution
makes it clear that only the governor, as described
above, may call the legislature into special session.
After establishing the times for the regular sessions,
this section concludes with the statement, "unless
the Governor of the State shall in the interim,
convene the Legislature by proclamation."

Article V, Section 9 of the Nevada Constitution quoted above also serves to illustrate two other facets of special legislative sessions. The purpose for the special session must be announced and the session is limited to that purpose, unless the governor specifies other topics. Other states allow a super-majority of the legislature to expand the matters that may be considered at the special session. Article IV, Section 76 of the Alabama Constitution provides that, "When the legislature shall be convened in special session, there shall be no legislation on subjects other than those designated in the proclamation of the governor calling such session, except by two-thirds vote of each house."

Section 36. Origination Clauses

A number of state constitutions require that bills for increasing taxes or raising revenue originate in the lower house of the state legislature, but that amendments can be proposed by the upper house. An example is Article III, Section 33 of the Wyoming Constitution. "All bills for raising revenue shall originate in the House of Representatives; but the Senate may propose amendments, as in case of other bills." Such provisions are obviously patterned after Article I, Section 7, Clause 1 of the United States Constitution. The Oklahoma Supreme Court in *Sullivan v. Williamson* (1908) justified such provisions by relying on the thoughts of Story in his treatise on the constitution. The gist of Story's position was that the federal House of Representatives was comparable to the British House of

Commons because both legislative houses were selected directly by the people. Under the English system, revenue bills originated in the House of Commons. Nonetheless, Story concluded the federal senate was given power to amend revenue raising measures and vote on whether they should ultimately become law. Story denigrated the importance of such provisions in state constitutions and suggested that while some states did not have such provisions, the ones that did were patterned after the federal one which allows the involvement of the upper house in amending and approving revenue bills. For this reason, the concept of what constitutes a revenue raising measure has been very narrowly construed. The Oklahoma Supreme Court in *Sullivan v. Williamson* (1908) cited a number of early federal decisions that limit the operation of origination clauses to those bills designed *specifically* to raise revenue. It would not apply to bills that just happen to create revenue although serving other purposes.

Modern cases continue to make just such distinctions. The Texas Supreme Court has held that Article III, Section 33 of the Texas Constitution which requires that all revenue raising measures originate in the House of Representatives "is confined to bills which levy taxes in the strict sense, and does not extend to bills for other purposes which incidentally create revenue." *Smith v. Davis* (1968). Thus, a bill which changed the procedure for assessing property for tax purposes in certain hospital taxing districts did not have to originate in the

House of Representatives. *Id.* The Delaware Supreme Court has held that a law authorizing school districts to levy real property ad valorem taxes for local school purchases did not come under the origination limitation which in Delaware is found in Article VIII, Section 2 of the Delaware Constitution. In its reasoning, the Court concluded that since the revenue was not available for use by the state, it was not governed by the origination clause. *See, Opinion of the Justices* (1967). Interestingly, Article VIII, Section 2 of the Delaware Constitution actually recognizes the limited applicability of its provisions. "[N]o bill from the operation of which, when passed into laws, revenue may incidentally arise shall be accounted a bill for raising revenue." Of course, the limiting interpretation placed on the Delaware origination clause by the Court is even more narrow in that it holds that even a revenue raising measure is not within the constitutional proscription unless it is general state revenue that is being raised. Apparently to alleviate definitional problems, Article VIII, Section 2 also provides that "nor shall any matter or cause whatever not immediately relating to and necessary for raising revenue be in any manner blended with it annexed to a bill for raising revenue."

Delaware's interpretation has not gone unchallenged. There is case law suggesting that statutes affecting ad valorem taxation, even though the revenues raised are by and for local government, do come within a state origination clause. In *Weissinger v. Boswell* (1971) a United States District Court, relying on Alabama case law, held that legislation lowering the ad valorem assessment rate had to originate in the House of Representatives.

Section 37. Elections, Qualifications, Disqualifications, Expulsion and Privileges of Legislators

Legislators in the United States are popularly elected. Article III, Section 2 of the Idaho Constitution is illustrative.

(1) Following the decennial census of 1990 and in each legislature thereafter, the senate shall consist of not less than thirty nor more than thirty-five members. The legislature may fix the number of members of the house of representatives at not more than two times as many representatives as there are senators. The senators and representatives shall be chosen by the electors of the respective counties or districts into which the state may, from time to time, be divided by law.

State constitutions differ widely in prescribing the way in which legislative electoral districts may be established. Under Article III, Section 2 of the Idaho Constitution, the legislature has virtual free reign over this process with the exceptions that there must be at least one senator from each county and the number of representatives may not exceed the constitutional limit. Not all state constitutions are so generous. For example, Article III, Section 1 of the Florida Constitution forbids multi-member legislative districts.

The legislative power of the state shall be vested in a legislature of the State of Florida, consisting of a senate composed of one senator elected from each senatorial district and a house of representatives composed of one member elected from each representative district.

Each house of a state legislature is usually recognized by the state constitution as the sole judge of the elections and qualifications of its own members. Article II, Section 8 of the Kansas Constitution is an example. It provides: "Each house shall be the judge of the elections, returns and qualifications of is own members." *See*, as another example of such provisions, *Henry v. Henderson* (1997). There is however, some uncertainty as to the scope of this power. In *Powell v. McCormack* (1969) the United States Supreme Court decided that this power exercised by the United States House of Representatives did not extend to refusal to seat a member who was actually elected and who otherwise met the qualifications for that office set out in the United States Constitution.

United States citizenship, age and district residency are the most common constitutional qualifications for election to state legislatures. Article III, Section 2 of the Wyoming Constitution is typical. In pertinent part, it provides that:

No person shall be a senator who has not attained the age of twenty-five years, or a representative who has not attained the age of twenty-one years, and who is not a citizen of the United States and of this state and who has not, for at least twelve months next preceding his election resided within the county or district in which he was elected.

The most common minimum age for the lower house of the state legislature is twenty-one, and the next common is twenty-five. In the case of the upper house, the most common minimum age is twenty-five with ranges of twenty-one to thirty. No state appears to have a maximum age established by its constitution. The words *resident of the district* and *inhabitant thereof* appear to be used interchangeably.

In some states, the citizenship requirement is direct, as in the provisions of Article III, Section 2 of the Wyoming Constitution referred to above. In others it is concealed. Article III, Section 9 of the Maryland Constitution imposes as a condition of membership of either house of the legislature that a person must be a citizen of Maryland who has resided there for one year. It also provides for district residency and minimum ages for senator and delegate. Maryland citizenship does not seem to be defined in the constitution. However, Article I, Section 12 of the Maryland Constitution provides that the holder of an elective office must, unless otherwise provided, be a registered voter. Article I, Section I of the Maryland Constitution provides that one must be a United States citizen in order to vote. So, a legislator is an elected officer, elected officers must be registered voters, and voters must be United States citizens.

The residency within a district requirement can take what to some might seem to be some strange twists and turns. Article V, Section 4 of the Arkansas Constitution which required that a state representative be "for one year preceding next his election a resident of the county or district" caused the Arkansas Supreme Court to disqualify a candidate who moved into the district less than a year before the election, even though he had thought of District 10 as his area of residence. He had worked in District 10, had his child educated there, received mail at a post office there, and had other ties to that district. *Jenkins v. Bogard* (1998).

The Pennsylvania Commonwealth Court has considered an unusual case involving military service. As the Court opined,

> Most telling of the evidence presented, however, is the Candidate's application for, and acceptance into, the early release/retirement program from his active duty commitment with the Army. By obtaining an assignment with the Reserves to the unit in Brookville, the Candidate and his wife were able to return to Western Pennsylvania. It is apparent that the Candidate took steps to return here even before his active duty service with the Army was satisfied. More importantly however, by obtaining the assignment with the Reserves, the Candidate actually increased the overall term that he was required to serve in the military. Thus, the Candidate actually increased the time he was committed to serve in the military for the opportunity to return to Western Pennsylvania.

Such an active manifestation of his intention that Pennsylvania is his domicile outweighs any evidence to the contrary. *Petition of Pippy* (1998).

Various things disqualify one from being a legislator. The following list is illustrative but not all inclusory.

1. Bribery conviction (Article IV, Section 10 of the North Dakota Constitution).

2. Being an active military serviceperson (Part II, Section 95 of the New Hampshire Constitution).

3. Dual office holding variously described as "lucrative" state office (Article III, Section 9 of the Nebraska Constitution), state office created during term (Article IV, Section 8 of the Nevada Constitution), and U.S. office (Article III, Section 7 of the New York Constitution).

4. Not accounting for previously held public funds (Article IV, Section 43 of the Mississippi Constitution).

5. Embezzlement of public money (Article IV, Section 60 of the Alabama Constitution).

6. Violating oath of office or refusal to take same (Article III, Section 8 of the South Dakota Constitution).

7. Forgery conviction (Article V, Section 9 of the Arkansas Constitution).

8. Conviction of infamous crime (Article III, Section 4 of the South Dakota Constitution).

9. Perjury conviction (Article IV, Section 10 of the North Dakota Constitution).

10. Accepting favors from railroad (Article IV, Section 37 of the New Mexico Constitution).

11. Subversion conviction (Article IV, Section 7 of the Michigan Constitution).

Some, such as Article 4, Section 44 of the Mississippi Constitution, state this type of requirement in more general terms, "conviction of an infamous crime." This has been found to "includ[e] all felonies other than those specifically excluded in subsection 3 of Miss. Const. Art. 4, sec. 44" *Mauney v. State ex rel. Moore* (1998).

Most state constitutions recognize the right of either house of the state legislature to expel or punish a member. *See, e.g.*, Article V, Section 10 of the Montana Constitution which authorizes each house to expel or punish a member for good cause shown if two-thirds of the membership concur in the punishment or expulsion.

There are a number of privileges commonly enjoyed by legislators that are sanctioned in state constitutions. Virtually everywhere legislators are privileged from arrest during the time the legislature is in session. *See, e.g.*, Article III, Section 15 of the Nebraska Constitution which recognizes the privilege along with certain commonly recognized exceptions: "Members of the Legislature in all cases except treason, felony or breach of the peace, shall be privileged from arrest during the session of the legislature, and for fifteen days next before the

commencement and after the termination thereof.''
Not all state constitutions are as liberal as Nebraska's regarding the existence of the privilege before and after the session. Article IV, Section 14 of the California Constitution limits the privilege to five days before and after the session. Article IV, Part III, Section 8 of the Maine Constitution does not establish a limit in terms of days but instead affords protection to legislators ''going to and returning from'' the legislative session.

Other privileges while perhaps less common are nevertheless significant. Article IV, Section 11 of the Nevada Constitution provides a privilege from ''arrest on civil process'' during the legislative session and for the fifteen days before the beginning of each session. Article V, Section 5 of the Rhode Island Constitution protects the legislator from having his property civilly attached during the session and for two days before and after the session.

It is quite common for state constitutions to provide that legislators shall not be questioned for any speech and debate during the legislative session. Obviously, such provisions are intended to promote candid debate without subjecting the speaker to accusations of defamation. Article IV, Section 10 of the Minnesota Constitution implements this policy as follows: ''For any speech or debate in either house they shall not be questioned in any other place.'' It has been held that these ''Speech and Debate Clauses'' preclude introduction of protected material in criminal prosecution of legislator. *State v. Neufeld* (1996). The Supreme

Court of Kansas, in *Neufeld*, also distinguished "arrest clauses" from "speech and debate clauses."

There are two different protections provided by these [provisions of the Kansas Constitution]. The Arrest Clause provides temporary protection from arrest for civil proceedings which may prohibit a legislator from attending a legislative session. Such protection does not apply to arrest for any criminal proceeding or to subpoenas for civil proceedings. [Case citation omitted.] The privilege created by the Speech and Debate Clause prohibits the admission into trial of evidence which is protected by the clause.... *Neufeld, supra.* Furthermore, the Court in *Neufeld* also held that "legislators are absolutely protected from the burden of defending lawsuits if the conduct upon which the suit is based falls within 'the sphere of legitimate legislative activity.'" [Case citation omitted.] *Neufeld, supra. See also Steiner v. Superior Court* (1996) which relates this rule or at least a similar one to the doctrine of separation of powers.

The question of the extension of "speech and debate clause" beyond its literal terms poses an interesting question. The Supreme Court of Kansas has held that "In determining whether particular activities other than literal speech or debate fall within the *'legitimate legislative sphere'* we look to see whether the activities took place 'in *a session of the House by one of its members in relation to the business* before it.'" [Case citation omitted.] *Neufeld, supra.*

Thus, an attempt by one legislator to blackmail another legislator into changing his vote on a certain matter was within the protections of the Clause. *Neufeld, supra.*

It has, however, been held that the protections of a "speech and debate clause" are not a bar to a court considering allegations of constitutional violations that supposedly occurred during legislative process. *Pennsylvania AFL–CIO by George v. Commonwealth* (1996).

Section 38. Legislative Compensation

In most states, legislative compensation is to be provided by law. *See, e.g.,* Indiana Constitution, Article IV, Section 29. Some constitutions add the stipulation that no legislature is to fix its own compensation. *See, e.g.*, Wyoming Constitution, Article III, Section 6. As if to guard against the self-interest of the legislators, a few state constitutions mandate an appointed citizen committee which reviews and sets the members' salaries. *See, e.g.*, Idaho Constitution, Article III, Section 23.

Not too many years ago state constitutions provided either the legislators' precise salary or set a limit which could not be exceeded. Today, owing perhaps to the mercurial nature of the economy, only a few state constitutions place a specific dollar limitation on legislative salaries. *See, e.g.*, Nebraska Constitution, Article III, Section 7 (not to exceed $1000 per month); Texas Constitution, Article III, Section 24 ($600 per month); Tennessee Constitution, Article II, Section 23 ($1800 per year); and

Rhode Island, Article VI, Section 3 ($5 per day, but only if "in actual attendance").

In addition to salaries, some state constitutions also address the subject of expenses. While, at one time, it was not unusual to find such limiting language in the constitutions as "to receive mileage one way by the shortest practicable route," (repealed Arizona section) today there seems to be more flexibility. Perhaps a few state constitutions still control the dollar amount of expenses; however, Texas' $30 a day limit as described in the First Edition has been changed so that the per diem is now set by the Texas Ethics Commission. *See*, Texas Constitution, Article III, Section 24.

These expenses are extended to special sessions, but some constitutions have a built-in session limiter. Under the Tennessee Constitution, Article II, Section 23, for example, legislators receive their usual per diem for special sessions, but the payments cease after thirty days. New York also provides an additional per diem for senators when they sit as a court of impeachment. *See*, New York Constitution, Article III, Section 6.

Few state constitutions provide for the method in which legislators are to be paid, *i.e.*, monthly, quarterly or yearly. Most constitutions delegate establishing the method of payment to the legislature. *See, e.g.*, Connecticut Constitution, Article III, Section 17.

The final compensation issue governed by many state constitutions is the prevention of legislative salary alterations. While increases or, less likely, decreases are not forbidden, the members who voted on the changes are generally not allowed to benefit from them. *See, e.g.*, Ohio Constitution, Article II, Section 31. However, some constitutions permit these members to collect the new salary at the session after the one which enacted the raise. *See, e.g.*, Wyoming Constitution, Article III, Section 6. In at least one case, legislators can change their salaries during the session, in addition to determining the effective date of the change. *See, e.g.*, South Dakota Constitution, Article XXI, Section 2. In this state, the change could take place during their term in office.

Section 39.　Single Subject Requirement

State constitutions usually prohibit a piece of legislation from applying to more than a "single overall idea" and matter properly germane to that idea. Many constitutional provisions describe the "single overall idea" as a single subject. Article IV, Section 13 of the Arizona Constitution is representative. It provides, "Every Act shall embrace but one subject and matters properly connected therewith." Other state constitutions employ the word *object* rather than *subject*. *See, e.g.*, Article IV, Section VII of the New Jersey Constitution which asserts: "[E]very law shall embrace but one object. . . . " As long as either word is used to mean the overall goal or idea to be achieved, rather than the method used to achieve it, they mean the same thing. However, the Florida Supreme Court has stated that the constitutionally mandated one subject can encompass a number of separate objects. *North Ridge General Hospital, Inc. v. City of Oakland Park* (1979). The Court of Errors and Appeals of New Jersey has said that the object is the primary subject of the law, while the product may be as "diverse as the object requires." *Jersey City v. Martin* (1941). Thus, it is probably fair to say that when the state constitution speaks in terms of a "single object" limitation, it most likely means the same thing as "single subject."

In *City of Oakland Park, supra,* the Florida Supreme Court determined that the subject of the law at issue was annexation of contiguous unincorporated territory by Oakland Park. One of the objects of that annexation was procurement of the land on which North Ridge General Hospital was located. The law had a number of objects but only one subject, annexation. In the Michigan Constitution, the word "object" appears to have the same meaning as "subject" in the Florida Constitution. Thus, in Michigan it has been held that the " 'object' of a law is its general purpose or aim. [Case citation omitted.]" *Township of Ray v. B & BS Gun Club* (1997). This view was reinforced when the Court opined in *Township of Ray* that a "violation [of Title–Object clause of Constitution] exists where the law contains *subjects* so diverse that they have no necessary connection." (Emphasis supplied.)

So, in Florida the "subject" and "object" are clearly delineated. This does not appear to be the case in Michigan. In other words, what is the equivalent of the Florida "object" in Michigan?

In general, it seems that legislatures are given a great deal of leeway in the application of what is generally called the single subject rule. That leeway can be described in many different ways. Perhaps the most common is found in the statement that, "The subject of a bill may be as broad as the legislature chooses, provided that the bill's provisions have a natural and logical connection. [Case citation omitted.]" *People v. Malchow* (2000). The Florida Supreme Court has described the necessary nexus as "natural" or "logical." *State v. Thompson* (1999). In a different case the same court commented that, "single subject requirement is satisfied if a 'reasonable explanation exists as to why the legislature chose to join the two subjects within the same legislative act.' " *Grant v. State* (2000) quoting *State v. Johnson* (1993). The Illinois Supreme Court has expressed the broad leeway somewhat differently from its comment in *Malchow, supra,* as when two subjects are so "unrelated" that "by no fair interpretation [can they] have any legitimate relation to one another. [Case citations omitted.]" *People v. Cervantes* (1999). A divided panel of the Indiana Court of appeals has said that the Indiana Supreme Court has taken a "laissez-faire" approach to determining whether a violation of the single subject requirement has occurred. [Case citation omitted.] *Indiana State Teachers Association v. Board of School Commissioners of the City of Indianapolis* (1997). Perhaps the leeway is best illustrated by a Minnesota appellate court when it commented that, "The common thread that runs through the various sections of a law need only be a 'mere filament' to withstand the single subject restriction. [Case citation omitted.]" *Masters v. Commissioner, Minnesota Department of Natural Resources* (2000). One of the most structured approaches to the single subject issue was used by the Supreme Court of Maryland. "Two matters can be regarded as a single subject, . . . either because of direct connection between them horizontally, or because they each have a direct connection to a broader common subject to which the act relates." *Maryland Classified Employees Association, Inc. v. State* (1997).

It has been suggested that it is possible to link the satisfaction of the single subject requirement to the parallel title requirement which is discussed in Section 39, *infra*. The Supreme Court of Washington has opined that "In general, violations of the single subject rule are more readily found where a restrictive title [as opposed to a "general title"] is used." *Amalgamated Transit Union Local 587 v. State* (2000).

The following two examples will help to illustrate the broad leeway regarding the single subject limitation that has been discussed above. The Supreme Court of Missouri has held that billboards could be considered germane to the subject of transportation, "assuming that 'transportation' [was] not too broad to identify a single subject, an argument neither made nor addressed here, ..." *C.C. Dillon Company v. City of Eureka* (2000).

A somewhat divided Commonwealth Court of Pennsylvania was faced with a House bill to amend the public utility code for the purpose of modifying the regulation of taxi cabs. In the Senate, it was changed to further amend the public utility code in the matter of "deregulation of the generation of electricity." As amended by the Senate it was enacted by both houses of the Legislature. Relying heavily on "the presumption of constitutionality" of legislation, and a somewhat analogous precedent from the Pennsylvania Supreme Court, the Court was "unconvinced that any clear violation of the [single subject requirement] occurred." *Fumo v. Pennsylvania Public Utility Commission* (1998). The Court in *Fumo* also found that "no clear constitutional violation occurred" in regard to a provision of the Pennsylvania Constitution regarding a "change in the original purpose of the law."*

The Pennsylvania Commonwealth Court also appears to have found the appropriation bills will be more closely scrutinized under the change of subject rule and *perhaps* under the single subject limitation as well. *See Pennsylvania AFL–CIO by George v.*

* The reader should note that these finding were made in the context of the "justiciability" of the claims. Although not entirely clear to the authors, it appears that the claims were held to be nonjusticiable because of the confluence of the rule of "presumption of constitutionality" of "legislative enactments" and the failure of the Court to find "clear constitutional violations". The opinion does not appear to be a majority one.

Commonwealth (1996).** *See also Department of Education v. Lewis* (1982).

At least one state has found that a single subject violation is cured by its "reenact[ment] for codification into the Florida Statutes," thus creating a "window period" for attacking the law which runs from the effective date of the law that violated the single subject rule to the point in time when it is codified as part of the Florida Statutes. *See Salters v. State* (2000). The authors have considerable difficulty with the reasoning that supports this rule unless one views it as some sort of judicially created curative act. This situation provides the opportunity to suggest that the single subject limitation applies to laws as enacted by the legislature not to the codified laws usually called statutes. As described by the Florida Supreme Court, "When laws passed by the legislature are being codified for publication in the Florida Statutes, [the single subject restriction] does not apply. The legislature is free to use whatever classification scheme it chooses. [The Constitution] does not require sections of the Florida Statutes to conform to the single subject requirement. The requirement applies to 'laws' in the sense of acts of the legislature." *Santos v. State* (1980).

In what appears to be an unusual treatment of a law found to be in violation of the single subject rule, the Supreme Court of Missouri has found that "when a bill violates the 'one subject' provision . . .

** *See Pennsylvania AFL–CIO by George v. Commonwealth* (2000) which criticized one aspect of the Commonwealth Court's holding while ultimately affirming the final holding.

the entire bill is unconstitutional unless court is convinced beyond a reasonable doubt that one of the bill's multiple subjects is its original, controlling purpose and that other subjects are not." If the Court is so convinced, it will sever that portion of the bill containing additional subject(s) and permit bill to stand with its primary core subject intact. *Carmack v. Director of Missouri Department of Agriculture* (1997), relying upon *Hammerschmidt v. Boone County* (1994).

The importance of the single subject limitation is, perhaps, best summed up by the Supreme Court of Washington's presumably invidious comparison between that limitation and what goes on in the Congress of the United States. "Our constitution also evidences a clear policy that bills should pertain to single subjects and should not be encumbered by 'riders' containing divergent subjects, as in the practice in Congress; our Framers vigorously opposed legislative logrolling." *Washington State Legislature v. Lowry* (1997).

The primary purpose of the single subject limitation is to prevent legislators from combining diverse subjects into one bill. Such combinations might occur for the purpose of garnering enough votes to insure passage of the entire bill, although each of the subjects standing alone might not otherwise be assured of the requisite numbers of votes for passage. The Supreme Court of South Dakota in *South Dakota Association of Tobacco and Candy Distributors v. State By and Through Department of Revenue* (1979) has described a particular diversity of subjects as having "no common basis except, perhaps, their separate inability to receive a favorable vote on their own merits." *Id.* In an earlier opinion, the same court in *State v. Morgan* (1891) succinctly identified the evil of multiple subject legislation.

> The practice of bringing together in one bill subjects diverse in their nature, and having no necessary connection, with a view to combine in their favor the advocates of all, and thus secure passage of several measures, no one of which could succeed upon its own merits, was one both corruptive to the legislator and dangerous to the state.

Another rationale for the single subject limitation was to prevent the attachment of riders to popular measures so that the former which might otherwise not be enacted might become law because of the popularity of the underlying act itself. Article IV, Section VII, Paragraph 4 of the Constitution of New Jersey explicitly recognizes this concern:

> To avoid improper influences which may result for intermixing in one and the same act such things as have no proper relations to each other, every law shall embrace but one object and that shall be expressed in the title. This paragraph shall not invalidate any law adopting or enacting a compilation, consolidation, revision or rearrangement of all or parts of the statutory law.

The benefits of this limitation may be more apparent than real in terms of preventing alliances for the purpose of securing enough votes to enact a law.

One has but to remember Bismarck's aphorism, "No man should see how laws or sausages are made," to realize that this type of limitation can perhaps be circumvented by the legislators' mutual agreement to support several pieces of legislation each of which complied with the single subject requirement.

However, although little discussed, this limitation would seem to be of greater importance in insuring the vitality of the governor's veto, since governors either have no line item veto or such veto power is limited to general appropriation bills. If a bill sent to the governor could contain multiple subjects, intolerable pressure could seemingly be brought on the governor by including a subject he might wish to veto along with other subjects.

Section 40.   Title Requirement

In addition to the single subject requirement, another very common constitutional limitation is that the subject must be briefly stated in the title to the act. Article II, Section 16 of the Kansas Constitution is of this category. It states: "[t]he subject of each bill shall be briefly expressed in its title."

In interpreting this provision, the Kansas Supreme Court has held that in satisfying this requirement the title need not contain all the specific details included in the law. *Brickell v. Board of Education* (1973). This is consistent with the stated purpose of the title requirement which has been described as "preventing surprise and evils of omnibus bills and surreptitious legislation." *Shaw v.*

State (1968). In *North Ridge General Hospital, Inc. v. City of Oakland Park* (1979), the title involved stated that the subject of the bill was annexation of unincorporated contiguous land by the city of Oakland Park. The Court held this was adequate to put legislators, and the public generally, on notice that any contiguous unincorporated land might have been included in the act. As suggested by a Michigan Appellate Court, "[T]he test is whether the title of the act gives the Legislature and the public fair notice. . . ." *Knauff v. Oscoda County Drain Commission* (2000). It was therefore not necessary to give the legal description of each parcel that was actually to be annexed to satisfy the title requirement. This reasonable notice, rather than "index" approach, is the prevalent method of applying constitutional title requirement to state legislative enactments. *See, e.g. H.J. Tucker and Associates, Inc. v. Allied Chucker and Engineering Company* (1999).

When a Kentucky Appellate Court opined that the title requirement in the Kentucky Constitution "requires that the title of an *act* agree with the body of the *act*, not that the title of a *statute* agree with the body of the *statute*," it appeared to have in mind the same distinction as that found in the preceding section between the single subject requirement applying to laws but not statutes (*Santos v. State*). *Cooksey Brothers Disposal Company, Inc. v. Boyd County* (1997) (emphasis in original).

Although, as we have seen in the preceding section, it has been suggested that the wording of the title may have some bearing on the existence *vel non* of a single subject, it seems to be a very general rule that a constitutional provision governing single subject and title "imposes two distinct procedural limitations by which the General Assembly may pass legislation: (1) a bill cannot contain more than one subject and (2) the subject of the bill must be clearly expressed in its title." *C.C. Dillon Company v. City of Eureka* (2000).

As with the single subject rule, the courts seem willing to give the legislature a great deal of leeway on the title requirement. They have spoken in terms of "invalidity [having to be] manifest" (*Kansas Public Employees Retirement System v. Reimer and Koger Associates, Inc.* (1997)), "matter utterly incongruous to the general subject of the statute is buried in the act." *Utilicorp United, Inc. v Iowa Utilities Board, Utilities Division, Department of Commerce* (1997)* and in terms of "deception," to the effect that it "must [be] demonstrat[ed] either that: (1) the legislators and the public were actually deceived as to the act's contents at the time of passage; or (2) the title on its face was such that no reasonable person would have been on notice as to the act's contents." *Common Cause/Pennsylvania v. Commonwealth* (1998).

This is not to suggest that almost anything goes. It has been held "that the words 'economic development' are too broad and amorphous to describe

* The use of the word "statute" is somewhat troubling in light of what was said by the Kentucky Court of Appeals in *Cooksey, supra*. Perhaps (hopefully?) by "statute" the Court meant the original law or act and not the state statutes.

subject of pending bill with the precision necessary to provide notice of its contents." *Carmack v. Director of Missouri Department of Agriculture* (1997).

Nevertheless, the benefit of the doubt (which might very well be called, as have many courts, the presumption of constitutionality) seems to go to the legislature. Washington has, *e.g.*, recognized both "general titles" and "restrictive titles." *See Amalgamated Transit Union Local 587 v. State* (2000). *See also* the reference to this case in the preceding section. Virginia has upheld a title that was "broader than the legislation specifically enacted." *Gilmore v. Landsidle* (1996).

Section 41.   General Laws and Limitations on Special and Local Legislation

The deeply rooted practice of enacting laws of limited application led to state constitutional provisions that either prohibit special and local legislation altogether or place severe limits on it. Frequently, it is necessary to distinguish general legislation from that which is special or local for purposes of such provisions. This is not always an easy task.

General laws need not be universal, but only uniform in their application. *See, e.g. Sheffield v. Rowland* (1999) and *State ex rel. Cotterill v. Beesenger* (1961), *infra*. Merely because a law does not apply to everyone or every location in the state does not prevent it from being a general law. *See, e.g. State v. Bonnewell* (1999). This is true provided the difference recognized by the classification is a reasonable one. *See, e.g. Ocala Breeders' Sales Company, Inc. v. Florida Gaming Centers, Inc.* (1999).

Early cases and writing of other authorities* made reference to the Latin origin of the words general and special, *genus* and *species*. The former meant an entire category while the latter meant part of a category. Whether or not something can be classified as a separate category turns on whether the classification that created the category is based on substantial differences. This determination is made by the Court after considering the purpose of the law. Thus, a law that taxed all mortgages created a valid category or *genus* since mortgages can fairly be considered different from other types of taxable property. However, a law that taxed mortgages only if they pertained to real property located in a single county did not create a valid category or *genus* since the difference between single and multiple county mortgages was not fairly related to the purpose of taxation. Such a law pertained to *species* and not *genus* and was therefore special. *Dundee Mortgage, Trust Investment Company v. School District Number 1* (1884). This distinction is not as simple as it might appear.

Even though Courts no longer refer to *genus* and *species*, the definitions have remained basically unchanged. In *State ex rel. Heck's, Inc. v. Gates* (1965), the Supreme Court of Appeals of West Virginia

* *E.g.*, Binney, "Restrictions upon Local and Special Legislation in the United States." Section II. "The Distinctions Between General, Local and Special Legislation," American Law Register and University of Pennsylvania Law Review, Old Series Vol. 41, New Series Vol. 32. 1893.

recognized that while ideally, a general law would apply to everyone and every place in the state, circumstances usually preclude such universal application of legislative power. The legislative purpose behind its Sunday closing law would have been unworkable without exceptions and thus, the classification created by the exceptions were based on real differences related to the purpose of the law.

Local laws are a type of special law that apply geographically to less than the entire state. At least in some states, local laws are distinguished from special laws even though both would in all likelihood share the same disabilities when compared to a general law. The following definitions seem to correctly describe the two types of what might be called, "non-general laws." "Local legislation is legislation that is arbitrarily applied to only one geographic area of the state, while special legislation arbitrarily separates from the operation of an act some person, place or thing from another." *Hall v. Tucker* (1999).

The Arkansas Supreme Court's use of the word "arbitrary" was, most likely, employed to distinguish local and special laws from general laws which classified "reasonably" rather than arbitrarily. *See infra* this section in paragraph containing reference to the *Sheffield, Bonnewell* and *Ocala Breeders* cases. Usually, local laws pertain to one of the state's political subdivisions such as a county or a municipal corporation. However, a law does not have to apply to the entire geographic area of the state in order to be a general law. As stated by the

Arkansas Supreme Court in *Hall v. Tucker, supra*, "The fact that a statute ultimately affects less than all of the state's territory does not *per se* render it local or special legislation." Counties, for example, may be classified by general law as long as there is a real difference between those included in the classification and those which are not. These determinations are made after consideration of the purpose for which the law was enacted. Therefore, an environmental law pertaining only to the coastal counties of a state is general if the environmental concerns addressed by the law are unique to the coastal counties. *See, Adams v. North Carolina Department of Natural and Economic Resources* (1978).

Some courts have chosen to measure a classification in a manner that raises questions about its general applicability under a balancing of interest test that is familiar in the equal protection context. "Application of the rational basis test requires us to determine whether a classification: (1) is genuine rather than illusory, and (2) is reasonably related to a legitimate government purpose." *City of Greenwood Village v. Petitioners for Proposed City of Centennial* (2000). The reader will note a curious, but by no means uncommon, oddity. The Colorado Supreme Court described the balancing test it is using as the "rational basis test." The oddity is the use of the word "reasonable" instead of the word "rational" in the quote from *City of Greenwood Village*. The Florida Supreme Court, not infrequently, has used the word "reasonable" in what it describes as the "rational basis test." At times the words are used, seemingly interchangeably, in the same case, although "reasonable" seems a somewhat higher level of scrutiny than rational. *See, e.g.*, *Rollins v. State* (1978). It is very tempting to suggest that what is going on is a somewhat higher level of judicial scrutiny masquerading as the rational basis test. This point of view can be defended because a good case can be made that, in *Rollins*, the outcome would have been different if the Court had really applied the word "rational." Reverting back to *City of Greenwood Village* for a moment, a partial answer to this issue *may possibly* be found in the comment by the Colorado Supreme Court that, "The prohibition against special legislation, however, is more than a redundant Equal Protection Clause, 'because in cases of enumerated prohibitions it involved a threshold question [of] whether the classification adopted by the legislature is a real or potential class, or whether it is logically and factually limited to a class of one and thus illusory,' " quoting *Curtiss v. GSX Corporation of Colorado* (1989).

What all of this appears to amount to is that since general laws need not be "universal," but rather, "uniform" in their application statewide (*See Sheffield v. Rowland* (1999)), a classification that is either "irrational" or "unreasonable" is one that is not of uniform application statewide and thus fails as a general law and is therefore to be restricted by all the limitations placed upon local or special laws or whatever a state chooses to call them.

Perhaps the most exhaustive analysis of whether a law enacted as a general law meets the requirement of uniform has been described by a Wisconsin Appellate Court. That court identified a "five part test." It did this in the context of a state constitutional provision that "No private or local bill [probably the same as special or local law] shall embrace more than one subject...." The five parts of the "test" are,

"First, the classification employed by the legislature must be based on substantial distinctions which make one class really different from another. Second, the classification adopted must be germane to the purpose of the law. Third, the classification must not be based on existing circumstances only. Instead, the classification must be subject to being open, such that other [members] could join the class. Fourth, when a law applies to a class, it must apply to all members of the class.... [Fifth] the characteristics of each class should be so far different from [the others] so as to reasonably suggest ... the propriety ... of substantially different legislation." *Group Health Co-op. of Eau Claire v. Wisconsin Department of Revenue* (1999), citing *City of Brookfield v. Milwaukee Metropolitan Sewerage District* (1988).

Compare this five part test with the one for general laws of local application–population acts found *infra*.

In addition to the requirement that a general law's classification must be reasonable in light of the purpose of its enactment, as indicated in *Eau Claire, infra*, a general law may not "freeze" its classification, *i.e.*, the class must be open-ended. *See also, Department of Legal Affairs v. Sanford–Orlando Kennel Club, Inc.* (1983). In the *Adams, supra*, case, involving the coastal counties of North Carolina, it was extremely unlikely that in the future other counties would qualify as coastal counties, but the law provided for that possibility.

The fewer the entities that fall within a classification, the greater the likelihood that the classification will be considered unreasonable, and the law labeled a local one. Nevertheless, there are instances where a classification was limited to one entity, and the statute was held to be general. *See, Sanford–Orlando Kennel Club, supra.*

General laws that classify localities cause particular problems. If a law is based on the peculiarities of geography, it may still qualify as a valid general law even though no other entities could satisfy the classification. *See, e.g., Caldwell v. Mann* (1946). Likewise, laws that classify by population may be valid general laws if the population classifications are reasonably related to the purpose of the law and the classifications are open-ended. Courts are generally liberal in discovering a reasonable relationship between a population classification and a law's purpose. Thus, a population classification was reasonable even though it provided for a unique type of criminal court procedure in only one county of the state. However, when the population classification was subsequently changed in such a fashion that again only that county was included, the Court determined that there was no reasonable relationship between the population and the purpose. Further, the Court determined that the legislature intended that no other county could even qualify for the classification. *Smith v. State* (1932).

At times, legislatures can try a court's traditional deference to legislative prerogative. The Florida legislature once enacted a ban on nudist colonies in all counties of the state having a population not less than 36,700 and not more than 38,000 according to the most recent federal census. Only one county in the state had a population that corresponded with the population brackets. In *State ex rel. Cotterill v. Bessenger* (1961), the Court invalidated the statute as an improper special law.

> [T]he thought immediately occurs whether there is a genuine reason to be concerned with the health, morals, and welfare of the public as affected by nudist colonies once a certain population is reached, then to consider these elements inconsequential if the population increases beyond the higher limitation, ...

Several common types of limitations on special and local legislation are found separately or in various combinations in state constitutions. However, there is wide diversity in such provisions on a state-to-state basis. The common thread is the desire to guard against the evil inherent in the practice of enacting legislation that benefits some but not all. *Keiderling v. Sanchez* (1977).

One of the most widely found types of limitation is that in Article V, Section 12 of the Montana Constitution: "The legislature shall not pass a special or local act when a general law is, or can be made, applicable." A literal reading of this provision suggests that a legislature could only enact a special or local law if its purpose could not reasonably be achieved by a general law. This literal approach was adopted by the Montana Supreme Court in *Grossman v. State Department of Natural Resources* (1984) when it held that a law authorizing various public works projects to be funded by revenue bonds in a number, but not all, of that state's political subdivisions was special or local. However, the law was constitutional because the legislature could not reasonably be expected to achieve its purpose by general law.

Application of this type of constitutional limitation, requires a two-step judicial process. This process was described by the Indiana Supreme Court in the following manner. "In analyzing a law ... we must first determine whether the law is general or special. If one law is general, we must then determine whether it is applied generally throughout the state. If it is special, we must decide if it is constitutionally permissible." *Williams v. State* (2000). As suggested, first a determination must be made that the challenged legislation is special or local. In many cases this presents no problem because such laws are frequently identified as such by the legislature. In *Grossman, supra,* since the legislation designated the public works projects by name, there could be no pretense that it was general. If this issue is not conceded, a judicial determination must be made as to whether the legislation is general or special. If the classification is found to be reasonable and of uniform application, it will be classified as general. *John R. Grubb, Inc. v. Iowa Housing Finance Authority* (1977).

Second, as also suggested by *Williams,* if the law in question is special or local, it must be determined whether the legislative purpose could have been achieved by a general law. This determination turns in large measure on the degree of deference given to the implicit legislative finding that its purpose could only be achieved by a special or local law. Unlike Montana's, some state constitutions emphasize that this issue is to be determined by the courts. Article IV, Section 13 of the Illinois Constitution is an example. "The General Assembly shall pass no special or local law when a general law is or can be made applicable. Whether a general law is or can be made applicable shall be a matter for judicial determination." The effect of such a provision would seem to preclude great deference to the legislative determination. The Supreme Court of Illinois read this provision in that fashion. *See, In re Belmont Fire Protection District* (1986). However, a comparison of the approaches of the Montana and Illinois courts suggests that the difference is not as great as it might otherwise appear. Even in Illinois, the courts apply the following standards: (1) all reasonable doubts are resolved in favor of the legislature, (2) the Court presumes that the legislature acted in accordance with its constitutional duty, and (3) the legislature has broad discretion. Thus, in *Melbourne Corporation v. City of Chicago* (1979) a law that had granted immunity from suit to local governments but not to the state was found to be a reasonable classification. The Court reached this conclusion because the legislature could have found that local government needed immunity while the state did not. The additional requirement that the legislature used, if possible, a general law resulted in a finding that the law was general.

Nevertheless, courts would appear to possess more liberty to invalidate laws as being special or local under the Illinois type of limitation. The Michigan Constitution and its predecessors have had an Illinois type provision for many years. In *Common Council of City of Detroit v. Engel* (1918) the Michigan Supreme Court deferred to the judgment of the legislature when it upheld a law that authorized only the library commission of the City of Detroit to issue bonds for library improvement. Generally, the courts are more willing to find that a general law cannot reasonably be made applicable when the legislature demonstrates, by enacting a special or local law, that it has already so concluded. The safeguards that frequently surround the enactment of special or local legislation, such as published notice or referendum, obviously play a role in a court's greater willingness to find that a general law is or cannot be reasonably made applicable. A legislature is in a weak position to assert that a general law cannot be made applicable when it has enacted what purports to be a general law. In such instances, courts frequently hold that a general law can be made applicable, but that the legislation at issue is not a general law.

Since the Montana and Illinois Constitutions, along with a number of others, are written in terms of present applicability as well as potential applicability ("is applicable" as contrasted with "can be made applicable") it could be argued that the inquiry might well be different if a special or local law involved a subject already covered by a general law. In the latter case, the inquiry might well be different if a special or local law involved a subject not now covered by a general law. Then the inquiry would be as it was in *Grossman, supra*, could the legislature have enacted a general law rather than a special or local one? In the former, the inquiry would focus on the existence of a general law already in place. The distinction turns out to be more apparent than real. The Montana Supreme Court in *Grossman, supra*, referenced an earlier decision, *State ex rel. Ford v. Schofield* (1917). At a time when the Montana Constitution contained the "can be made" but not the "is" language, the Court held that a local law creating a new county was valid even though a general law dealing with the creation of counties already existed. As a result, the dispositive question appears to be the ability of the legislature to achieve its purpose by general law.

Whatever deference courts might extend to legislatures when a state constitution prohibits special or local laws where a general law may be made applicable, none exists when a law is determined to be special or local, and the state constitution prohibits such laws in certain areas. Article II, Section 28 of the Washington Constitution is of this variety. It provides as follows:

The legislature is prohibited from enacting any private or special laws in the following cases:

1. For changing the names of persons, or constituting one person the heir at law of another.

2. For laying out, opening or altering highways, except in cases of state roads extending into more than one county, and military roads to aid in the construction of which lands shall have been or may be granted by congress.

3. For authorizing persons to keep ferries wholly within this state.

4. For authorizing the sale or mortgage of real or personal property of minors, or others under disability.

5. For assessment or collection of tax, or for extending the time for collection thereof.

6. For granting corporate powers or privileges.

7. For authorizing the apportionment of any part of the school fund.

8. For incorporating any town or village or to amend the charter thereof.

9. From giving effect to invalid deeds, wills or other instruments.

10. Releasing or extinguishing in whole or in part, the indebtedness, liability or other obligation, of any person, or corporation to this state, or to any municipal corporation therein.

11. Declaring any person of age or authorizing any minor to sell, lease, or encumber his or her property.

12. Legalizing, except as against the state, the unauthorized or invalid act of any officer.

13. Regulating the rates of interest on money.

14. Remitting fines, penalties or forfeitures.

15. Providing for the management of common schools.

16. Authorizing the adoption of children.

17. For limitation of civil or criminal actions.

18. Changing county lines, locating or changing county seats, provided this shall not be construed to apply to the creation of new counties.

Illinois has abandoned such provisions as archaic. *Anderson v. Wagner* (1979). However, the rationale for such provisions has been enunciated by the Supreme Court of North Carolina in *Idol v. Street* (1951). The purpose of limitations was to require legislation for the state as a whole "rather than as a conglomeration of discordant communities." It made no difference "how praiseworthy or wise" such a law might be. *Id.* The Florida Constitution only contains prohibitions on special law in certain areas. *See*, Florida Constitution, Article III, Section 11. It contains no provision prohibiting a special law where a general law can be made applicable. As a result, the state legislature has carte blanche to enact special or local laws outside of the prohibited areas unless some other state or federal constitutional provision is violated.

In addition to the more common types of constitutional provisions that preclude special or local legislation discussed above, certain constitutional provisions specifically require uniformity in certain instances. In *St. Louis Teachers' Credit Union v. Marsh* (1979), the Missouri Supreme Court held that a statute limiting interest rates charged by credit unions violated the section of the Missouri Constitution which required interest rates to be uniform as to all lenders. Presumably this special provision was necessary to preclude a court finding that there was a reasonable basis for classifying credit unions for special law treatment. In *Mountain Fuel Supply Company v. Emerson* (1978) the Wyoming Supreme Court found that a law which voided indemnity agreements only in the well drilling and mining industries was a reasonable classification and thus, a general law. Even though other occupations were equally hazardous, the legislature was not precluded from dealing with the limited aspect of the problem.

Finally, it is possible for a state constitution to mandate that a particular subject only be affected by general law. For example, Article IV, Section 13 of the Alaska Constitution provides that judicial salaries may only be diminished during a term of office if accomplished "by general law applying to all salaried officers of the State."

In addition to these limitations, state constitutions often require the publication in a newspaper of general circulation of intention to seek the enactment of special or local legislation as a condition of a special or local law's validity.

Article V, Section 26 of the Arkansas Constitution provides a model of this type of provision:

No local or special bill shall be passed, unless notice of the intention to apply therefor shall have been published in the locality where the matter or thing to be affected may be situated, which notice shall be at least thirty days prior to the introduction into the General Assembly of such bill and in the manner to be provided by law. The evidence of such notice having been published shall be exhibited in the General Assembly before such act shall be passed.

Such published notice serves a purpose similar to the title requirement of legislation; persons affected by the proposed special legislation are placed on notice that its enactment will be proposed to the legislature. This theoretically allows persons singled out by such legislation to apprise the legislature of their views. Since notice is the purpose, such provisions are interpreted like title requirements. This principle is illustrated by *North Ridge General Hospital, Inc. v. City of Oakland Park* (1979). The title of the special law which was upheld as providing reasonable notice provided:

A bill to be entitled: An act relating to the city of Oakland Park, Broward County; extending and enlarging the corporate limits of the City of Oakland Park by including previously unincorporated land into said corporate limits; providing an effective date.

The published notice, also upheld by the Court to present a reasonable notice, read as follows:

NOTICE OF PROPOSED LEGISLATION TO WHOM IT MAY CONCERN:

Notice is hereby given of intention to apply to the 1975 session of the Legislature of the State of Florida for the passage of an act relating to the enlarging and extending of the corporate limits of the city of Oakland Park by including previously unincorporated land into said corporate limits; providing an effective date.

BROWARD COUNTY LEGISLATIVE DELEGATION
By: (s) *[signature of attorney]*
Attorney for the Delegation
April 14, 1975

Both notices were similar and both gave constitutionally adequate notice to the legislature and the public of the contemplated action.

Some state constitutions permit the legislature to dispense with the publication requirement if a referendum on the issue is required in the affected area before the special law becomes effective.

For example, Article III, Section 10 of the Florida Constitution provides that "Such [published] notice shall not be necessary when the law, except the provision for referendum, is conditioned to become effective only upon approval by vote of the electors of the area affected."

CHAPTER 6

THE JUDICIAL BRANCH

Section 42. Court Structure: Sources and Patterns

All state constitutions contain provisions providing for the complete or partial organization of the state's judicial branch. If the intent of the drafters of the Constitution was to prohibit the legislative creation of additional types of courts, the legislature is not constitutionally free to alter that basic structure. *See, generally, Simmons v. Faust* (1978). However, if the state constitution does not expressly or implicitly prohibit the legislature from creating additional courts, then the legislature is free to do so. *Woodmansee v. Smith* (1971). In *Woodmansee, supra*, the then existing provisions of the Vermont Constitution, while not specifically providing for the organization of the state's judiciary, referred to justices of the Supreme Court, and judges of the County Court, Chancery Court, Probate Court and Justice Court. In addition to creating this judicial structure, the legislature had created a separate tier of courts called district courts. Against assertions that the district court system was constitutionally invalid, the Vermont Supreme Court, finding no express or implied limitation on the legislature's authority to create additional courts, upheld the

135

legislature's authority to create the district courts. In reaching this result, the Court refused to apply the maxim *expressio unius est exclusio alterius* to the extent it would have required the Court to hold the mere listing of certain judges in the constitution would preclude the legislature from creating additional courts. As discussed in Chapter 2, the maxim *expressio unius est exclusio alterius* should be applied sparingly and with great caution, to a limiting document such as a state constitution. Even in these instances, it should only be applied when it will effectuate the intent of the constitutional provision. Had the Court in *Woodmansee, supra,* applied the maxim, the Court would have been compelled to declare the district court system invalid because it was not provided for in the constitution.

Article VI, Section 1 of the Illinois Constitution simply states that: "The judicial power is vested in a Supreme Court, an Appellate Court and Circuit Courts." In determining whether this type of provision is intended to prohibit a legislature from creating any additional courts, the courts will generally examine the intent of the drafters of the provision. In the absence of a negative implication from this inquiry, the courts will generally conclude that the legislature is free to create additional or specialized courts. *See, Woodmansee, supra.* However, in certain states, the constitutional draftsmen deprived the judiciary of the authority to proceed with such an investigation of intent. For example, Article V, Section 1 of the Florida Constitution unambiguous-ly conveys the drafters' intent as to the authority of the legislature to create additional courts:

Section 1. Courts.—The judicial power shall be vested in a supreme court, district, courts of appeal, circuit courts and county courts. No *other courts may be established* by the State, any political subdivision or any municipality.... (Emphasis added)

The rationale given for the existence of such provisions is the promotion of a unified court system. *State v. Matthews* (1967). In the absence of such a provision, and subject to the constitutional limits on special legislation discussed in Chapter 5, the legislature would possess the power to create a non-uniform court system. In other words, some counties or cities could have specialized courts not found in comparable governmental entities. To prevent the legislature from establishing this type of confusing judicial structure, many constitutions mandate a uniform court system. For example, Article V, Section 1 of the Florida Constitution provides:

Section 1. Courts.—The judicial power shall be vested in a supreme court, district courts of appeal, circuit courts and county courts. No other courts may be established by the state, any political subdivision or any municipality. The legislature shall, by general law, divide the state into appellate court districts and judicial circuits following county lines. Commissions established by law, or administrative officers or bodies may be granted quasi-judicial power in matters connected with the functions of their offices. The legislature may establish by general law a civil traffic hearing officer system for the purpose of hearing civil traffic infractions. The legislature may, by general law, authorize a military court-martial to be conducted by military judges of the Florida National Guard, with direct appeal of a decision to the District Court of Appeal, First District.

It is possible for a state legislature to abolish an existing court. Thus, the Indiana legislature could abolish Superior Court but it could not do so during the judge's term of office without "violat[ing] the separation of powers provision of the Indiana Constitution." *State v. Monfort* (2000). Under this provision, the legislature is denied authority to create any additional courts, other than municipal courts. In contrast, many state constitutions grant broad authority to the legislative branch to create additional courts which are not enumerated within the state constitution. For example, Article VII, Section 1 of the Montana Constitution provides as follows: "The judicial power of the State is vested in one supreme court, district court, justice courts and such other courts as may be provided by law." Under this explicit type of provision, the Montana legislature possesses broad discretion in creating additional courts or specialized courts without the need for the Montana judiciary to probe the original intent of Article VII, Section 1 of the Montana Constitution. Article VI, Section 1 of the Michigan Constitution represents a hybrid approach to this issue. Under this provision, the legislature possesses authority to create additional courts, but only with a super majority.

The judicial power of the State is vested exclusively in one court of justice which shall be divided into one supreme court, one court of appeals, one trial court of general jurisdiction known as the circuit court, one probate court, and courts of limited jurisdiction that the legislature may establish by a two-thirds vote of the members elected to and serving in each house.

However, even in states which constitutionally prohibit the legislature from creating additional levels of courts or specialized courts, there may be no limit on the number of courts within each level that may be created by the legislature. For example, Article V, Section I of the Florida Constitution limits judicial power to "a Supreme Court, district courts of appeal, circuit courts, and county courts." The use of the plural for all court levels, except the Supreme Court, logically suggests that, subject to constitutional limitation, it is within the discretion of the legislature to determine the appropriate number of courts at each level.

Moreover, the limitation on the judicial branch found in Article V, Section 1 of the Florida Constitution does not preclude legislative creation of executive bodies that perform quasi-judicial functions. These bodies are occasionally referred to as legislative courts. Article V, Section 1 of the Florida Constitution is an example of a provision expressly recognizing that quasi-judicial power in executive agencies is not governed solely by provisions relating to the judiciary:

Commissions established by law or administrative officers or bodies may be granted quasi-judicial power in the matters connected with the functions of their office.

Many state constitutions prescribe the number of justices of the Court of last resort. However, the constitutions usually leave the number of judges in the other courts to be legislatively determined. Most courts of last resort consist of five, seven or nine justices.

State constitutions frequently require a quorum of the court of last resort. *See, e.g.,* Article V, Section 2 of the Nebraska Constitution. Some constitutions impose majority requirements for a decision or a particular type of decision. For example, Article V, Section 2 of the Nebraska Constitution provides as follows:

The Supreme Court shall consist of seven judges, one of whom shall be the Chief Justice. A majority of the judges shall be necessary to constitute a quorum. A majority of the members sitting shall have authority to pronounce a decision except in cases involving the constitutionality of an act of the Legislature. No legislative act shall be declared unconstitutional except by the concurrence of five judges.

Thus, while a simple majority may rule on most issues, a vote of five of the seven judges will be required to declare a legislative act invalid.

Certain constitutions authorize the court of last resort to sit in divisions. Article V, Sections 7 and 9 of the Missouri Constitution contains the following provisions relating to divisions in the Supreme Court.

Section 7. *Supreme court and court of appeals may sit in divisions.* The Supreme Court may sit en banc or in divisions as the Court may determine ... Each division of the Supreme Court ... shall be composed of not less than three judges, at least one of whom shall be a regular judge of the Court. A majority of a division shall constitute a quorum thereof, and all orders, judgments and decrees of a division, as to causes and matter pending before it, shall have the force and effect of those of the Court.

* * *

Section 9. *Transfer of causes to supreme court en banc.* A cause in the supreme court shall be transferred to the court en banc when the members of a division are equally divided in opinion, or when the division shall so order, or on application of the losing party when a member of the division dissents from the opinion therein, or pursuant to supreme court rule.

Many constitutions authorize their collegial courts to sit either *en banc* or as panels. Commonly, these panels or divisions are composed of three judges as illustrated by Article V of the Missouri Constitution referenced above. Some state constitutions require their courts to sit *en banc in* specified instances. By way of illustration, Article V, Section 8 of the Louisiana Constitution generally provides for Louisiana Courts of Appeal to sit in three-judge panels. However, the Court is required to sit *en banc* in the following instance:

A majority of the judges sitting in a case must concur to render judgment. However, in civil matters only, when a judgment of a district court is to be modified or reversed and one judge dissents, the case shall be reargued before a panel of at least five judges prior to rendition of judgment, and a majority must concur to render judgment.

By the intentional omission of specific details concerning court structure, state constitutions generally provide the legislature with great discretion concerning the boundaries and jurisdiction of courts. Such discretion is generally found in provisions relating to intermediate appellate courts and trial courts. Nevertheless, minimal limits may be placed on the legislature's discretion. For example, Article V, Section 11 of the Nebraska Constitution allows the legislature to change the boundaries of appellate judicial districts. However, this same provision limits the legislature by stating that the boundaries "shall be formed of compact territory bounded by county lines."

Most state constitutions require that the judges reside within the geographical boundaries of the judicial district in which they sit. However, many state constitutions usually modify this requirement to prevent the ousting of a judge from office by a territorial change in the boundaries of the judicial district. In addition, some constitutions divide their state into districts and require that Supreme Court Justices be elected from these districts. This resembles legislative re-districting because such districts are frequently modified to reflect population shifts evidenced after each ten-year federal census.

The most common court structure is for a state to have one court of last resort, a level of lower or intermediate appellate courts and two or more levels of trial and specialized courts of original jurisdiction. The court of last resort is frequently called the Supreme Court, while the intermediate court is often called the Court of Appeals. The trial and specialized courts have varying designations which include: District Courts, County Courts, Circuit Courts, Municipal Courts, Magistrate Courts, Probate Courts and Juvenile Courts. Graphically, this structure would appear as follows:

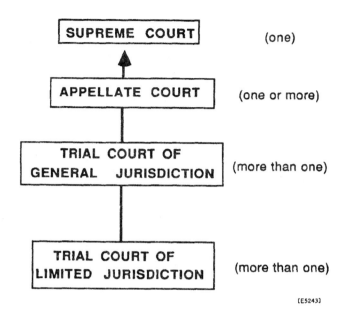

Although not precisely identical to this graphic representation, this type of judicial structure has been adopted in North Carolina and Florida. *See,* North Carolina Constitution, Article IV, Section 2; and Florida Constitution, Article V, Section 1.

In examining state constitutions, three other general judicial structures commonly appear. A graphic representation of the second general category would be as follows:

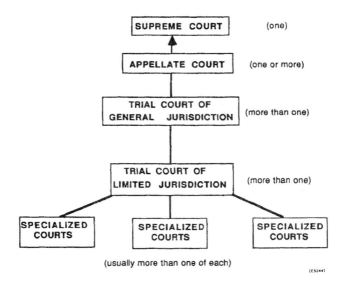

(usually more than one of each)

While generally similar to the first category, because of the presence of both a Supreme Court and an Intermediate Appellate Court, the second category contains an additional layer of trial courts of limited jurisdiction or specialized courts. This type of court structure can be found in a number of states including Michigan and Maryland. *See,* Maryland Constitution, Article IV; and Michigan Constitution, Article VI.

A third type of general court structure is represented by states which possess a simpler structure consisting only of a Supreme Court, trial courts of general jurisdiction and trial courts of limited jurisdiction. Graphically, this structure appears as follows:

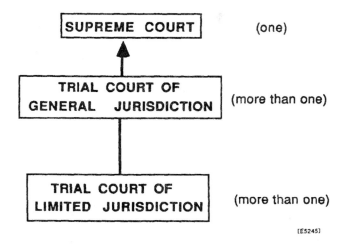

This third type of structure has been adopted by a number of states including Nevada and Utah. *See,* Nevada Constitution, Article VI; Utah Constitution, Article VIII.

The fourth general category of court system can graphically be represented as follows:

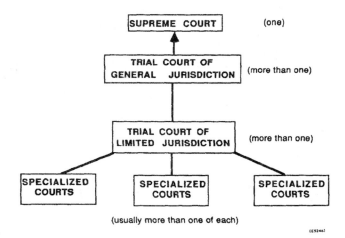

(usually more than one of each)

(E5246)

Under this structure, there is a Supreme Court, but no Intermediate Appellate Courts. While the courts of original jurisdiction are trial courts of general jurisdiction, an additional layer of trial courts of limited jurisdiction or specialized courts are present. This pattern is found in a number of states, including Delaware. *See,* Delaware Constitution, Article IV.

There is nothing magical about these general categories, and much variation exists from state-to-state within each category. Some states simply cannot be classified. For example, under the Oklahoma court structure there exists a Supreme Court and a Court of Criminal Appeals. These parallel courts are both courts of last resort and supreme in their respective areas. In addition, the Oklahoma court system contains civil courts of appeal. However, these courts of appeal do not receive appeals from the state's trial courts. Instead, these courts are "helper" courts and cases are assigned to these courts for review by the Supreme Court. *See, generally,* Article VII of the Oklahoma Constitution. Graphically, this structure appears as follows:

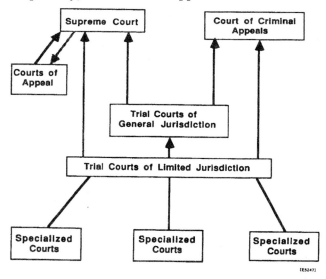

Within these common court structures, the Supreme Court is usually one of limited appellate jurisdiction, and little or no original jurisdiction. The Supreme Court's jurisdiction is usually based on the importance of the issue or the need for uniformity in precedent or both. As an illustration, Article V, Section 5 of the Louisiana Constitution provides that the Supreme Court is granted appellate jurisdiction over cases in which a law or ordinance has been declared unconstitutional or where the death penalty has been imposed. The Louisiana Constitution also grants discretionary jurisdiction to the Supreme Court to entertain certified questions from the lower level appellate courts in Article V, Section 11. Louisiana's Constitution also specifies the scope of review in all cases properly brought before the Supreme Court. *See,* Article V, Section 5 of the Louisiana Constitution.

The proper relationship between levels of appellate courts was addressed by the Court of Appeals of Wisconsin in *State v. Grawien* (1985). In *Grawien,* the intermediate appellate court was asked to overrule precedent, previously established by the Wisconsin court of last resort, the Wisconsin Supreme Court. However, the Court of Appeals refused to so act. In its opinion, the Court described the functions of the two levels of appellate courts. In that court's view, the intermediate appellate court serves as an "error correcting" court. *Id.* The court of last resort serves as a "law declaring" court. *Id.* In other words, the intermediate level appellate court's primary function is to insure that the actions of the court of first instance were free from harmful error.

On the other hand, the court of last resort is not principally concerned with protecting litigants from the errors of the trial courts, although this may be the indirect result of their rulings. Thus, the court of last resort hears only those cases involving issues of law that need to be resolved for the public good. Article VII of the Wisconsin Constitution implements this dichotomy in the following fashion:

Supreme Court: jurisdiction. Section 3.

(1) The supreme court shall have superintending and administrative authority over all courts.

(2) The supreme court has appellate jurisdiction over all courts and may hear original actions and proceedings. The supreme court may issue all writs necessary in aid of its jurisdiction.

(3) The supreme court may review judgments and orders of the courts of appeals, may remove cases from the courts of appeals and may accept cases on certification by the court of appeals.

Court of Appeals. Section 5.

. . . .

(3) The appeals court shall have such appellate jurisdiction in the district, including jurisdiction to review administrative proceedings as the legislature may provide by law, but shall have no original jurisdiction other than by prerogative writ. The appeals court may issue all writs necessary in aid of its jurisdiction and shall have supervisory authority over all actions and proceedings in the courts in the districts.

In *State v. Grawien* (1985), the trial court ruled on certain search and seizure issues. These issues were then appealed to the court of appeals. That court was compelled to determine whether the trial court erroneously interpreted governing search and seizure law. While the existing precedent of the

Wisconsin Supreme Court would have required a
particular result, a recent United States Supreme
Court decision arguably established a lower standard of protection in search and seizure issues than
the existing Wisconsin Supreme Court precedent.
Noting that the interpretation of federal search and
seizure law and the Fourth Amendment to the
United States Constitution had been modified by
the United States Supreme Court subsequent to the
Wisconsin Supreme Court's existing precedent, the
Court was faced with the dilemma of possibly over-
ruling the State Supreme Court's precedent. Confronted with this choice, the Court, finding it lacked
authority to overrule Wisconsin Supreme Court precedent, and acting in accord with its role as an
"error-correcting" court, determined the issues consistently with existing Wisconsin Supreme Court
precedent. The Court then certified the case to the
Wisconsin Supreme Court, the "law declaring"
court. The rationale for the certification of the case
was to afford the Wisconsin Supreme Court an
opportunity to consider the United States Supreme
Court's new interpretation of the Fourth Amendment. As the existing Wisconsin precedent was
more protective than federal law, the Wisconsin
court was not bound by the federal precedent. (For
a discussion of the Adequate and Independent State
Ground Doctrine, *see* Chapter 3.) The Wisconsin
Supreme Court denied certification, leaving the existing search and seizure precedent intact. *See,
State v. Grawien* (1985). In failing to review the
case, the Wisconsin Supreme Court indirectly ruled

on the search and seizure issue, by effectively upholding existing Wisconsin search and seizure law which provided greater protection for the citizens of Wisconsin than the protection provided by the federal constitution. Through this indirect declaration of law, the Court reaffirmed existing precedent.

In some state constitutions, certain levels of courts serve dual roles with both trial court and appellate court responsibilities. For example, Article VI, Section III of the New Jersey Constitution allocates trial court jurisdiction to the Superior Courts of that state, but also establishes an Appellate Division of that court:

> 2. The *Superior Court* shall have original general jurisdiction throughout the State in all causes.
>
> 3. The *Superior Court* shall be divided into an Appellate Division, a Law Division, and a Chancery Division.... (Emphasis added)

In Article VI, Section V of the New Jersey Constitution, this Appellate Division of the Superior Court is authorized to hear appeals from lower trial courts:

> 2. Appeals may be taken to the *Appellate Division of the Superior Court* from the law and chancery divisions of the Superior Court and in such other causes as may be provided by law.
>
> 3. The Supreme Court and the *Appellate Division of the Superior Court* may exercise such

> original jurisdiction as may be necessary to
> the complete determination of any cause on
> review. (Emphasis added.)

When a court plays this dual role, it performs the
function of "error-correcting." While certain states
do not appear to have intermediate Courts of Appeal, frequently intermediate appeals are heard by
courts serving this dual type of Trial/Appellate role.
See, generally, Mississippi Constitution, Article 6.

Beneath Appellate Courts are dual purpose courts
of original jurisdiction or trial courts. Frequently,
by constitution or statute, these courts are divided
into separate divisions for civil and criminal matters. Such courts may also hear specialized matters
such as family, probate and juvenile law. In many
states, another tier of trial courts possessing either
limited jurisdiction or hearing specialized matters
such as family matters, probate and juvenile law
may be established.

Historically, the primary trial courts were divided
into law courts and equity or chancery courts. The
judges of the chancery courts were commonly referred to as Chancellors. The jurisdiction of this
type of court depended upon whether law or equity
was involved. In many states, this distinction is
fading or has been abolished altogether. While the
New Jersey Constitution divides the Superior
Courts into Appellate, Law and Chancery Divisions,
the distinction between law and equity is blurred
when justice requires. Article VI, Section III(4) of
the New Jersey Constitution provides as follows:

Subject to rules of the Supreme Court, the Law Division and the Chancery Division shall each exercise the powers and functions of the other division when the ends of justice so require, and legal and equitable relief shall be granted in any cause so that all matters in controversy between the parties may be completely determined.

The Mississippi Constitution provides a similar solution in Article 6, Section 147:

No judgment or decree in any chancery or circuit court rendered in a civil cause shall be reversed or annulled on the ground of want of jurisdiction to render said judgment or decree, from any error or mistake as to whether the cause in which it was rendered was of equity or common-law jurisdiction; but if the Supreme Court shall find error in the proceedings other than as to jurisdiction, and it shall be necessary to remand the case, the Supreme Court may remand it to that court which, in its opinion, can best determine the controversy.

Many state constitutions have simply abolished the two different courts, so that the principal trial court hears both law and equity issues.

Section 43. Judicial Power: Source and Nature of Jurisdiction

The reader should note that questions of a court's judicial power and jurisdiction will come up again in a somewhat different context in the Chapter on Separation of Powers. It is possible for a court's jurisdiction or judicial power to be traced back to what amounts to inherent power and thus beyond the reach of state legislature. Thus, one State Supreme Court has held that a court's "inherent equitable power," "derived from the historic power of equity courts, cannot be taken away or abridged by the legislature." *Smithberg v. Illinois Municipal Retirement Fund* (2000). This case appears to bear out the authors' belief that a state's inherent power (*see* Chapter 1) is historically divided between the three traditional branches of government. Thus, as a general proposition it is correct to say that state constitutions, to the extent that they address courts, judicial power or jurisdiction, do not grant power to state courts, but rather merely *allocate* judicial power to the judiciary and then limit inherent judicial power further by allocating it among courts created by the constitution. This idea of allocating inherent judicial power to the judiciary seems to be borne out by the following comment, "[t]he courts possess the entire body of the intrinsic judicial power of the state . . . ." *State v. Monfort* (2000) quoting *State ex rel. Kostas v. Johnson* (1946) quoting yet another case. The view has also been taken that inherent judicial power vests in the judiciary even absent any constitutional "allocation." *State v. Buckner* (2000). The creation of courts by state constitutions may be, as discussed in section 41, a limitation on any legislative attempt to do so. State constitutions may (also as discussed in section 41) allocate to the legislature a role in court creation. State constitutions may also choose to allocate to the legislature a role in the allocation of judicial power or jurisdiction among the state courts. In *Smithberg, supra*, there can be little doubt that by constitutional amendment the equitable power of the trial court could be "taken away or abridged." When courts say, as they frequently do, that the constitution grants a certain power to a state court, they are not being as precise as they should be because of power is inherent how can it be granted?

Most state constitutions contain provisions relating to the jurisdiction of the courts specified within the constitution. However, such provisions vary radically from state-to-state. The most common pattern is to allocate to the legislature the authority to prescribe the jurisdiction of the respective courts. Article X, Section 2 of the Rhode Island Constitution illustrates this variety of clause in its most pristine form: "The inferior courts shall have such jurisdiction as may from time to time be prescribed by law. Chancery powers may be conferred on the Supreme Court, but on no other court to any greater extent than is now provided by law."

At the other extreme are constitutions which specify in considerable detail the precise jurisdiction of certain courts. Most commonly, these provisions exist to describe the limited jurisdiction of the court of last resort of the state. Article 6, Section 4 of the Nevada Constitution, describing the jurisdiction of the Nevada Supreme Court, is descriptive of this pattern.

The Supreme Court shall have appellate jurisdiction in all civil cases arising in district courts, and also on questions of law alone in all criminal cases in which the offense charged is within the original jurisdiction of the district courts. The court shall also have power to issue writs of *mandamus*, *certiorari*, *prohibition*, *quo warranto*, and *habeas corpus* and also all writs necessary or proper to the complete exercise of its appellate jurisdiction. Each of the justices shall have power to issue writs of habeas corpus to any part of the state, ... (Emphasis in original).

Buckwalter v. City of Lakeland (1933). Even with a relatively clear constitutional *allocation* of certain judicial power or jurisdiction to a court the role of the legislature in regard to that judicial power on jurisdiction can vary. Much, of course, depends on the exact wording of the relevant provisions of the state constitution. Nevertheless, consider the following views of two different state courts.

"[T]he legislature may put reasonable restrictions upon the constitutional function of the courts–provided that such legislatively imposed restrictions do not defeat or materially impair the exercise of the courts functions." Referring to *Superior Court v. County of Mendocino* (1996). *People v. Lynch* (1999). "[A]s a general rule, whatever power is conferred upon the courts by the Constitution cannot be enlarged or abridged by the Legislature." *Allen v. Butterworth* (2000), citing *State ex rel. Buckwalter v. City of Lakeland*. The reader should note the unfortunate use of the words "conferred upon" rather than the proper "allocated to." One court has used the term "constitutional obligations" of the judiciary which seems closer to "allocate" than "confer." *Best v. Taylor Machine Works* (1997).

A rule similar to the one in *Allen v. Butterworth* has been held to apply even when the court in question was created by the legislature "even though there [was] no constitutional requirement that they be established in the first place." *State v. Monfort* (2000).

A hybrid of these types of provisions exists in several states. Under this variation, the basic confines of jurisdiction are constitutionally provided, but a certain amount of discretion exists for legislative regulation of this jurisdiction. Article 7, Section 4 of the Arkansas Constitution typifies this approach. It provides:

> The Supreme Court, except in cases otherwise provided by this Constitution, shall have appellate jurisdiction only, which shall, be coextensive with the state, under such restrictions as may from time to time be prescribed by law. It shall have a general superintending control over all inferior courts of law and equity; and, in aid of its appellate and supervisory jurisdiction, it shall have power to issue writs of error supersedeas, certiorari, habeas corpus, prohibition, mandamus and quo warranto, and other remedial writs, and to hear and determine the same. Its judges shall be conservators of the peace throughout the

State, and shall severally have power to issue any of the aforesaid writs.

The appropriate exercise of jurisdiction may depend to a large extent on the court structure discussed in the preceding section. Where both an intermediate appellate court and a court of last resort exist, appellate jurisdiction may exist in both forums, but the jurisdiction of the court of last resort may fairly be described as "law-declaring" rather than "error-correcting." *See, State v. Grawien* (1985). Although this policy is effectuated by different methods from state-to-state, this "law-declaring" function of the court of last resort is normally emphasized by either court decision or constitutional provision. A typical allocation of appellate jurisdiction which recognizes this distinction is found in Article V of the Missouri Constitution. Under Section 3 of that Article, the Supreme Court of Missouri is given exclusive jurisdiction in certain specified matters of great public importance. All other appellate jurisdiction is allocated to the court of appeals:

The supreme court shall have exclusive appellate jurisdiction in all cases involving the validity of a treaty or statute of the United States, or of a statute or provision of the constitution of this state, the construction of revenue laws of this state, the title to any state office and in all cases where the punishment imposed is death. The court of appeals shall have general appellate jurisdiction in all cases except those within the exclusive jurisdiction of the supreme court.

In addition to its specified exclusive jurisdiction, the Missouri Supreme Court has jurisdiction over other matters considered by the Court of Appeals where it is asserted that the matter involved is of great public importance, or modifies existing precedent. Section 10 of Article V of the Missouri Constitution implements this jurisdiction in the following language.

Cases pending in the court of appeals shall be transferred to the supreme court when any participating judge dissents from the majority opinion and certifies that he deems said opinion to be contrary to any previous decision of the supreme court or of the court of appeals, or any district of the court of appeals. Cases pending in the court of appeals may be transferred to the supreme court by order of the majority of judges of the participating district of the court of appeals, after the opinion, or by order of the supreme court before or after opinion because of the general interest or importance of a question involved in the case, or for the purpose of reexamining the existing law, or pursuant to supreme court rule. The supreme court may finally determine all causes coming to it from the court of appeals, whether by certification, transfer or certiorari, the same as on original appeal.

The combined effect of these two sections is to establish limited exclusive jurisdiction for the Supreme Court, while at the same time creating a mechanism whereby that court can exercise limited general appellate jurisdiction. Because of the selectivity of this limited general appellate jurisdiction, the court is theoretically free to perform a unifying function, both as to the judiciary and the precedent of the state.

These types of jurisdictional limitations on the Supreme Court are quite common. Many state constitutions recognize other areas where final Supreme Court review is deemed appropriate. A number of states consider the regulation of public utilities by a statewide agency of such importance that it is subject to review by direct appeal to the court of last resort. Article IV, Section 12(1) of the North Carolina Constitution authorizes this type of review if the legislature enacts enabling legislation: "The Supreme Court also has jurisdiction to review, when authorized by law, direct appeals from a final order or decision of the North Carolina Utilities Commission." Another area where Supreme Court review is constitutionally recognized in some states is bond validation proceedings. *See, e.g.,* Florida Constitution, Article V, Section 3(b)(2).

Although generally falling under the nomenclature of separation of powers, legislative (or executive) interference with judicial power or jurisdiction of courts is obviously part of the discussion in this section also. The Supreme Court of Wisconsin has devised what may be the most complete system of looking at this problem. "[Supreme Court] must first determine whether the subject matter of the statute is within powers constitutionally granted [allocated?] to the legislature." The court must then ask "Whether the subject matter of the statute falls within powers constitutionally granted [allocated?] to the judiciary." Last, it must be asked if the subject matter of the statute is within ... an area of shared powers. Such a "statute is constitutional if it does not unduly burden or substantially interfere with either branch." *State v. Horn* (1999).

It was held in *State v. Burchfield* (1999) that although *Horn* was limited to its facts, "it provides the direction and guidance necessary to decide the issue presented here."

The "law-declaring" versus "error-correcting" dichotomy found in states with both Intermediate Appellate Courts and a court of last resort creates a patchwork of jurisdiction whereby certain cases are appealable directly to the Supreme Court from the trial court level. For example, under Article V, Section 3 of the Missouri Constitution referenced above, an appeal from a case in which the death penalty was imposed is directly to the Supreme Court, without consideration of the issue by the Court of Appeals. The same result would be true if the trial court's ruling involved any of the exclusive jurisdictional subjects contained in that section. In all other appellate matters, Supreme Court review could only occur if the matters were first considered by the Court of Appeals, and if one of the jurisdictional requirements of Article V, Section 10 of the Missouri Constitution were satisfied.

Many courts of last resort possess limited original jurisdiction. This jurisdiction may exist either independently or to assist the court in the exercise of its other jurisdiction. Commonly, this original jurisdiction is exercised through a writ proceeding. Article V, Section 5 of the South Carolina Constitution is representative and provides as follows: "The Supreme Court shall have power to issue writs or orders of injunction, mandamus, quo warranto, prohibition, certiorari, habeas corpus, and other original and remedial writs."

In a court structure consisting of both a court of last resort and an intermediate appellate court, the intermediate court hears most cases which are appealed from the trial and specialized courts. In addition, the courts may also review decisions of statewide administrative agencies. Frequently, such courts also possess the original jurisdiction to issue various writs. Article IV, Section 3 of the Ohio Constitution typifies the range of jurisdiction commonly afforded intermediate appellate courts:

(1) The courts of appeals shall have original jurisdiction in the following:

    (a) *Quo Warranto;*

    (b) *Mandamus;*

    (c) *Habeas Corpus;*

    (d) Prohibition;

    (e) *Procedendo;*

    (f) In any cause on review as may be necessary to its complete determination.

(2) Courts of appeals shall have such jurisdiction as may be provided by law to review and

affirm, modify, or reverse judgments or final
orders of the courts of record inferior to the
court of appeals within the district and shall
have such appellate jurisdiction as may be
provided by law to review and affirm, modify,
or reverse final orders or actions of administrative officers or agencies.

The legislative control provided by this provision
is important for several reasons. First, the limiting
provision insures no conflict between the appellate
jurisdiction of the intermediate appellate court and
the court of last resort. Second, the provision allows
for the allocation of appellate jurisdiction between
the intermediate appellate court and the lower
courts. Thus, even though the lower courts are
principally trial courts, they can be allocated appellate jurisdiction over courts below them. Third, the
legislature can allocate the review of administrative
agencies between the intermediate appellate courts
and the principal level of trial courts. Generally, the
intermediate appellate court reviews statewide
agencies and the principal trial court reviews local
government agencies.

The principal level of trial courts review major
civil and criminal cases. In addition, many decide
specialized issues such as probate matters. They
also frequently have appellate jurisdiction over the
courts beneath them and over some administrative
agencies. For example, Section 112(5) of the Kentucky Constitution provides as follows: "The Circuit
Court shall have original jurisdiction of all justicia-
ble causes not vested in some other court. It shall

have appellate jurisdiction as may be provided by law."

Generally, these mixed trial court/appellate court function provisions have been held valid. In *Village of Monroeville v. Ward* (1969)*, the court held that the legislature could confer appellate jurisdiction on a trial court to hear appeals from a trial court of more limited jurisdiction.

Where the principal trial court serves as an appellate court for courts of limited jurisdiction beneath it, decisions made in its appellate capacity can usually be reviewed only by common law certiorari. A writ would be proper in the intermediate appellate court, in the event there is no intermediate court, then in the court of last resort. *See generally, People v. Meyers* (1979). Review by common law certiorari is not a second appeal, but rather, is a limited review to test (1) whether the courts below had jurisdiction, and (2) whether there was a departure from the essential requirements of law. Furthermore, it is a discretionary type of review.

In many states there exists a tier of courts performing trial court functions, but possessing limited original jurisdiction. This jurisdiction is circumscribed by the jurisdiction of the principal level of trial courts in the state, and is frequently determined by statute. In Kentucky, district courts qualify as trial courts of limited jurisdiction, while circuit courts are the principal trial courts of general jurisdiction. Article 113(6) of the Kentucky Constitution

* Reversed on other grounds, *Ward v. Village of Monroeville* (1972).

describes the jurisdiction of the district courts as follows: "The district court shall be a court of limited jurisdiction and shall exercise original jurisdiction as may be provided by the general assembly."

A court structure consisting of a court of last resort, an intermediate appellate court, trial courts of general jurisdiction, and trial courts of limited jurisdiction can be generally summarized as follows. The court of last resort is a court of limited appellate jurisdiction, with extremely limited original jurisdiction. The intermediate appellate court is one of general appellate jurisdiction, which is generally described as including all appellate jurisdiction not exercised by the court of last resort or any other court. It also possesses general writ jurisdiction. The principal trial court's original jurisdiction is generally described as all such jurisdiction not exercised by another court. This general trial court's appellate jurisdiction is usually over courts of limited jurisdiction. These lower courts generally have no appellate jurisdiction, frequently no writ jurisdiction, and limited original jurisdiction. Graphically, this system could be described as follows:

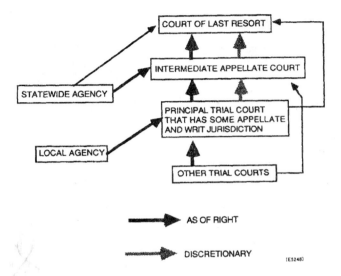

Section 44.   Judicial Power: Rule Making

Many state constitutions allocate rule making power to the court of last resort. An example of this can be found in Article VI, Section 21 of the Colorado Constitution. It provides:

The supreme court shall make and promulgate rules governing the administration of all courts and shall make and promulgate rules governing practice and procedure in civil and criminal cases, except that the general assembly shall have the power to provide simplified procedure in county courts for claims not exceeding five hundred dollars and for the trial of misdemeanors.

In viewing the source of this rule making authority, it has been argued that such provisions are merely "a declaration of the inherent powers of the judicial branch of government." *See, Page v. Clark* (1979); *See also, Miller v. State* (1977). This position is not universal since it has also been asserted that this type of provision is "a grant of power which would not otherwise exist...." *See, Page v. Clark* (1979).

In some states, rule making power is divided between the court of last resort and the legislature. For example, in Article IV, Section 15 of the Alaska Constitution, rule making power is primarily allocated to the Supreme Court. The section continues "[t]hese rules may be changed by the legislature by two-thirds vote of the members elected to each house." The Florida Constitution is similar. While it does not permit legislative amendment of the rules, it does permit legislative repeal. Article V, Section 2(a) of the Florida Constitution provides "[t]hese rules may be repealed by general law enacted by two-thirds vote of the membership of each house of the legislature."

Difficulties arise when it becomes important to distinguish between procedural matters which are subject to judicial rule making authority, and substantive matters which are properly legislative concerns. In different settings, courts have struggled to distinguish these concepts. In *State v. J.A., Jr.* (1979) a Florida Appellate Court distinguished these concepts as follows:

Substantive law prescribes duties and rights under our system of government, and the legislature is responsible for enacting such law. Procedural law concerns the means and methods to apply and enforce those duties and rights, and the supreme court determines procedural law through the promulgation of rules. (Citation omitted). Substantive law creates, defines and regulates rights, while procedural law is the legal machinery by which substantive law is made effective. (Citation omitted).

In *Suchit v. Baxt* (1980), a New Jersey court argued for an outcome determinative test:

If the rule can determine in and of itself the outcome of the proceeding, it is generally substantive. If it is but one step in the ladder to final determination and can effectively aid a court function, it is procedural in nature and within the Supreme Court's power of rule promulgation.

In spite of attempts to draw clear distinctions between these terms, it is generally recognized that a definitional approach is futile. "[I]t is simplistic to assume that all law is divided neatly between 'substance' and 'procedure.' A rule of procedure may have an impact upon the substantive result and be no less a rule of procedure on that account." *Busik v. Levine* (1973). In *Busik, supra*, the court held that a judicial rule authorizing prejudgment interest in tort actions was within the court's procedural rule making power. In *Laudenberger v. Port Authority of Allegheny County* (1981), another prejudgment interest case, the Pennsylvania Supreme Court held that such a rule was within its rule making power, and in doing so recognized that: "Most rules of procedure will eventually reverberate to the substantive rights and duties of those involved." *Id.*

Evidence is an area with perhaps the most potential for overlap between matters of substance and procedure. As a general rule, most courts have concluded that evidentiary matters are principally procedural and thus within the jurisdiction of the judiciary. *State ex rel. Collins v. Seidel* (1984); *Vogel v. State* (1980).

Where the judiciary believes that the legislature has invaded the rule making jurisdiction of the court by enacting legislation, it is argued that the court should consider adopting the offensive statute as a procedural rule, to avoid a confrontation with the legislature. *See, Adams v. Rubinow* (1968). Cooperation between the judicial and legislative branches in this area has been encouraged. *State v. Mitchell* (1983). When cooperation is not possible, the court possesses the power to declare unconstitutional a statute that invades the court's rule making authority. For example, in *State v. Connery* (1983), the court held that a court rule governing the time in which a notice of appeal had to be filed superseded an earlier statute on the same subject.

Courts regard their rule making power as inviolable. In *Goldberg v. Eighth Judicial Dist. Court* (1977) the court stated that:

Pursuant to [the doctrine of separation of powers], it is clear that the judiciary, as a co-equal branch of government, has inherent powers to administer its affairs [citation omitted] which include rule making and other incidental powers reasonable and necessary to carry out the duties required for the administration of justice. Any infringement by the legislature upon such power is in degradation of our tripartite system of government and strictly prohibited. (Citation omitted).

Not all state constitutions expressly allocate exclusive rule making authority to the judiciary. Article V, Section 14 of the Iowa Constitution typifies a provision which appears to allocate this authority to the legislature: "It shall be the duty of the General Assembly to provide for the carrying into effect of [the judicial] article, and to provide for a general system of practice in all Courts of this State." Despite this provision, the Iowa Supreme Court in *Iowa Civil Liberties Union v. Critelli* (1976) held that this provision did not allocate exclusive rule making power to the legislature because the court possessed inherent power to make rules. Nevertheless, if the legislature established a particular rule of practice or procedure, then it could not be superseded by a judge made rule. In Washington, the legislature has statutorily authorized the Supreme Court to adopt practice and procedure rules. *State v. Fields* (1975). This was necessary because the Washington Constitution appears to be silent on that exact point. However, in *Fields, supra*, the Supreme Court asserted that it could have enacted rules under its own inherent rule making power.

In Connecticut, a hybrid rule prevails. The legislature possesses no authority to make rules of practice and procedure for the two courts created by the Constitution, the Supreme Court and the Superior Court. As to the other courts, which are creations of the legislature, the legislature has limited rule making power. In *Adams v. Rubinow* (1968), this authority was described as follows: "[The legislature] has the power to make reasonable rules of administration, practice and procedure provided that they do not significantly interfere with the orderly operation of the court while it remains in existence as a court."

Section 45.   Judicial Power: Advisory Opinions

In the absence of an express constitutional provision creating jurisdiction in the court of last resort to issue advisory opinions, it is generally held that there is no authority to issue such opinions. *See, e.g., In re Constitutionality of House Bill No. 222* (1936). However, a number of state constitutions including Colorado, Florida, Maine, Massachusetts, New Hampshire, Rhode Island and South Dakota contain provisions authorizing the court of last resort to issue advisory opinions.

Under Chapter III, Article II of the Massachusetts Constitution, as amended by Article LXXXV, the Supreme Judicial Court of Massachusetts may issue advisory opinions in the following instances: "Each branch of the legislature, as well as the governor or the council, shall have authority to require the opinions of the justices of the supreme judicial court, upon important questions of law, and upon solemn occasions."

While such power appears virtually unlimited, the court has limited its jurisdiction in such matters. The court only exercises its jurisdiction in instances where the requesting official or branch has pending before it a question which raises legitimate doubts concerning its authority to act, and where resolution of that doubt is necessary to enable it to properly act. *See, In re Opinion of the Justices* (1929).

Section 46.   Judicial Power: Lawyer Governance and the Regulation of the Practice of Law

Many state constitutions allocate to the court of last resort the regulation of the practice of law. For example, Article VIII, Section 4 of the Utah Constitution provides in pertinent part: "The Supreme Court by rule shall govern the practice of law, including admission to practice law and the conduct and discipline of persons admitted to practice law." However, in instances where the state constitutions do not expressly provide for the regulation of the state bar, including admission to the practice of law, power to regulate such activities has been found in the inherent power of the courts. *See, Enquire Printing and Publishing Company, Inc. v. O'Reilly* (1984). For example, in Iowa the Supreme Court has "claim[ed] and exercise[d] the inherent power to admit those who practice law before our courts and assume[d] the responsibility to discipline them." *Sonksen v. Legal Services Corporation* (1986). Likewise, in *Laffey v. Court of Common Pleas* (1983), the court held that this power is the exclusive property of the court of last resort and may not be exercised by a lower court.

Occasionally, a legislature may enact statutes which authorize non-lawyers to perform acts which arguably resemble the practice of law. In *Bennion, Van Camp, Hagen & Ruhl v. Kassler Escrow, Inc.* (1981), the Supreme Court of Washington held that the legislature could not statutorily authorize real estate agents to:

> [S]elect, prepare, and complete documents and instruments relating to such loan, forbearance, or extension of credit, sale, or other transfer of real or personal property, limited to deeds, promissory notes, deeds of trust, mortgages, security agreements, assignments, releases, satisfactions, reconveyances, contracts for sale or purchase of real or personal property, and bills of sale . . . .

The Court distinguished what appeared to be similar situations in several other states, including Minnesota, Georgia, Wisconsin, and Rhode Island because of unstated differences in their constitutions and because the statutes at issue were not as broad as the challenged Washington statute. *Bennion, Van Camp, Hagen & Ruhl v. Kassler Escrow, Inc.* (1981).

The Georgia case cited in *Bennion* was *Georgia Bar Association v. Lawyers Title Insurance Corpora-*

tion (1966). In that case, the Georgia Supreme
Court considered a Georgia statute allowing land
title companies to:

> [p]repare such papers as it thinks proper, or
> necessary, in connection with a title which it
> proposes to insure, in order, in its opinion, for it
> to be willing to insure such title, where no charge
> is made by it for such papers . . . . *Id*.

The Court's reasoning recognized the long judicial involvement by the legislature "in aiding the
judiciary in the discharge [of the judicial function of
regulating the practice of law]," and held that the
legislature had not usurped the judicial function to
regulate the practice of law. *Id*.

A different approach was taken by the Supreme
Court of Minnesota in *Cowern v. Nelson* (1940)
another case cited in *Bennion*. *Cowern, supra*, held
that a similar provision in the laws of Minnesota
did not authorize the practice of law. The Minnesota statute, in banning the unauthorized practice of
law, provided that it did not "prohibit anyone,
acting as a broker for the parties or agent of one of
the parties to a sale or trade or lease of property or
to a loan, from drawing or assisting in drawing,
with or without charge therefor, such papers as may
be incident to such sale, trade, lease, or loan." *Id*.
The Court recognized it was not possible to clearly
delineate the boundary between the practice of law
and that which "may also be done by others without wrongful invasion of the lawyers' field." *Id*. As
a result, in many instances, a determination in this

area may turn on whether the conduct authorized by the legislature was actually the practice of law, rather than whether the legislature could authorize a lay person to practice law.

Questions concerning this issue are not limited to the question of whether lay persons may practice law. The Florida Supreme Court has held that the Florida legislature may not grant immunity from disciplinary proceedings to lawyers under investigation for alleged disciplinary infractions. *Ciravolo v. The Florida Bar* (1978). This holding left unanswered the question of whether the use of such nonimmunized testimony in attorney disciplinary proceeding violates the self-incrimination provisions of the federal constitution.

The judiciary jealously guards its prerogatives in this area. The Florida Supreme Court, while recognizing the laudatory purpose of legislation that made licensing examination accessible to blind and deaf persons taking those exams, nevertheless held that any attempt to apply such statutory modifications to the bar examination would violate the court's inherent and constitutionally recognized role in regulating the profession of law. *In re Florida Board of Bar Examiners* (1977).

A somewhat different twist to this issue occurred in Pennsylvania where that state's Commonwealth Court held that the Lobbying Disclosure Act which applied to both lawyers and non-lawyers could not be applied to the former, "when [he or she was] performing such a service on behalf of their clients,

... " because to do so would be an invalid attempt to regulate "the practice of law." *Gmerek v. State Ethics Commission* (2000).

Section 47. Qualifications Required by Constitution for Judicial Office

The most common qualifications for judicial office found in state constitutions pertain to age, United States citizenship, state residency, and admission to the practice of law in that state, sometimes for a specific length of time. The most common ages are 25, 30 and 35, although not as many state constitutions impose age requirements for their judicial officers as they do for the office of governor. One reason for this is that legislatures are more involved in establishing qualifications for judicial office than gubernatorial office. There would not appear to be any federal Fourteenth Amendment equal protection infirmity with respect to such minimum age requirements. (*See* the discussion of the mandatory retirement cases later in this chapter.) United States citizenship and state residency, usually for set periods of time, are common constitutional requirements for judicial office. Neither requirement appears to offend existing federal equal protection analysis. In instances of this type, the federal courts have traditionally deferred to the states involving issues concerning the qualifications for holding policy making positions at the state level. *See, e.g., Foley v. Connelie* (1978). Most state constitutions also impose durational state bar membership as a pre-requisite for judicial office. In certain instances, the length of bar membership requirements required may vary, depending on which court is involved. Section 122 of the Kentucky Constitution contains most of the requirements for judicial office discussed above. It provides:

> To be eligible to serve as a Justice of the Supreme Court or a Judge of the Court of Appeals, Circuit Court or District Court a person must be a citizen of the United States, licensed to practice law in the Courts of this Commonwealth, and have been a resident of this Commonwealth, and of the district from which he is elected for two years next preceding his taking office. In addition, to be eligible to serve as a Justice of the Supreme Court or a Judge of the Court of Appeals or Circuit Court a person must have been a licensed attorney for at least eight years. No District Judge shall serve who has not been a licensed attorney for at least two years.

The eligibility section of the Kentucky Constitution quoted above refers only to Supreme Court justices, court of appeals judges and district judges. The Kentucky Constitution also provides for county judges and justices of the peace, both of which are described as conservators of the peace. *See*, Kentucky Constitution, Sections 140 and 142. Since the Constitution does not describe their qualifications for office, the establishment of qualifications for these positions is left to the legislature.

Many state constitutions do not explicitly require that judges be either lawyers or members of the state bar. The existence of non-lawyer judges has raised issues as to whether such a judge may administer his office consistently with due process standards. However, the ability of a judge to meet due process standards does not appear to turn on bar membership or eligibility to practice law. *Treiman v. State ex rel. Miner, Jr.* (1977); *People v. Sabri* (1977).

A number of state constitutions provide for mandatory retirement of judges at a set age. Article V, Section 23(B) of the Louisiana Constitution is an example. "Mandatory Retirement. Except as otherwise provided in this section, a judge shall not remain in office beyond his seventieth birthday." In 1979, a federal district court held that a similar provision of the Pennsylvania Constitution violated the due process and equal protection guarantees of the United States Constitution. *Malmed v. Thornburgh* (1979). This was reversed by the United States Third Circuit Court of Appeals when it ruled that Pennsylvania's mandatory requirement standards met the minimal rationality due process and equal protection standards. *Malmed v. Thornburgh* (1980). As a result, it would appear that such provisions do not violate the United States Constitution.

Section 48. Selection and Retention of Judges

State constitutional provisions relating to the selection and retention of judges vary from state-to-state. Generally, judges are selected by the Gover-

nor, a Judicial Nominating Commission, the electorate, or a combination of these entities.

While at one time most state court judges were
elected, there is now a definite trend toward the
selection or nomination of judges through the medi-
um of a commission which screens the qualifications of potential judges. Article VI of the Colorado
Constitution contains a number of relatively common provisions implementing a Judicial Nominating Commission. Under Section 24 of that article, a
judicial nominating commission is created for the
State Supreme Court and intermediate appellate
court; and a separate judicial nominating commission for each judicial district in the state. The
commissions are composed of both lawyers and non-
lawyers. Under Section 20 of Article VI of the
Colorado Constitution, where a vacancy exists at a
court level, these commissions forward to the governor a list of two or three nominees to fill the
vacancy. Ultimately, it is the governor's decision,
provided he acts timely, as to which of the nominees
on the list is appointed to fill the vacancy.

While most commonly judges are initially selected
in this fashion, most state constitutions require a
judge to be regularly subjected to review by the
electorate. Such elections are generally nonpartisan,
and are of a retentive rather than elective nature.
In such elections, the voters are asked either to
retain the judge for another term or to reject the
judge. Some state constitutions actually contain the
ballot language required. For example, Article VI,
Section 38 of the Arizona Constitution, which estab-

lishes a system whereby a sitting judge must file to indicate his desire to be retained in office, the Constitution provides as follows:

The name of any justice or judge whose declaration is filed as provided in this section shall be placed on the appropriate official ballot at the next regular general election under a nonpartisan designation and in substantially the following form:

Shall _____, (Name of Justice or Judge) of the _____ Court be retained in office? Yes___ No___ (Mark X after one).

If the judge is not retained, then at the conclusion of his term the office becomes vacant. Even in a system where all or part of the judiciary is elected, when a vacancy occurs in the elected judicial office, the governor fills the vacancy either until the end of the term or until the next election.

Section 49. Discipline and Removal of Judges

Many state constitutions contain express provisions authorizing the removal of judges from office and other forms of discipline. The traditional method of removal of judges is the process of impeachment. This process contemplates investigation and filing of impeachment charges by the lower house of the state legislature. Normally, the impeachment is followed by a trial on the charges in the Senate or upper house with the Chief Justice of the Supreme Court presiding. Impeachment is discussed in more detail in Chapter 11, and will not be discussed further other than in comparison to other more modern methods of discipline and removal.

Impeachment is an inefficient method of disciplining a judge or removing him from office because of its time consuming nature and expense. As a result, it has become common for state constitutions to provide more efficient alternative methods for dealing with these concerns. Representative of this trend is Article IV, Section 17(2) of the North Carolina Constitution. It provides:

Additional method of removal of Judges. The General Assembly shall prescribe a procedure, in addition to impeachment and address set forth in [Section 17(1)] for the removal of a Justice or Judge of the General Court of Justice for mental or physical incapacity interfering with the performance of his duties which is, or is likely to become, permanent, and for the censure and removal of a Justice or Judge of the General Court of Justice for wilful misconduct in office, wilful and persistent failure to perform his duties, habitual intemperance, conviction of a crime involving moral turpitude, or conduct prejudicial to the administration of justice that brings the judicial office into disrepute.

Prior to the enactment of Section 17(2), there had been two methods of removing judges from office under the North Carolina Constitution: (1) impeachment for misbehavior in office, and (2) "address" which allowed the legislature by a two-thirds vote of each house to remove a judge for physical or mental incapacity. The Supreme Court of North Carolina indicated in *In re Peoples* (1978), that the driving force behind Section 17(2) was the need for a workable alternative to the "cumbersome and antiquated" machinery of impeachment. The court observed that no judge had been removed by impeachment at least since 1868, and no judge had ever been removed by "address."

The response by the North Carolina legislature in implementing Section 17(2) is typical of the evolving alternatives to impeachment found in other states. The Legislature created a Judicial Standards Commission which investigates charges of judicial misconduct of the type found in Section 17(2) other than allegations of mental or physical incapacity. This Commission makes recommendations to the State Supreme Court pertaining to the potential discipline of a judge. *In re Peoples, supra.*

Some state constitutions themselves create the mechanism for the discipline and removal of judges. Section 121 of the Kentucky Constitution establishes a commission of this variety:

Retirement and Removal. Subject to rules of procedure to be established by the Supreme Court, and after notice and hearing, any Justice of the Supreme Court or Judge of the Court of Appeals, Circuit Court or District Court may be retired for disability or suspended without pay or removed for good cause by a commission composed of one Judge of the Court of Appeals, selected by that

Court, one Circuit Judge and one District Judge selected by majority vote of the Circuit Judges and District Judges, respectively, one member of the Bar appointed by its governing body, and two persons, not members of the Bench or Bar, appointed by the Governor. The commission shall be a State body whose members shall hold office for four-year terms. Its actions shall be subject to judicial review by the Supreme Court.

This section is intended to be an alternative to impeachment because the removal of judges (described as "civil officers") by impeachment is authorized in Section 68 of the Kentucky Constitution. The California Supreme Court in *McComb v. Commission on Judicial Performance* (1977), described discipline and removal of judges through a Qualification Commission as "a constitutional alternative to the impeachment process."

In Texas there are four different constitutionally described means of disciplining and removing judges. They are described in *Matter of Carrillo* (1976). The first is impeachment. The second is an action by the Texas Supreme Court upon recommendation by the Judicial Qualification Commission. These two are consistent with the procedures in North Carolina and Kentucky, which have already been discussed. The third is removal by the governor on the address of two-thirds of each house of the legislature. As described in Article XV, Section 8 of the Texas Constitution, this procedure is not limited to physical and mental disability, but rather is designed to cover "wilful neglect of duty, incompetency, habitual drunkenness, oppression in office, or other reasonable cause which shall not be sufficient ground for impeachment. . . . '' The provision requires notice of the grounds of address and an opportunity to be heard prior to removal. The fourth method is by Supreme Court action upon charges filed by lawyers practicing before the judge in question. As provided in Article XV, Section 6 of the Texas Constitution, the fourth method pertains only to district courts, the principal trial court of that state. Under its provisions, at least ten lawyers practicing in that particular court, who are licensed to practice before the Supreme Court, must present grounds for removal based upon their knowledge or upon written oaths of creditable witnesses. They include ''incompeten[ce] to discharge the duties of his office, . . . [guilt] of partiality, or oppression, or other official misconduct, or . . . habits and conduct . . . [of such a nature] as to render him unfit to hold such office, or . . . [negligent failure] to perform his duties as judge; or [failure] to execute in a reasonable measure the business in his courts. . . .''

CHAPTER 7

SEPARATION OF POWERS

Section 50. Separation of Powers as a Concept

Although certainly not exclusively an American phenomenon, the separation of governmental powers into three branches is a hallmark of the American system of government. The doctrine is based on the belief that the concentration of power in one branch of government risks despotism. *See e.g. United States v. Morrison* (2000), *Kasler v. Lockyer* (2000) and *Holmberg v. Holmberg* (1999). It is interesting to note that it has been stated that "[t]he doctrine of the separation of powers [is not meant to] promote efficiency . . . ." *Quoting Myers v. United States* (1926) (Brandeis, J., dissenting). *State Auditor v. Joint Committee on Legislative Research* (1997). The same court again quoting from Justice Brandeis dissenting opinion in *Myers* made the point in a different case that "The purpose [of separation of powers] [is] not to avoid friction, but, by means of the inevitable friction incident to distribution of governmental powers among three departments [branches], to save the people from autocracy." *Missouri Coalition for Environment v. Joint Committee on Administrative Rules* (1997).

186

Another court, however, has viewed separation of powers as "a practical measure to efficiently facilitate the administration of state government by the assignment of numerous labors to designated governmental authorities," *Wegleitner v. Sattler* (1998) (citing case). The doctrine has been described as "compliment[ing] the notion of checks and balances...." *Opinion of the Justices* (1997). The separation of power doctrine finds its philosophical support in the writings of a number of political philosophers who influenced the development of government in the United States. Despite the pervasiveness of the Doctrine in the American system, the degree to which legislative, executive and judicial power are to be confined to those branches of government has never been totally clarified. In the intellectual confrontation between Justices Sutherland and Holmes in *Springer v. Government of the Philippine Islands* (1928), Justice Sutherland, writing for the majority, argued for strict lines of demarcation between the branches of government "unless otherwise expressly provided or incidental to the powers delegated to each branch." *Id.* Justice Holmes, in dissent, countered that "however we may disguise it by veiling words we do not and cannot carry out the distinction between the legislative and executive branches with mathematical precision and divide the branches into watertight compartments...." *Id.*

Consider roughly the same idea expressed by a state court. It appears to the majority, if indeed not the unanimous, view.

> Although the purpose of the doctrine of separation of powers is to protect one branch of government against the overreaching of any other branch, common boundaries exist among the branches, and the doctrine does not require a "hermetic sealing off" of the branches of government one from another. *State v. Gilfillan* (2000), referencing *State v. Prentiss* (1989).

The same idea has been put a bit differently by the Supreme Court of Wisconsin.

> Shared powers lie at the intersections of ... exclusive core constitutional powers. These " '[g]reat borderlands of power' " are not exclusive to any one branch. [Citing cases.] "While each branch jealously guards its exclusive powers, our system of government envisions the branches found in the borderlands." [Citations omitted.] *State v. Horn* (1999).*

Courts have, however, held that the Separation of Powers Doctrine must be "strictly construed." *Scheer v. Zeigler* (2000), citing *Vaughn v. Knopf* (1995). The nexus between strict construction and the idea of overlap may be explained by this comment from the Supreme Judicial Court of Massachusetts, "while the limitations of [separation of powers] must be scrupulously observed, 'separation of powers does not require three "watertight compartments" within the government.' " *Commonwealth v. Gonsalves* (2000) citing *Opinion of the Justices* (1948).

---

* *Horn* has been limited to its facts, *see Horn* and *State v. Burchfield* (1999).

The United States Constitution does not contain a specific provision dealing with separation of powers. Nonetheless, the federal judiciary has found the separation of powers doctrine implicit in the constitutional structure which grants power to the legislature, the executive and the judiciary. State constitutions also allocate the state's inherent power to legislature, executive and judiciary. As a result, the Separation of Powers Doctrine would also appear to be implicit at the state level. One court has described separation of powers as " 'embedded in the constitutional framework of [its] state government....' " *State ex. rel. Ohio Academy of Trial Lawyers v. Sheward* (1999), citing *State v. Warner* (1990).

It is interesting to note that state courts have differed as to the similarity between separation of powers at the state and federal levels of government. Compare the opinion of the Supreme Court of Kansas that "as to doctrine of separation of powers, however, the Kansas Constitution is almost identical to the federal constitution," (*Gleason v. Samaritan Home* (1996) (cited case omitted)) to the view of the Supreme Judicial Court of Maine that " 'the separation of governmental powers mandated by the Maine Constitution is much more rigorous than the same principle as applied to the federal government.' " *New England Outdoor Center v. Commissioner of Inland Fisheries and Wildlife* (2000), citing *State v. Hunter* (1982).

However, most state constitutions also contain a specific mandate providing for separation of powers.

Typical of these is Article III, Section 1 of the New Jersey Constitution: "The powers of government shall be divided among three distinct branches, the legislative, executive, and judicial. No person or persons belonging to or constituting one branch shall exercise any of the powers properly belonging to either of the others, except as expressly provided in this Constitution." In spite of the fact that this provision appears to restate the Sutherland view in *Springer, supra*, the reality of its interpretation seems closer to the Holmes view expressed in his *Springer, supra* dissent. In interpreting this provision the New Jersey Supreme Court has held that this constitutional command is not an absolute, does not preclude cooperation between the branches, and is basically designed to insure the existence of a system of checks and balances to prevent excessive concentration of power in one branch of government. *State v. Leonardis* (1977).

Issues concerning separation of powers tend to fall into categories involving either the usurpation of power by one branch of government by another or attempts by one branch to delegate its power to another. *See State ex. rel. Shepherd v. Nebraska Equal Opportunity Commission* (1997). Since all state governments are composed of three branches, a simple calculation would suggest that there are six potential categories of attempted usurpation and invalid delegation. The judiciary could attempt to usurp executive and/or legislative power or delegate its power to either or both of those branches. The legislature could attempt to usurp judicial and/or executive power or delegate its power to either or both of these branches. The executive could attempt to usurp legislative and/or judicial power or delegate its power to either or both of these branches. The remaining sections of this chapter will consider what the authors believe to be the more important of these problems of usurpation and delegation.

Section 51. Judicial Deference to and Usurpation of Legislative Power

It is axiomatic that a court should not substitute its views of proper legislative policy for the views of the legislature on that subject. *See Community Memorial Hospital v. County of Ventura* (1996). This axiom is frequently utilized to encourage judicial self-restraint. Most agree that a court should never interpret a statute to thwart legislative intent even though that intent is silly, unless the silliness somehow results in a finding that the statute is unconstitutional on some recognized theory. *See Indiana Wholesale Wine and Liquor Company, Inc. v. State ex. rel. Indiana Alcoholic Beverage Commission* (1998). Consistent with this theory of judicial restraint is its corollary that a court should only declare a law unconstitutional if it clearly fails to pass constitutional muster. *See Quinton v. General Motors Corporation* (1996). The oft-cited dissent of Justice Holmes in *Lochner v. New York* (1905) vividly captures this concept. Holmes stated that a judge's disagreement with even a "shocking" law should not affect the outcome as to its constitutionality. Rather, the inquiry should be whether "a rational and fair man necessarily would [find that the law violated] fundamental principles as they have been understood by our people and our law." *Id.* Neither the "calculus of effects, the manner in which a particular law reverberated in a society" nor the "financial consequences of legislation" are, absent constitutional infirmity, the business of the courts. Such issues are properly the responsibility of the legislature. *Eielson v. Parker* (1980) and *Wilson v. Nepstad* (1979).

Cases restating these fundamental concepts are legion. The Maine Legislature once enacted a statute that allowed hearing aid dealers to require no more than one half of the purchase price at the time of purchase and established a method for the balance to be paid after the customer's satisfaction was reasonably assured. While suggesting possible disagreement with the method selected by the legislature to effectuate its goals, the Court observed that the choice of means belonged to the legislature "no matter how much the Court might have preferred some other procedure." *National Hearing Aid Centers, Inc. v. Smith* (1977).

In *Matter of Lembo* (1977), the Passaic County Department of Public Works did not have sufficient work to keep its bridge and highway construction inspectors occupied. When the firm responsible for cleaning the courthouse cancelled its contract with the county, the inspectors, including Mr. Lembo, were assigned to perform the cleaning until other arrangements could be made. Lembo objected on the basis that it would require him to perform duties outside his formal job requirements. As a result, he was fired by the county, but subsequently reinstated by the Civil Service Commission. This reinstatement was upheld by the Appellate Division of the New Jersey Superior Court.

Previously, the New Jersey Legislature had delegated implementation of policy regarding "out-of-title" transfers at the local government level to the civil service commission. The commission had interpreted its rules to exclude "out-of-title" transfers, even temporary ones. The Court upheld the commission in spite of the possibility that the no transfer policy would (1) "impede achievement of the overriding policy of the Civil Service Act to provide efficient and economic public service," *Id.*, and (2) cause "toleration by a public employer of a superfluous work force." *Id.* The Court also criticized the apparent unwillingness of the commission to incur the consequences of attempting to eliminate the inefficiency and waste of public resources caused by superfluous work force but described them as "symptoms of a general social and political malaise, the remedy of which is the primary responsibility of the body politic and not the courts." *Id.* The Court thus refused to substitute its judgment for that of the legislature and the commission.

Courts frequently assert that proper deference to the legislation is required of the judiciary. "Judicial deference is not indicative of the avoidance of a duty but to the contrary is the performance thereof with an appreciation that judicial interference with the legislative process should occur only when there is an unavoidable and legally compelled reason to do so." *Americans United v. Rogers* (1976). Nevertheless, courts frequently justify this deference by concluding that they actually agree with the legislature determination at issue. In *Matter of Lembo* (1977), the New Jersey Appellate Court felt obligated to justify itself by finding a valid basis for the no transfer policy. This analysis would have been necessary had the case involved a constitutional issue. All the Court was asked to do was interpret the statute and rule. Instead of simply deferring to legislation, as arguably it was required to do, the Court examined the provisions at issue until it could find an acceptable justification for the result.

The problem of the usurpation of legislative power by the judiciary can arise in strange contexts. It is reasonably clear that courts cannot generally order a legislature to legislate. *Serrano v. Priest* (1976).* However, when the failure of the legislature to act violates the constitution, other problems are presented. One solution where public school financing was involved was to enjoin the operation of the school financing system. *Id.* Another unique judicial response to this situation was to declare that if the legislature did not act within a specified period to provide for a constitutionally required system of collective bargaining for public employees, the Court would create such a system by judicial decree. *Dade County Classroom Teachers Associa-*

* A change in the California Constitution *may* have affected this case in the context used here. *See Crawford v. Huntington Beach Union High School District* (2002).

tion, Inc. v. Legislature (1972). Both responses to the unconstitutional legislative inactivity would seem to be appropriate judicial reactions to the problems presented.

Section 52.   Judicial Usurpation of Legislative Power: Problems of Statutory Construction

The presumption of the constitutionality of a statute, and the related rule that a statute should be interpreted in such a way as to be constitutional can be considered a rule of statutory interpretation. *Indiana Wholesale Wine and Liquor Company, Inc. v. State ex. rel. Indiana Alcoholic Beverage Commission* (1998). As these rules raise issues of possible judicial usurpation of legislative power they will be discussed in this section. The presumption of constitutionality is an expression of judicial deference to the legislature. In a way, this deference reflects a concern for proper separation of power between the branches of government. Despite this frequently enunciated concern, courts in attempting to interpret the legislature may well be tempted to actually infringe upon the constitutional domain of the legislature by *rewriting* a law in order to declare it constitutional. This, of course, a court should not do. " 'If there are two reasonable interpretations of a statute, one of which is constitutional and the other not, we will choose that path which permits upholding the statute....' " *Indiana Wholesale Wine and Liquor Company, Inc. v. State ex. rel. Indiana Alcoholic Beverage Commission* (1998), citing *Boehm v. Town of St. John* (1996). "On the other hand, separation of powers prevents a court from effectively rewriting a statute to save it from constitutional infirmity." *Indiana Wholesale, supra.* Citing *Grody v. State* (1972).

While perhaps not intending to say what its words rather clearly suggest, the Colorado Supreme Court once opined that, "*Absent constitutional infringement*, it is not our province to rewrite the statutes." *Dove Valley Business Park Associates, Ltd. v. County Commissioner of Arapahoe County Colorado* (1997) (emphasis supplied.) Perhaps the statement can be considered *obiter dicta*, perhaps the Court didn't mean it, but if it did then it is swimming against a very strong tide. A related problem arises when courts succumb to the temptation to assist the legislature by judicially rewriting a statute in order to avoid an absurd result. *Town of Loxley v. Rosinton Water Sewer and Fire Protection Authority, Inc.* (1979). Nor, should a court rewrite a statute "to reach what court thinks would be a just result. (Citations omitted; internal quotation marks omitted.)" *Paul v. McPhee Electrical Contractors* (1997). It has, however, been stated that

   "The literal meaning of the words of a statute may be disregarded to avoid absurd results (citation)" "but this 'exception should be used most sparingly by the judiciary and only in extreme cases else we violate the separation of powers principle of government (citation).' "

People v. Pecci (1999), generally citing *Unzueta v. Ocean View School District* (1992).

While courts should be concerned with the separation of power issue, when they interpret statutes this issue should not be obsessive. Instead, they should be governed by a rule of reason. The Florida Supreme Court has described an approach to this problem in *Brown v. State* (1978). While "[I]n appropriate instances a court may authoritatively construe a statute so that it does not conflict with the federal or state constitution [or presumably so that it does not reach absurd results], we cannot condone judicial excision of [sic] statute's overbreadth or clarification of its ambiguities where ... there is no statutory language to support restructuring." *Id.* At times, "restructuring" is very tempting. In *Town of Loxley v. Rosinton Water, Sewer and Fire Protection Authority, Inc.* (1979), Alabama statutory law allowed municipal corporations to expand their water and sanitary sewer systems beyond their corporate limits. In the case this resulted in the creation of situations which, to quote an argument of one of the parties, "would create a chaotic result by allowing public water systems to compete [with each other] thus rendering some public water systems economically unfeasible as a result of such competition." *Id.* As a result, the utility contended "the true intent of the legislature is to require a municipality to obtain permission of the county commission before being allowed to expand its water system into designated service area of an authority such as Rosinton." *Id.* The utility supported its position by arguing that "the legislature would have corrected this possible chaotic condition if such situation had been brought to its attention." *Id*. Resisting this argument, the Alabama Court responded, "It is clearly not this court's function to usurp the role of the legislature and correct defective legislation or amend statutes under the guise of construction." *Id*. The Court went on to say that "[t]he purpose of interpretation is not to improve a statute but rather to explain the express language used in the statute." *Id*.

Apart from the separation of powers issues that lurk in court interpretation of statutes, there is the much vexed question of the growth of the common law in an era of legislatures. For example, while the Florida Supreme Court replaced the common law rule of contributory negligence with a new common law rule of comparative negligence, the Maryland Court of Special Appeals found that "In the final analysis, whether to abandon the doctrine of contributory negligence in favor of comparative negligence involves fundamental and basic public policy considerations properly to be addressed by the legislature." Compare *Hoffman v. Jones* (1973) with *Stewart v. Hechinger Stores Company* (1997) quoting *Harrison v. Montgomery County Board of Education* (1983). The Supreme Court of Tennessee appeared to have sided somewhat with the view taken by the Florida Supreme Court.

It is primarily for the Legislature to determine the public policy of this state; however, where there is no declaration in the constitution or the statutes and the area is governed by common law doctrines, it is the province of the courts to consider the public policy of the state as reflected in old, court-made rules. *Cary v. Cary* (1996).

Section 53. Judicial Usurpation of Executive Power

Just as courts cannot order the legislature to legislate, they cannot order the governor to sign legislation presented to him by the legislature. *Serrano v. Priest* (1976).* As the California Supreme Court stated in another case, "Judges must be as vigilant to preserve from judicial encroachment those powers constitutionally committed to the executive as they are to preserve their own constitutional powers from infringement by the coordinate branches of government." *People v. Superior Court of Contra Costa County* (1977).

One of the most prevalent areas of conflict concerning alleged judicial usurpation of executive power arises where it is alleged that the judiciary is interfering with sentences of imprisonment. Once a person convicted of crime is validly sentenced, the judicial function ceases. Thereafter, the individual may receive relief through executive clemency whether that clemency is awarded by the governor or some other part of the executive branch of government. Thus,

[T]he district court usurped the constitutional duties of the executive branch of government when it removed [defendant] from the custody of

* A change in the California Constitution *may* have affected this case in the context used here. *See Crawford v. Huntington Beach Union High School District* (2002).

the Department of Corrections and granted him probation, ... *State v. Heyrend* (1996).

Also, where a defendant must be resentenced because of constitutional defects in the original sentencing procedure, the judge cannot resentence that individual to a particular mandatory minimum sentence, where the governor had, in the meantime, commuted that mandatory minimum sentence. "The Governor's power to commute sentences, on recommendation of the Board of Pardons, is exclusive, and courts may not in any way impinge on the exercise of this power." *Commonwealth v. Gaito* (1980).

Under Indiana law, the Parole Board, part of the executive branch of government, has discretion to determine whether a person convicted of committing a crime while on parole should be required to serve the sentence for the crime for which he was on parole. A state trial court usurped the power of the executive branch when it ordered that the sentence for the crime committed, while on parole, be served consecutively with the sentence for the first crime. *Hurt v. State* (1977).

This type of judicial usurpation may occur in many different contexts. Absent violation of constitution or statute, "the administration of the state institutions and county jails is an executive and not a judicial one." *Robinson v. Peterson* (1976). Of course, courts do not infringe on the power of the executive branch when they order that branch to comply with the constitution in its operation of jails and prisons. The sanctity of executive power from judicial encroachment assumes that executive power is being exercised in a manner consistent with the constitution.

The Supreme Court of California has held that even though the honoring of an extradition demand from another state is essentially a ministerial act, separation of powers precludes a court from using the writ of mandamus to cause the governor to comply with the demand. *State of South Dakota v. Brown* (1978). This may or may not be valid because it relied to a certain extent on *Commonwealth of Kentucky v. Dennison* (1861) which was recently overruled in *Puerto Rico v. Branstad* (1987).

In another setting, the Supreme Court of Florida has held that a judge may not dictate to the executive branch of government the type of medical treatment to be provided to a defendant once the defendant has been assigned to the executive branch for treatment. *State ex. rel. Department of H.R.S. v. Sepe* (1974). Also, "judicial inquiries into the private motivation on reasoning of administrative decision makers is a substantial intrusion into the functions of the other branches of government." *Medical Licensing Board of Indiana v. Provisor* (1996).

In another instance, "[a] prosecutor is not subject to judicial supervision in determining what charges to bring and how to draft accusatory pleadings, but is protected from judicial oversight by the doctrine of separation of powers." . . . *State v. Iowa District*

Court for Johnson County (1997) quoting *American Jurisprudence 2d.*

Section 54.   Executive Usurpation of Legislative Power

Legislative power is the power to say what the law is. The executive branch in "faithfully executing the law" cannot amend the law. Perhaps the most frequent example of executive encroachment on the legislative prerogative is an attempt by an executive or administrative agency to alter the law it is applying. When litigated, such results are futile. "[A]n administrative rule is powerless to alter a statute enacted by the General Assembly." *Jones v. Connor* (1983). Thus, where the legislature has not placed a particular limit on the right of people to receive certain government benefits, an administrative agency may not do so based on its own perceptions of what is good public policy. As a result, the Wisconsin Department of Health and Social Services could not deny benefits because of what it considered to be a questionable transfer of assets by parties seeking those benefits when the legislature had not prohibited such a transfer. *Sinclair v. Department of Health and Social Services* (1977). Likewise, the pension board of a fire protection district does not have the power to change pension eligibility requirements established by the legislature. It can, of course, engage in "the application of statutory criteria to a specific set of circumstances." *Agee v. Trustees of Pension Board of Cunningham Fire Protection District* (1974). Another example of this type of impermissible executive encroachment problem is *Blood Service Plan Insurance Company v. Williams* (1966). In that case, even though Blood Service Insurance Company had complied with all the statutory requirements for engaging in the insurance business, the Insurance Commissioner refused to grant the license because of

> ... (a) the unique character of the Company's operation which required blood bank agency facilities which it does not now possess and (b) the reasonably anticipated impact on the operation of the blood bank program in this state in the reduction of the number of blood donors because of the cash benefits payable to blood banks under the company's insurance contracts. *Id.*

Although the concerns of the Insurance Commissioner may have been valid, the Court held he was not at liberty to add to the statutory criteria.

Results are not quite as easily predicted where the executive branch attempts to frustrate the lawmaking power by refusing to spend monies appropriated by the legislature. One court has held that the governor, acting through the state budget director, cannot refuse to spend funds appropriated by the legislature for certain projects. Conceding that separation of powers should not create a "captious, doctrinaire and inelastic classification of government functions," the Court of Appeals of New York has held that to allow the governor to impound appropriated monies in the asserted defense of fiscal integrity is to invade the province of the legislature. *County of Oneida v. Berle* (1980). The Court intimated that if the governor was allowed to impound appropriated funds, he would have an unoverridable item veto. The Court also suggested that, had the impoundment been in the furtherance of a constitutional obligation to maintain a balanced budget, the impoundment might have been within the governor's powers. *Id*.

In contrast, the Supreme Judicial Court of Massachusetts has held that, while the governor cannot refuse to spend appropriated moneys in such a way as to frustrate the legislature's objectives in appropriating the funds, the governor can, without impermissibly invading legislative prerogative, spend less than the full amount appropriated in order to further the "efficient and effective operation of government." *Opinion of the Justices to the Senate* (1978).

As might be expected, it appears to be a general rule that an agency cannot find a statute unconstitutional. Thus, "the Department [of State Revenue] has no authority to strike down tax statute." *State v. Sproles* (1996).* At least one court has found an exception to this. The Alaska Supreme Court held that,

The Division of Elections, as an executive branch agency, would have authority to 'abrogate statute

* On a related point, in *Common Council v. Matonovich* (1998) it was held that the holding in *Sproles* "that taxpayers may not avoid the administrative process and the tax court by filing a lawsuit in circuit court is limited to those cases involving taxes administered by the Department of Revenue."

which is clearly unconstitutional under a United States Supreme Court decision dealing with a similar law, without having to wait for another court decision specifically declaring the statute unconstitutional.' *O'Callaghan v. State Director of Elections* (2000) quoting *O'Callaghan v. Coghill* (1995).

Section 55.   Executive Usurpation of Judicial Power

One of the more blatant attempts by the executive branch to invade the province of the judiciary occurred when a governor of Florida asked for an advisory opinion of the Florida Supreme Court. In the request, the governor asked the Court whether he possessed the power to "review the judicial accuracy and propriety of a [judge], and to suspend him if it does not appear [to the Governor that the judge] has exercised proper judicial discretion and wisdom." *In re Advisory Opinion to the Governor* (1968). As understood by the Court, the governor was asking whether he possessed the power "to remove for incompetency a member of the judicial branch for judicial labor apparently unsatisfactory to some segment of the populace." *Id.* The Court rebuffed this invasion by the executive into the judicial branch and advised the governor that appeal was the exclusive remedy by which to test the correctness of a judge's decisions. *Id.*

Attempts by the executive branch to usurp judicial power are rarely as outrageous as a governor seeking the Court's permission to remove a judge because the governor does not like the judge's decisions. Nevertheless, such attempts are many and varied. For example, once a court has interpreted a statute to mean one thing, an administrative agency is not at liberty to find that it means something else. *Board of County Commissioners v. Industrial Commission* (1982).* The Supreme Judicial Court of Massachusetts has likewise held that, "The duty of statutory interpretation is for the courts, not for an administrative agency." *Briggs v. Commonwealth* (1999) quoting *Casey v. Massachusetts Electric Company* (1984) (which quotes yet another case). This concept is tempered by the notion that "Although an agency's interpretation of a statute it administers is entitled to 'serious consideration' if it is reasonable and does not contradict the plain language of the statute, . . . such an interpretation is a legal determination that does not bind the courts, . . . *Firemen's Pension Commission v. Jones* (1997), citing *Tarrant Appraisal District v. Moore* (1993), *Texas Rivers Protection Association v. Texas National Resources Conservation Commission* (1995) and *Cantu v. Central Education Agency* (1994)."

There is related concept (which might actually belong in the section on judicial encroachment on the executive). It is the doctrine of primary jurisdiction which has been described as a rule that "coun-

* Reversed on what were apparently other grounds. The Colorado Supreme Court did not reach the issue of "whether Rule 2.7 is a valid exercise of administrative authority." *Industrial Commission v. Adams County Board of County Commissioners* (1984).

sels that a court should not substitute its judgment for an agency's when dealing with a subject that is vested within the agency's expertise and discretion." *Kirk v. U.S. Sugar Corporation* (1999). " 'It does not [however] defeat the court's jurisdiction over the case, but coordinates the work of the court and the agency by permitting the agency to rule first and giving the court the benefit of the agency's views. . . .' " *Flo-Sun, Inc. v. Kirk* (2001) (cited case omitted). It has also been held that the carrying out of the quasi-judicial functions of agency does not necessarily encroach on the proper function of courts. *Barber v. Jackson County Ethics Commission* (1996).

Of course, judicial attempts to protect that branch against perceived encroachment by the executive can be carried to illogical extremes. Consider *Reznor v. Hogue* (1982) where a local trial court became embroiled in a dispute with a county about the form that court reporters would have to file in order to be reimbursed for a full forty-hour week. The trial court refused to require its employees to list the number of hours worked each day. This decision was based on the theory that previously, it had been sufficient for the reporter to indicate that he was present for that day. As a result, the county, the executive branch, refused to pay the judicial employees for a full forty-hour week without the hourly accounting. This executive action was upheld as "not interfer[ing] with the power of the judiciary to supervise court personnel." *Id*.

Section 56. Legislative Usurpation of Judicial Power

At least one court has established a rather elaborate three part test "to determine whether legislation unconstitutionally intrudes upon judicial power." *See State v. Horn* (1999)* in Section 42, *supra.* Consider, also, the two part "either-or" test described by the Supreme Court of Connecticut.

[A] two part inquiry has emerged to evaluate the constitutionality of a statute that is alleged to violate separation of powers principles by impermissibly infringing on the judicial authority.... "A statute will be held unconstitutional on those grounds if: (1) it governs subject matter that not only falls within the judicial power, but also lies exclusively within judicial control; or (2) it significantly interferes with the orderly functioning of the Superior Courts judicial role." *State v. Angel C.* (1998). Quoting *State v. Campbell* (1992) and *Bartholomew v. Schweizer* (1991) and indicating the omission of citations and internal quotation marks.

Of course, legislative encroachment on the judiciary can take numerous forms some of which are illustrated below.

The legislature, in the exercise of its power to appropriate money, cannot frustrate the inherent power of a court properly exercising its judicial functions. For example, the Supreme Court of Ohio

----
* *Horn* has been limited to its facts, *see Horn* and *State v. Burchfield* (1999).

declared that an impermissible legislative encroachment on the judiciary occurred when legislative
appropriations to the judiciary were placed within
the sole discretion of the County Commissioners
subject only to review by mandamus proceedings.
State ex rel. Johnston v. Taulbee (1981). The effect
of this type of appropriation was to remove the
burden of proof from the county commission and
place it on the judge challenging the appropriation.
The Ohio Supreme Court declared this legislative
action violative of separation of powers.

> This Court has often said that a legislative body
> has a duty to provide for the needs of constitu-
> tional Courts, as determined by those Courts,
> which needs may exceed, but may not be limited
> by, legislative provision thereof.... The public
> interest is served when Courts co-operate with
> executive and legislative bodies in the complicated
> budgetary process of government. However, such
> voluntary co-operation should not be mistaken for
> a surrender or diminution of the plenary power to
> administer justice which is inherent in every
> Court whose jurisdiction derives from the Ohio
> Constitution. *Id.*

Of course, not every legislative involvement with
the funding of the judiciary violates separation of
powers.

> [I]f the legislature's appropriation to the court
> system unduly burdens or substantially interferes
> with the judiciary, the court may declare such act
> unconstitutional, thus ensuring that the judiciary

can preserve its constitutional duty to oversee the administration of justice. The lapse of funds from the court automation program to the general purpose revenue fund was not, however, such a situation. *Flynn v. Department of Administration* (1998).

Not only must legislative bodies refrain from usurping the judicial function through inadequate funding, they also cannot interfere in other areas of judicial power such as: the regulation of lawyers; the exercise by a court of sound discretion in deciding cases; and, the establishment of rules of court procedure. The Supreme Court of Washington declared unconstitutional a statute that authorized escrow agents to engage in the limited practice of law in real estate transactions. The Court held that the regulation of the practice of law was an inherent power of the judiciary and that the legislature violated separation of powers when it attempted to allow non-lawyers to practice law. *Bennion, Van Camp, Hagen and Ruhl v. Kassler Escrow, Inc.* (1981). *See also Gmerek v. State Ethics Commission* (2000) *supra* Section 45.

When acts of the legislature use the word "shall" in regard to the issuance of discretionary writs, courts are faced with the choice of finding that the statute invades the judicial function or that "shall" really means "may." When this occurs, the courts often interpret "shall" to mean "may" because to do so would uphold the statute. "While we may agree that the legislature may not command the issuance of a discretionary writ, we take the view, as do other courts, that such language of the statute as would seem to require courts to issue injunctive writs in such circumstances merely authorizes rather than commands such relief." *Farmington v. Scott* (1965).

As with many areas of encroachment, and indeed with state constitutional law itself, the role of the legislature in making rules of practice and procedure will differ. Consider the following variations.

In Florida, the Florida Supreme Court's constitutionally allocated rule making power has been described as that court's "exclusive authority to 'adopt rules for the practice and procedure in all courts, . . .' " *Allen v. Butterworth* (2000).

In Massachusetts, "the Legislature . . . may establish and define methods of criminal practice and procedure." *Commonwealth v. Pyles* (1996).

Where the Supreme Court, rather than the legislature has the power to make rules for practice and procedure, the distinction between substance and procedure becomes important, because substantive matters are for the legislature. *See State v. Gilfillan* (2000) where in Arizona it was held that "the burden of proof is substantive, not procedural." (Case citations omitted.) "Therefore, a legislative enactment that changes the burden of proof does not violate constitutional standards." The same court also commented that "while rules of evidence generally are regarded as procedural, a statutory evidentiary rule may supplement the rules promulgated by the court." (Case citation omitted.)

The difference between substance and procedure has been defined in the following way. "Substantive law prescribes duties and rights under our system of government, and the legislature is responsible for enacting such law. Procedural law concerns the means and methods to apply and enforce those duties and rights, and the Supreme Court determines procedural law through the promulgation of rules." *State v. J.A., Jr.* (1979) citing *Benyard v. Wainwright* (1975).

Substance and procedure may, however, overlap. "Legislative policymaking and judicial rulemaking may overlap to some extent as long as there is no substantial conflict between statute and rule." *People v. Diaz* (1999).

The ability of the legislature to meddle with a court's contempt power may vary. Compare the following observations: "The power to punish for contempt does not depend on constitutional or legislative grant. Because such power interferes in the judicial branch of government, the legislative may not restrict its use." *People v. Warren* (1996). "Although the legislature is not entitled substantially to impair or destroy the court's contempt power, the legislature may prescribe reasonable procedures for the exercise of that authority." *Hiber v. Creditors Collection Service of Lincoln County, Inc.* (1998). Although the observations of the two courts can be read to suggest different views regarding the impact that a legislature may have on a court's contempt power, it should be noted that *Warren* did not appear to involve rules of procedure as did *Hiber*.

Section 57. Delegation of Legislative Power

It is frequently stated that a legislative body cannot delegate its law-making power to another branch of government, nor its law-making power to the private sector. This rule is based on the explicit or implicit requirement of "separation of powers" found in most state constitutions and in no way is predicated on the command of the federal constitution. *Gamel v. Veterans Memorial Auditorium Commission* (1978). The rule is founded in the desire to insure a representative form of government and to protect accountability in the law-making process. *People v. Parker* (1976). These two interests are related in that representative democracy presumes that the lawmakers will be accountable to the electorate. However, when the legislature does not delegate the power to say what the law is, but merely the authority to implement it, the recipient of the authority does not have to be directly accountable to the electorate. *Metropolitan Development and Housing Agency v. Leech* (1979).

Practically speaking, a legislative body cannot make laws detailed enough so that they can mechanically be carried into effect by the executive branch of government. As a result, the legislature is not able to enact legislation sufficiently encompassing to deal with every possible application of the law. In recognition of this reality, courts permit the legislative branch of government to delegate some authority to the executive to interpret and apply the law. Therefore, "when the Legislature itself cannot practically or efficiently perform the functions required, it has the authority to delegate some agency to carry out the purposes of such legislation." *Ex parte Granviel* (1978). In *Granviel, supra,* the Court explained that this meant that "generally, a legislative body, after declaring a policy and fixing a primary standard, may delegate to the administrative tribunal or officer the power to prescribe details, . . . such as to establish rules, regulations or minimum standards reasonably necessary to carry out the expressed purpose of the act." *Id*. However, this is not and apparently cannot be a "bright line" rule. "[T]he sufficiency of adequate standards depends upon the complexity of the subject matter and 'the degree of difficulty involved in articulating finite standards.'" *Avatar Development Corporation v. State* (1998) citing *Askew v. Cross Key Waterways* (1978) and *Brown v. Apalachee Regional Planning Council* (1990). For this reason, the rule is much easier to describe than to apply. It has caused courts to engage in absurd line drawing, hair splitting and a not inconsiderable amount of legal fiction in distinguishing between law-making and the mere provision of administrative detail. *See, e.g., Town of New Milford v. SCA Services of Connecticut, Inc.* (1977). The theory of executive supplementation by rule making has been described as allowing the executive or administrative agency to determine the existence of facts under which the law will become operative. *State ex rel. Douglas v. Sporhase* (1981).*

Section 58.   Delegation of Judicial Power

While not as common a concern as delegation of legislative power, it is possible for courts to engage in activity that allows another branch of government to improperly exercise judicial power. Questions of delegation of judicial power to the private sector also may arise. Judicial delegation problems arise less frequently than legislative delegation issues because a court simply does not have as much occasion to need assistance in carrying out its duties. Since the legislative branch makes law and the executive branch sees that that law is carried out, the legislature must rely heavily on the executive to supplement that law in its everyday operation. Not infrequently, this relationship results in the legislature relinquishing actual law making power to the executive branch.

From time to time, courts seek assistance from the executive branch and the private sector. Just as the legislature can avoid unconstitutional delegation of legislative power by including restrictive guidelines, the Court can limit improper delegation of judicial power by imposing restrictions. This is illustrated in one of the most frequent problem areas, probation. As a court is generally the only branch of government that can award probation, it is also the only branch that can impose conditions

* Reversed on other (Commerce Clause) grounds. *Sporhase v. Nebraska ex rel. Douglas* (1982).

for probation. However, it is not always possible for a court to supervise probation. Supervision is generally not considered a function of the judicial branch. Just as the executive branch must carry out the execution of the laws enacted by the legislature, it must also operate the probation system. "Probation is supervision and control with hope of rehabilitation. While only the Court can set conditions of probation, the judge cannot personally supervise; he cannot set forth a complete guidebook of directions in an order of probation. Instead, he properly delegates to the probation supervisor the giving of specific instructions necessary for effective and successful supervision." *Draper v. State* (1981).

Perhaps the most frequent type of judicial delegation problem occurs as a result of the interplay between the judiciary and executive in the decision whether or not to impose probation in the first instance. A court can, without violating separation of powers, seek the recommendation of the executive branch that has expertise in this area. A recommendation must be no more than that. If it appears that the executive branch has actually decided either the awarding of probation, or the terms and conditions under which it will be awarded, then "separation of powers" has been violated. *People v. Kendall* (1985) and *Garcia v. State* (1985).

The delegation problem can take many forms. It has, for example, been held that " 'the trial judge has broad discretion in maintaining courtroom security.' [Citations omitted.] The exercise of that discretion 'may not be delegated to courtroom security personnel.' " (Citation omitted.) *Lovell v. State* (1997).

Compare this to the Missouri case, infra, where separation of powers was not found to be violated. On the other hand, it has been held that "According to the Texas Constitution, the judicial power of the state is vested in [named courts]." (Citation omitted.) "Furthermore, the concept of judicial power, as it pertains to a district or other trial court, encompasses the authority to hear facts, decide issues of fact, decide questions of law, enter judgment in accordance with the facts and law, and enforce those judgments once entered." *Tabor v. Hogan* (1997). (Cited cases omitted.)

In compliance with the provisions of a state statute, the circuit judges of the twenty-first judicial circuit, sitting en banc created a "traffic court" as a "division of the circuit court." In effect, the traffic court was to be the trier of fact in certain types of traffic cases. "The circuit judge then enters a judgment on [those] findings."

The Missouri Supreme Court upheld this "delegation." First, "The delegation of functions normally associated with the judiciary, such as determining facts, applying the law, and entering judgments, does not violate the separation of powers clause [of the Missouri Constitution] because the provision primarily separates powers not functions." (Citing *Asbury v. Lombardi* (1993)).

Second, the Court held that "the authority that the constitution places exclusively in the judicial department has at least two components—judicial review and the power of courts to decide issues and pronounce and enforce judgements." (Citing *Chastain v. Chastain* (1996)). The traffic court system "does not delegate to a traffic judge either of these two exclusive functions." This part of the statute was upheld "as construed and applied in the twenty-first judicial circuit, however, [by the entry of a judgment by a circuit judge]." It was the "approval" found in the "entry of judgment" that kept the traffic court system within the bounds of separation of powers. *Dabin v. Director of Revenue* (2000).

CHAPTER 8

LOCAL GOVERNMENT

Section 59. Introduction

State constitutions generally tend to be highly individualistic. As a result, it is often difficult to neatly characterize constitutional provisions into categories which are meaningful. These observations are particularly apropos in regard to state constitutional provisions relating to local government. By way of illustration, certain constitutions are almost totally devoid of any provisions expressly referring to or regulating local government. *See, e.g.,* Vermont Constitution; New Hampshire Constitution. On the other hand, other constitutions contain detailed provisions dealing with a myriad of restrictions and regulatory limitations relating to local government. Perhaps the most unusual example of this type of extensive regulation is found in the Oklahoma Constitution. In Section 8 of Article XVII (comprising approximately 35 pages of text) of that constitution the geographical boundaries of all 77 counties located within the state are described in detail. While an earnest attempt will be made to identify and discuss common state constitutional local government provisions, fair warning is given that this area defies precise categorization.

219

Despite these shortcomings, all state constitutional limitations upon local government operate upon the basic assumption that counties, municipalities, school districts and all other forms of local government derive their governmental authority to act from the people through the state.

It is very difficult to generalize as to all the different types of local government units. In the course of teaching a course on the Florida Constitution for many years, we have found it both convenient and accurate to say that there are, in general, two types of *general purpose* local government units, municipal corporation and counties and many different types of *special purpose* local government units such as, *e.g.,* school districts. This dichotomy will probably be generally true throughout the fifty states, but there are bound to be differences. Even in Florida, there are units that can be either special purpose or general purpose that are not separate entities, but rather are creatures of the county. They are known as Municipal Purpose Taxing Units and are separate *taxing units* even though not separate entities for any other purpose. *See, e.g., Gallant v. Stephens* (1978). But, as we said, it is very hard to generalize. The Supreme Court of Arkansas has even held that "a county is a municipal corporation!" *Stilley v. Henson* (2000). Therefore, unless express constitutional provisions exist allocating certain governmental power to local government, all local governments are subject to the plenary authority of state government. In one of this principle's earliest and best known formulations, the Iowa

Supreme Court in discussing the authority of a municipal corporation to act, stated that local government "possesses and can exercise the following powers and no others: first, those granted in express words; second, those necessarily implied or necessarily incident to the powers expressly granted; third, those absolutely essential to the declared objects and purposes of the corporation—not simply convenient, but indispensable." *Merrian v. Moody's Executors* (1868). In a case decided over 100 years later which cited *Merrian*, the Iowa Supreme Court opined that a city ordinance may or may not be preempted by a state law on the same subject. *City of Council Bluffs v. Cain* (1983).

As a result of this principle of local government law, an analysis of whether an entity of local government possesses governmental authority to act is a different inquiry than determining whether the state possesses the power to act. As suggested in the Introduction to this work, we must view state government as a government of inherent power possessing all power necessary to govern unless such power is denied to the state by the federal or state constitution. However, local governments are more properly viewed as governments of delegated powers, whether the delegation comes from the legislature, the constitution or a combination of the two. As a result, we generally must find some explicit, implicit or inferable authority to authorize local government to act in a given area before we may assert that the entity has operated in a valid manner. The constitutional or statutory delegation of governmental power to entities of local government may be broad or narrow; uncomplicated or detailed.

Section 60. Limitations on Revenue Practices and Expenditures by Local Government

Some of the most common constitutional restrictions on the operation of local government are regulation of fiscal practices. During the first century of American legal history such restrictions were quite rare. However, during the latter portion of the nineteenth century state and local government unsuccessfully participated in the financing of internal improvements such as canals and railroads. The absence of any effective state regulation of local governmental involvement in these projects combined with sporadic economic downturns and political corruption nurtured a reform movement which sought the enactment of constitutional provisions regulating such matters.

By way of example, the Florida Supreme Court opined that,

During The Florida Boom of the 1920's, millions of dollars in bonds were issued and sold by various local government units in the state. When the boom was over, financial chaos prevailed. There were few areas of the state that did not default in their public obligations. For the purpose of preventing future irresponsible and excessive public debts, the Florida Constitution was amended in 1930 to require that all local bonds be approved at a freeholder election by a majority of the freeholders at an election participated in by a majority of the qualified freeholders in such local district.* *State v. City of St. Augustine* (1970).

These are enduring concerns. As a Texas Appellate Court put it, "Framers' intent in creating constitutional limitations on municipal debt was to protect city's financial standing and its other creditors; ..." *Municipal Administrative Services, Inc. v. City of Beaumont* (1998).

As to counties, the concerns should be similar, although the following comment by the West Virginia Supreme Court seems to reflect the general notion that counties are considered somewhat more political subdivisions of the state than are municipal corporations. (*See, e.g. City of Miami v. Lewis* (1958)).

"[The] critical issue for determining whether [county's financial] obligation violates constitutional debt restrictions is whether issuance of obligations will affect financial integrity of existing tax structure." *State ex rel County Commission of Boone County v. Cooke* (1996).

Many of these resulting provisions are discussed in detail in Chapter 9 of this work dealing with Revenue and Taxation. Nonetheless, descriptions of these types of provisions will generally be summarized in this chapter.

* With a few exceptions, the limitation of bond validation referendums to freeholders, that is to say property owners, has been declared invalid by the United States Supreme Court. *See, e.g. Phoenix v. Kolodziejski* (1970).

(a) Prohibition on the Extension of Local Governmental Credit to Private Businesses or Individuals

Among the most common constitutional restrictions on the activities of local government are provisions prohibiting the extension of governmental credit to private concerns. Article 8, Section 4 of the Idaho constitution is a section which is fairly representative of provisions of this type. It provides in relevant part that:

No county, city, town, township, board of education, or school district, or other subdivision, shall lend, or pledge the credit of faith thereof directly or indirectly, in any manner, to, or in the aid of any individual, association, or corporation, for any amount or for any purpose whatever, or become responsible for any debt, contract in liability of any individual, association or corporation in or out of this state.

While such provisions appear quite restrictive on the surface, most courts have judicially exempted the issuance of revenue bonds from the operation of such sections. *See, e.g., State v. City of Riviera Beach* (1981). However, even in states which originally extended such provisions to apply to revenue bonds, either subsequent decision or constitutional revision has ultimately exempted revenue bonds from such restrictions. For example, in Idaho the Supreme Court in 1960 held that Article VIII, Section 4 of the Idaho Constitution prohibited a city from issuing revenue bonds to finance the acquisition and construction of facilities to be leased to private businesses. *See, Village of Moyie Springs, Idaho v. Aurora Manufacturing Co.* (1960). Subsequent to this decision the Idaho Constitution was amended to specifically authorize the issuance by government of non-recourse revenue bonds. *See,* Idaho Constitution, Article 8, Section 5.

The exemption of revenue bonds from limitations on pledging the public credit can play out in strange ways. Florida presents an interesting example. Prior to the adoption of the 1968 Constitution, Florida's constitutional limitation on pledging the public credit included the words "obtaining money for" the private sector. These words were left out of the prohibition of pledging public credit in aid of the private sector ("any corporation, association, partnership or person"). As explained by the Florida Supreme Court, the extreme limitation on pledging the public credit that existed prior to the adoption of the 1968 Constitution, "Florida was placed at a competitive disadvantage" because of a change in federal law "which made the interest on industrial revenue bonds exempt from federal income tax." *Linscott v. Orange County Industrial Development Authority* (1983). This resulted in two different changes in the 1968 Constitution. The first, dropping the words "obtaining money for" has already been mentioned. The second was the placing in the Constitution an exception for local government revenue bonds for "(1) airports or port facilities or (2) industrial or manufacturing plants." What did not seem to have dawned on the drafters of the 1968 changes is that by deleting the words "obtaining money for" revenue bonds were no longer with the ban on the pledging of the public credit because a true revenue bond, sometimes called a "non-recourse revenue bond" pledges no public credit. All that is pledged are the revenues from the project funded by the bonds. This apparent truism seemed to be timely recognized by the Florida Supreme Court in *Nohrr v. Brevard County Educational Facilities Authority* (1971) but not its full potential impact. *Nohrr* ended up doing two things. First, it recognized the "airport and port facility/industrial or manufacturing plant" exceptions. They, "*ipso facto* did not involve the lending or use of a public units taxing power or credit. . . ." As an exception it works well enough but seems rather silly since as the Court in *Nohrr* recognized non-recourse revenue bonds do not pledge the public credit. In spite of that recognition, the Court earlier in its opinion had held that revenue bond projects not within the four exceptions "would, of course, have to run the gauntlet of prior case decisions to test whether the lending or use of public credit was contemplated, and if so 'whether the purpose of the project serves a paramount public purpose. . . .'" This "paramount public purpose" standard was the way around the prohibition on an *actual pledge of* the public credit in the aid of the private sector. Then, in discussing the actual facts of the case, the Court *seemed* to say that if non-recourse revenue bonds were involved, only a public purpose, not a paramount public purpose was necessary. On this point, the *Nohrr* opinion is not a model of clarity.

This lack of instructive clarity was driven home by a decision of the Florida Supreme Court that appeared to lose all sight of *Nohrr*'s *seemingly apparent* ruling that if no pledge of the public credit was involved, as it would not be if non-recourse revenue bonds were involved, then only a public purpose, not a paramount one, was needed. In *Orange County Industrial Development Authority v. State*, the Florida Supreme Court held in a case not involving an "airport or port facility" or an "industrial or manufacturing plant" (an expansion of a T.V. broadcasting facility was at issue) that even though non-recourse revenue bonds were involved and thus no pledge of the public credit, nevertheless, the expansion of a T.V. broadcasting facility was not a "paramount public purpose" and thus the bonds violated the Florida Constitution.

This mistake was apparently corrected in *Linscott, supra* when the Court held that only a public purpose is required when no pledge of the public credit is involved as in non-recourse revenue bond financing. This takes us back to what was apparently done in *Nohrr, supra* but still begs the question of where in the Florida Constitution *any type of* public purpose is required for non-recourse revenue bond financing?

Assuming arguendo that a public purpose is and should be required for non-recourse revenue bond financing, that concept, public purpose was pushed to what surely must be the edge of the envelope in *Northern Palm Beach County Water Control District v. State* (1992). There the Florida Supreme Court approved non-recourse revenue bonds for improvement of roads within a gated community. It was enough, the Court said that "the roadway improvements at issue will provide access to ... water management facilities and aid in the development of reclaimed lands," the "District would retain ownership of the roadways in question" and the legislature had found this to be a public purpose. There was a vigorous dissent on the basis of denial of public access within the gated community (money from the non-recourse revenue bonds would also pay for the construction and maintenance of three gate houses to be installed by security personnel to block all public access to the private Club.) As to the designation of the project a "public one" by the legislature, the dissenting justice quoted from Lewis Carroll's *Through the Looking Glass*. In part, the quote ran,

"But 'glory' doesn't mean 'a nice knock-down argument,'" Alice objected. "When I use a word," Humpty Dumpty said, in a rather scornful tone, "it means just what I choose it to mean—neither more nor less." "The question is," said Alice, "whether you can make words mean so many different things." *Id*.

The exceptions for "airport and port facilities" and industrial or manufacturing plants' has also been interpreted in what might be called a generous fashion. In *State v. Jacksonville Port Authority* (1975) the Supreme Court held that both a "food distribution center" for Publix Supermarkets and a "laundry facility" for a commercial laundry, Dixie Uniform Supply, qualified under the "industrial or manufacturing plants" exception. As to the latter, the Court emphasized that it was "not designed to serve the consuming public generally, as would, for example, an ordinary commercial laundry; it will not even maintain a cash register."

(b) Limitations on Local Government Debt

Fueled by a large number of local governmental bond defaults in the nineteenth century, state constitutions were revised to regulate the amount of constitutionally permissible local indebtedness. Basically, these restrictions were of three general types or a combination of these basic categories.

The first and most common restriction of this type is a simple percentage limitation on the amount of permissible local indebtedness. Under a provision of this type, local indebtedness is limited to a fixed percentage of the assessed valuation of all property subject to ad valorem taxation located within the jurisdiction of the issuing governmental entity. *See, e.g.,* Kentucky Constitution, Section 158.

A second common method of limiting local indebtedness is a constitutional provision prohibiting the incurment of local indebtedness in excess of the current year's revenue of the local entity. For example, Article XIV, Section 3 of the Utah Constitution provides that "[N]o debt in excess of the taxes for the current year" shall be created for the current year without a referendum. The Utah Supreme

Court has interpreted the word taxes as used in that provision to mean revenue. *Muir v. Murray City* (1919).*

A third common method of limiting permissible governmental debt is through the imposition of referendum requirements. In their purest form, such provisions prohibit the issuance of local debt until the electorate in the affected area consents to the debt. For example, Article IX, Section 9 of the Alaska Constitution provides: "No debt shall be contracted by any political subdivision of the state, unless authorized for capital improvements by its governing body and ratified by a majority vote of those qualified to vote and voting on the question."

Finally, it is not uncommon for restrictions of these types to appear in hybrid form. For example, under Article IX, Section 8 of the Arizona Constitution no local government may become indebted in any amount in excess of "six per centum of the taxable property" within the issuing entity without the approval of the qualified electorate within the issuing entity.

(c) Miscellaneous Restrictions

The fiscal reform fervor that culminated in the adoption of constitutional limitations on local government's ability to incur debt arose in part due from the public's desire to prevent any further governmental corruption scandals. As a result, many state constitutional provisions restricting local officials in fiscal matters are anti-corruption

* Overruled on other grounds. *State v. Spring City* (1953).

provisions. Article X of the Oklahoma Constitution is a good catalogue of a number of these provisions. Article X, Section 5 of the Oklahoma Constitution provides that the power of taxation shall never be "surrendered, suspended, or contracted away." Section 11 of Article X of the Oklahoma Constitution requires the disqualification from office of any governmental officer profiting in any manner from public funds. Section 15 of Article X prohibits the state from making a donation by gift or otherwise to any enterprise. Section 16 of Article X requires that local government only borrow money for speci-fied purposes.

Similar provisions are found in many state constitutions. Article 14, Section 1 of the Wyoming Constitution requires officers of most entities of local government to be paid "fixed and definite salaries" which are required to be "in proportion to the value of the services rendered and the duty performed." Section 161 of the Kentucky Constitution prohibits the compensation of any local officials from being changed after their appointment or election.

While the referenced provisions certainly are not exhaustive, they are illustrative of the types of restrictions on local officials contained in a number of state constitutions.

Section 61. Provisions Pertaining to Counties Other Than Home Rule Provisions

Absent specific state constitutional provisions providing to the contrary, a state legislature possesses plenary power over local government including counties. *Commissioners of Laramie County v. Albany County Commissioners* (1875). As a result, in the absence of constitutional restrictions, a state legislature possesses power to create, reorganize, and abolish counties. In order to promote local autonomy over local affairs and encourage uniformity, a number of state constitutions contain provisions which allocate specific governmental powers to counties, thereby protecting this level of government from the caprice of the state.

As one of the basic units of government in the American system, counties are specifically recognized in many state constitutions. A few state constitutions specifically provide that the pre-statehood county structure of the state shall continue. For example, Article 11, Section 1 of the Washington Constitution provides that "the several counties of the Territory of Washington existing at the time of the adoption of this constitution are hereby recognized as legal subdivisions of the state." Some state constitutions merely require that the state be divided into political subdivisions referred to as counties. *See, e.g.*, Florida Constitution, Article VIII, Section 1.

As far as provisions pertaining to creation of additional counties or reorganization of existing counties, constitutional provisions vary. For example, Article 13, Section 1 of the Arkansas Constitution prohibits the legislature from reorganizing existing counties or creating new counties with "an area of less that six hundred square miles nor less than five thousand inhabitants." Such provisions are not unique to Arkansas. *See, e.g.*, Maryland Constitution, Article XIII, Section 1. Article XVII, Section 4 of the Oklahoma Constitution combines area and population restrictions with minimum wealth requirements as prerequisites for reorganization. Under that provision the legislature is prohibited from creating a new county unless the targeted area is in excess of four hundred square miles, with a population in excess of 15,000 and has a taxable wealth in excess of "two and one-half million dollars, as shown by the current tax rolls." Article XI, Section 1, Paragraph II of the Georgia Constitution limits the number of permissible counties in that State to 159. Generally, any merger, division, or consolidation of existing counties must be approved by a referendum in the affected counties. *Id*. Many state constitutions simply limit the legislative authority to create new counties. For example, Article IX, Section 2 of the Montana Constitution provides that no county boundaries may be altered unless approved "by a majority of those voting on the question in each county affected."

Where county boundaries are changed, or new counties created, many state constitutions require an allocation of the existing indebtedness of the previous county. For example, Article XI, Section 3 of the Washington Constitution provides that: "Every county which shall be enlarged or created from territory taken from any other county or counties shall be liable for a just proportion of the existing debts and liabilities of the county or counties from which such territory shall be taken."

A number of state constitutions contain specific provisions relating to the consolidation or merger of counties. Article VIII, Sections 4 and 5 of the South Carolina Constitution authorizes the legislature to provide for the merger of parts or all of adjoining counties. However, the legislative act must be requested by either the governing bodies of the affected areas or by citizen petition. In either eventuality a referendum is required in the affected area.

Curiously, constitutional provisions restricting the relocation of county seats are more common than might be expected. Under Article XI, Section 2 of the Utah Constitution, a county seat may not be removed or relocated until "at a countryside general election two-thirds of those voting on the proposition vote in favor of moving the county seat." A provision of this type may only be presented to the electorate once every four years. *Id*.

Section 62. Limitations on Special Laws That May Affect Local Government

A number of state constitutions promote local autonomy by prohibiting the legislature from enacting "special laws" pertaining to certain local affairs. As the area of general vs. special law is dealt with extensively in the Chapter 5, only cursory attention will be given to that issue in this Chapter.

Article III, Section 23 of the South Dakota Constitution presents a flavor of provisions of this particular type. Under that section, the legislature is prohibited from enacting special laws which pertain to specified subject matters. These prohibitive areas include *inter alia*: locating or changing county seats, regulating county and township affairs, incorporating or amending the charter of towns, cities and villages, and provisions relating to the management of common schools.

Article III, Section 56 of the Texas Constitution contains a similar provision. Under this section the legislature is prohibited from enacting special laws which create offices or prescribe "the powers and duties of officers, in counties, cities, towns, elections or school districts."

An alternative type of provision is represented by Article XII, Section 2 of the Minnesota Constitution. Under that provision, any special law relating to a local governmental unit, may only become effective after approval "by the affected unit expressed through the voters or the governing body and by such majority as the legislature may direct."

Clearly such provisions exist to encourage the legislature to enact uniform statewide general laws in these areas. Such provisions promote uniformity and also operate to limit the ability of the legislature to single out an entity of local government for preferential or detrimental treatment.

Section 63. Home Rule Provisions

As indicated in the introduction to this chapter, local governments, as subdivisions of the state, draw their legal authority to act from the state itself. Therefore, in the absence of constitutional provisions allocating specific power to entities of local government, such entities are viewed as being subject to the whim of the legislature. *See, e.g., City of Trenton v. New Jersey* (1923). The most significant type of state constitutional provision allocating governmental power to local government, and thereby insulating local government affairs from absolute domination by the state legislature, are charter or home rule provisions.

The legal effect of a home rule provision is to alter the traditional judicial inquiry. In the absence of home rule provisions, a local entity of government must be explicitly or implicitly empowered by provision of law to enable it to act. Except as restricted by statutes, home rule governments are presumed to possess all necessary governmental power to act. Further, the charter becomes the organic law of the local entity and functions like a constitution. Home rule constitutional provisions are diverse. Nonetheless, a few general observations may be made.

(a) *Provisions Relating to Specified Cities or Counties*

A number of state constitutions make explicit provisions for certain identified cities or counties. A classic illustration of this kind of provision is Article XI of the Maryland Constitution. Presumably because of the perceived specialized needs of that metropolis, the Maryland Constitution contains detailed provisions relating to the powers of the City of Baltimore. These provisions are diverse. Sections 1–9 of Article XI provide for the structure of Baltimore City government and enunciate certain restrictions on city government. Articles XI–B, XI–C, XI–D, and XI–G deal respectively with Land Development, Off Street Parking, Port Development, and Residential Rehabilitation and Commercial Financing Loans.

In similar fashion, Article XX of the Colorado Constitution allocates special powers to the City of Denver, and Article VIII Section 6(f) of the Florida Constitution continued constitutionally favored treatment for the metropolitan government of Dade County. While such provisions may appear beneficial because they recognize the peculiar needs of the affected entity, they frequently cause conflict with more general constitutional provisions. Such conflicts invariably must be determined by judicial resolution. *See, e.g., State ex rel. Dade County v. Dickinson* (1969).

(b) *Provisions Allocating Home Rule Power to All Municipalities or Counties*

A few state constitutions eschew any charter requirement as a prerequisite for home rule power. For example, Article XVIII, Section 3 of the Ohio Constitution provides that municipalities "shall have authority to exercise all powers of local self-government." In *Village of Perrysburg v. Ridgway* (1923), the Ohio Supreme Court recognized that Article XVIII, Section 3 allocated all powers of local government to municipalities thereby depriving the

legislature authority to act in such matters. The
Court also concluded that this power resided in
each municipality regardless of whether the municipality had exercised its option under Article XVIII,
Section 7 of the Ohio Constitution to adopt a charter to govern municipal affairs.*

The Illinois Constitution presumptively allocates
"home rule unit" status to all counties in Illinois
which have a "chief executive officer elected by the
electors of the county." *See*, Illinois Constitution,
Article VII, Section 6. However, a qualifying county
may affirmatively elect by referendum not to be a
home rule unit. *See*, Illinois Constitution, Article
VII, Section 6(b).

(c) Constitutional Provisions Requiring a Charter

The most common type of state constitutional
provision authorizing home rule requires the adoption of a charter by the local government. This
charter serves a function similar to that served by
the constitution at the state level. *See generally,
Hudson Motor Car Co. v. City of Detroit* (1937).

The Colorado Constitution is representative of
this general type and it contains provisions for
charter home rule at both the county and municipality level. Article XIV, Section 16 of that constitution authorizes home rule at the county level. This
section requires the legislature to provide by general law a method by which the electors of a county

* The case was limited to a situation where "the powers of
home rule sought to be exercised were not at variance with
general law." *State v. Wagner* (1960).

"may adopt, amend and repeal a county home rule charter." *Id*. Any county home rule charter or amendment or repeal of an existing charter must be approved by a majority of the registered electors of the affected county.

Article XX, Section 6 of the Colorado Constitution authorizes any city or town with a population in excess of two thousand inhabitants to "make, amend, add to or replace the charter of said city or town, which shall be its organic law." A charter adopted pursuant to the Colorado Constitution shall supercede, within its territorial limits, "any law of the state in conflict therewith." *See*, Article XX, Section 6 of the Colorado Constitution. A city or town operating pursuant to such home rule power is constitutionally allocated "all other powers necessary, requisite or proper for the government and administration of its local and municipal matters." *See*, Colorado Constitution Article XX, Section 6.

(d) *What Constitutes Local Matters for Purposes of Home Rule Provisions*

It is axiomatic that a state may not interfere with the local affairs of entities of local government operating under home rule provisions. *See, e.g., City of Sapulpa v. Land* (1924). However, frequently, the most difficult issue presented for resolution is whether a particular matter qualifies as a matter of state or local interest. In describing this dichotomy, the Arizona Supreme Court concluded "there is a twilight zone wherein it is difficult to discern with positive assurance that legislation is of general concern, or is merely of local or municipal concern." *City of Tucson v. Arizona Alpha of Sigma Alpha Epsilon* (1948).

In attempting to formulate a workable judicial rule to distinguish between matters of state and local concern, the Supreme Court of Oregon has indicated its decisions will be made "solely upon the basis of our knowledge of the manner in which local and state governments operate and the relative importance of the function in question to the cities and to the state as a whole." *State ex rel. Heinig v. City of Milwaukie* (1962).* Thus, the Court attempts to determine what interest is "predominant" or "paramount." *City of Beaverton v. International Association of Fire–Fighters, Local 1660* (1975).

Other courts attempt to distinguish between state and local matters by reference to an agent-proprietary distinction. To the extent local government acts as the agent of the state, it is considered a matter of state concern. To the extent local government acts in a proprietary capacity, it is considered a matter of local concern. *Apodaca v. Wilson* (1974).

Section 64. School Districts

A number of state constitutions contain provisions relating to education. As discussed in Chapter

* The Oregon Supreme Court has held that "[T]he *Heinig* formula should [not] be extended beyond the context of laws for city government in which it was formulated." *City of La Grande v. Public Employees Retirement Board* (1978). It is unclear to us the effect this will have on the purpose for which we used *Heinig*.

11, such provisions arguably create a constitutionally protected interest in education which may be asserted by members of the public. *See, e.g., Serrano v. Priest* (1976).*

On a much more fundamental level, a number of state constitutions provide specifically for the governmental structures which are responsible for delivering educational services to the public. For example, Article VIII, Section 203(2) of the Mississippi Constitution provides for a nine member appointed State Board of Education which is responsible to "manage and invest school funds according to law, formulate policies according to law for implementation by the State Department of Education, and perform such other duties as prescribed by law."

Provisions as to local school districts vary. Under Article IX, Section 4 of the Florida Constitution, each county presumptively constitutes a school district with provision for consolidation of contiguous counties into one school district upon approval by referendum in the affected area. Each school district is governed by a five member school board which is constitutionally responsible to "operate, control and supervise all free public schools within the school district." Under Article IX, Section 5 of the Florida Constitution, provision is made for an elective Superintendent of Schools in each district, with an option for the appointment of the superintendent by the School Board.

* A change in the California Constitution *may* have affected this case in the context used here. *See Crawford v. Huntington Beach Union High School District* (2002).

In other states, school districts' boundaries are not as strictly tied to county boundaries. In many instances, discretion is placed in the hands of the legislature to make such decisions. For example, Article IX, Section 14 of the California Constitution allocates to the legislature the power, by general law "to provide for the incorporation and organization of school districts." Likewise in Colorado, the authority to establish school districts is placed in the legislature. Under Article IX, Section 15 of the Colorado Constitution, the General Assembly is directed to "provide for organization of school districts of convenient size."

Many of the constitutional provisions, discussed elsewhere in this chapter, which promote local autonomy are made expressly applicable to school districts. Article XVI, Section 6 of the Wyoming Constitution prohibits inter alia any school district from loaning its credit or making donations "to or in aid of any individual, association or corporation." Under Article III, Section 32 of the Pennsylvania Constitution, the General Assembly is denied the authority to enact local or special laws "regulating the affairs of . . . school districts." Under Article IX, Section 8 of the Arizona Constitution, the indebtedness which a non-unified school district may incur is limited to "six per centum of the taxable property" within the school district, unless there is a referendum authorizing additional debt.

In addition, some state constitutions contain explicit provisions concerning education which presumably are intended to promote local autonomy over education, while constitutionally guaranteeing minimum educational standards. Under Article XII, Section 5 of the New Mexico Constitution, school attendance is constitutionally compelled. "Every child of school age and of sufficient physical and mental ability shall be required to attend a public or other school during such period and for such time as may be prescribed by law." Under Article IX, Section 8 of the Missouri Constitution, all governmental aid to religious or sectarian schools is expressly prohibited.

A number of state constitutions contain provisions providing special treatment for designated institutions of higher learning. For example, Article X, Section 5 of the Hawaii Constitution expressly provides for the creation of the University of Hawaii and a Board of Regents to govern the University.

CHAPTER 9

REVENUE AND TAXATION

Section 65. Federal Constitutional Limitations

The authority of the sovereign states to establish and operate systems of taxation for the purpose of collecting revenue to fund state and local governmental functions is affected by a number of provisions of the federal constitution. Specifically, the United States Supreme Court has judicially tested state revenue provisions against the following provisions of the federal constitution.

1. The Commerce Clause. *See, e.g., Bacchus Imports, Ltd. v. Dias* (1984).

2. The Export Import Clause. *See, e.g., Michelin Tire Corp. v. Wages* (1976).

3. The Supremacy Clause. *See, e.g., Maryland v. Louisiana* (1981).

4. The Due Process Clause of the Fourteenth Amendment. *See, e.g., Standard Pressed Steel Co. v. Washington Dept. of Revenue* (1975).

5. The Equal Protection Clause of the Fourteenth Amendment. *See, e.g., Exxon Corp. v. Eagerton* (1983).

6. The Privileges and Immunities Clause of Article IV, Section 2 of the United States Constitution. *See, e.g., Austin v. New Hampshire* (1975).

While this list appears onerous at first glance, the federal courts have historically exhibited great deference towards the states in local revenue matters. This deference has apparently been motivated by federalism concerns. In permitting the states the ability to indulge certain discriminations in local revenue matters, federal courts frequently observe that the states are afforded the widest possible latitude within the limits of the constitution in tax matters. *Carmichael v. Southern Coal & Coke Co.* (1937). This deferential policy is further evidenced by the fact that Congress has denied jurisdiction to the federal trial courts in most instances pertaining to state and local tax matters. *See*, 28 U.S.C. § 1341 (2002). Thus, while federal constitutional concerns should not be totally overlooked, historically they have been less likely to have an impact on local tax matters than in other areas.

A.   RESTRICTIONS ON LONG TERM INDEBTEDNESS

Section 66.   Constitutional Limitations on Issuance of State Bonds—Introduction

In the early years of the Republic, state constitutions did not impose restrictions on the use of long term debt to fund governmental activities at the state level. This constitutional silence was primarily due to the fact that the power of state government to borrow freely was widely accepted. Moreover, governmental borrowing was primarily limited to short term debt and war financing. This changed in 1817 when the state of New York financed the construction of the Erie canal. Revenues from the operation of the canal swiftly exceeded debt service costs. Buoyed by this success, other states commenced construction of other internal improvements. State borrowing grew dramatically.

From 1837 through 1840, the American economy experienced a deep depression. In 1840, many of the state public improvement projects ceased construction due to economic setbacks. As a result, the states felt the dual wrath of declining revenues occasioned by the depression and unrelenting debt service requirements. Consequently, many states found themselves with non-income producing, partially completed projects, with the obligation to fully repay the outstanding indebtedness. From 1841 to 1842, nine separate states, including Florida, Illinois, Indiana, Michigan and Pennsylvania, were unable to resist the economic pressures and defaulted on their bonds. For example, the state of Mississippi alone defaulted on $7,000,000 worth of state bonds in 1841. The state continued to repudiate the bonds, and in 1875 the Mississippi Constitution was amended to include a specific provision prohibiting the state from repaying any of these bonds. *See*, Mississippi Constitution of 1875, Article XII, Section 5.

These developments fueled a popular movement for revenue reform at the state level. As a result of the relative success of this movement, most state constitutions currently contain some restrictions on the issuance of state debt. Generally, state constitutions can be categorized into four separate classes pertaining to regulation of state indebtedness. Each of these categories will be described below.

Section 67. Public Purpose Limitations

Most states, either by express constitutional provision or by judicial construction, require that the credit of the state can only be pledged for activities which serve a public, rather than a private, purpose. The difference between these two concepts is frequently difficult to determine, and has served as the focus of much litigation. *See, e.g., Common Cause v. State* (1983). This general restriction is often discussed in conjunction with another provision, which is found in most state constitutions which prohibits the state, or any of its subdivisions, from "giving or lending its credit in the aid of any individual, association, or corporation." *See, e.g.*, Massachusetts Constitution, Article LXII, Section 1. While these provisions are similar in many ways, it is ill advised to assume they are identical in reach. Generally, the public purpose limitation has been construed to apply to any obligation bearing the state's name, even if the credit of the state has not technically been pledged. Thus, revenue bonds which do not affect the credit of the state must still satisfy the public purpose test. Given that state taxes and credit are not threatened, the courts are generally quite liberal in finding this requirement satisfied.

On the other hand, the constitutional restriction prohibiting the extension of credit to private citizens and businesses is only triggered when the credit of the state has been pledged. Thus, where revenue bonds are involved, this more specific provision would not appear to be applicable. *See, e.g., State v. City of Miami* (1980).

In addition, many state constitutions contain provisions which prohibit the state from becoming an owner or a stockholder of a private entity and prohibit the state from making donations or gifts to private entities. *See, e.g.*, Oklahoma Constitution, Article X, Section 15. Furthermore, state constitutions contain specific provisions dealing with state indebtedness. While these four separate categories will be summarized, be advised that each constitution will vary and in certain instances combine elements of each category.

Section 68.   States With No or Minimal Restrictions on the Issuance of State Debt

A number of state constitutions, primarily centered on the east coast, have no provisions addressing state indebtedness, or only the requirements discussed in the preceding section that state bonds must comply with a public purpose requirement. However, a few of the state constitutions do contain restrictions on the extension of state credit to private entities. Most of these states have constitutions which predate the 1840 depression, and apparently did not experience the fiscal constitutional reform zeal that developed in other states. These states include Connecticut, New Hampshire, Vermont and Massachusetts.

The Connecticut Constitution does not contain any constitutional provisions specifically dealing with state indebtedness. Nonetheless, the courts of that state have construed Article 1, Section 1 of Connecticut's Constitution, which provides that no individual is entitled to "exclusive public emoluments or privileges," as imposing a public purpose limitation on the issuance of state bonds. *See, Roan v. Connecticut Indus. Bldg. Com'n* (1963).

Section 69. States With Legislative Super Majority Requirements

A common type of substantive constitutional restriction on state indebtedness imposes super majority requirements on the legislature when it incurs indebtedness. Such provisions require the legislature to approve any state indebtedness by a larger margin than a simple majority. For example, Article VIII, Section 3 of the Delaware Constitution provides that, with certain exceptions, in the event of war, insurrection or the refinancing of existing state debt, the state cannot incur indebtedness, unless it is approved by a three-fourths majority of each house of the Delaware legislature.

Occasionally, legislative super majority requirements are combined with other types of restrictions.

For example, Article VII, Section 13 of the Hawaii Constitution limits the amount of general obligation bonds that the state may issue. Specifically, total payments on state bonds are limited in any fiscal period to a percentage of the average general fund revenues of the state for the preceding three years. Despite this provision, the limitation can be exceeded if the governor declares an emergency and a two-thirds majority of each house of the legislature consents to the issuance of bonds in excess of these limits.

Section 70.   Referendum Requirements

Another common type of constitutional restriction on state indebtedness is a referendum requirement. Basically, these provisions require the electorate to approve contemplated state indebtedness before the credit of the state can be extended. An illustration of this type of restriction is Article IX, Section 8 of the Alaska Constitution. Under that provision, the state can only incur indebtedness where bonds are authorized by law for either capital improvements or veteran housing loans. In essence, the constitution limits the permissible purposes for which bonds may be issued. The provision continues to require that the electorate must ratify any contemplated bond issue within the purposes permitted by the constitution. To be valid, a bond issue must be ratified by a majority of qualified voters participating in an election. Excluded from the ratification requirements are bonds incurred in war, repelling invasion and insurrection, and in meeting natural disasters. Most states with referendum requirements provide for the same or similar exclusions.

Another common exclusion from referendum requirements are bonds which merely refinance existing indebtedness. *See, e.g.*, Alabama Constitution, Section 213. Some states permit refinancing bonds but limit their use to those instances where the refinancing will result in a reduced interest burden to the state. *See, e.g.*, Florida Constitution, Article VII, Section 11.

Section 71. States Prohibiting State Debt but Providing Exceptions for Certain Purposes

Another type of constitutional restriction on state indebtedness found in many state constitutions is an absolute prohibition on state indebtedness. These are generally accompanied by provisions permitting the incurring of state debt for limited purposes. A good illustration of this type of clause is found in Article XI, Section 7 of the Oregon Constitution. This section specifically provides that the legislature cannot lend the credit of the state or create any debt or liability which, when aggregated with all other state debt, would exceed the sum of $50,000. Excluded from the operation of this section are debts incurred in time of war, or when repelling invasion or suppressing insurrection. Excluded from the section is indebtedness incurred "to build and maintain permanent roads." *Id*. However, all the aggregate road building state debt may not exceed 1% of the "true cash value of all the property of the state taxed on an ad valorem basis." *Id*. This provision is typical of this type of restriction, because it initially prohibits all state debt, excludes emergencies, makes provision for minimal debt to provide for small deficits, and then permits debt for a preferred state purpose, *i.e.*, road building.

Article XIII, Section 1 of the Nebraska Constitution is a similar type of clause. Specifically, it prohibits all state debt above the aggregate sum of $100,000. This limit is specifically permitted "to meet casual deficits or failures in the revenue." Excluded from the operation of the clause is debt incurred during wartime or in repelling invasion or suppressing insurrection. Despite these provisions, the state can incur debt, with the consent of a three-fifths vote in the legislature, for road construction or water conservation and management projects.

Section 72. Summary of State General Obligations Bonds

Although each of the four categories discussed above overlap and have local variations in each state constitution, a few conclusions can be drawn. First, the most common category of restrictions on state bonds are those requiring a popular referendum. One can assume from this assertion that the extent of state indebtedness can be peculiarly subject to popular control. Actually, this is an inaccurate statement. All the restrictive constitutional provisions discussed above are only applicable where the state incurs a debt or otherwise extends its credit. Other financing devices, such as state issued revenue bonds, have been judicially determined not to constitute an extension of credit by the state. Thus, through this device, which will be discussed in more detail below, states have been able to finance projects through bond issue while circumventing the rather rigid restrictions discussed above.

Section 73.   Revenue Bonds

By 1900, most states had enacted rigid prohibitions against the creation of state debt and the extension of the credit of the state. Faced with a need to identify sources of revenue, state legislatures enacted methods of borrowing that effectively challenged the limits of the constitutional restrictions on debt. These efforts were subsequently judicially tested. As revenue bonds are exceptions to these provisions, their development is in many ways a history of judicial construction of state constitutional restrictions on debt.

One of the first cases to deal with this issue was *In re Canal Certificates* (1893). Colorado, like most states, has rather restrictive constitutional provisions on state indebtedness. In financing the construction of a canal, legislature had authorized the responsible state agency to pay expenses with certificates of indebtedness. Under the enacting legislation, the certificates were to be paid from a fund created by the income produced by the canal. The statute specifically provided that the certificates would never be a claim against the state. Under other circumstances, the indebtedness would have violated the constitutional restrictions on state debt. However, under the circumstances, the Court concluded that the certificates did not constitute state debt because they were payable only out of the special fund and the statute prohibited the certificates from ever becoming a claim against the state. As a result, the certificates could be issued, without violating the constitutional restrictions.

From this simple beginning, virtually every state that had constitutional restrictions on the issuance of state debt adopted some variation of this "special fund doctrine" in identifying revenue bonds as an exception to state constitutional debt restrictions. Currently, the special fund doctrine can be summarized as holding that debts which are not serviced out of general funds and which are not backed by the full faith and credit of the state are not debts within the meaning of the constitutional restrictions on state debt.

There are as many variations of the scope of this doctrine as there are states. For example, in Texas the "special fund doctrine" was extended to allow a statute donating to a flood district half of the state ad valorem tax collected in the county to be used by the district to control flood waters. This was determined not to violate that state's restriction on state indebtedness. *Harris County Flood Control District v. Mann* (1940). In Oklahoma, the irrevocable pledging of a portion of the gasoline tax was originally determined sufficient to violate the constitutional restrictions on state debt. *Boswell v. State*

(1937). In contrast, identical arrangements were determined not to violate constitutional restrictions in Alabama and Idaho. *See, Scott v. Alabama State Bridge Corp.* (1936); and *Lyons v. Bottolfsen* (1940).

Certain states have even elevated this doctrine to constitutional proportions. For example, Article XIII, Section 1 of the Nebraska Constitution explicitly excludes from the state debt restrictions, revenue bonds issued by the Board of Regents of the University of Nebraska, or the Board of Trustees of the Nebraska state colleges and the state Board of Education, for the provision of education and related services within the state. Under Article VII, Section 11(d) of the Florida Constitution, revenue bonds are expressly exempted from the constitutional restrictions, provided the project is authorized by law.

Section 74. Constitutional Restrictions on Debt of Local Government

As discussed above, state constitutional provisions restricting the issuance of state debt were primarily a response to dramatic bond defaults that occurred during the depression of 1837 on some rather substantial internal improvement projects. Perhaps due to these restrictions, local governments began to finance many of the projects that state government was prohibited from financing. During the economic crises of the 1870's, many local governments experienced difficulties repaying these obligations, especially so-called "railroad aid bonds." In response to this crisis, popular pressures resulted in the amendment of many state constitutions placing restrictions on the issuance of debt by local levels of government. Although these provisions vary significantly from state to state, they can generally be divided into three separate categories of restriction.

Section 75. Limitation on Local Debt Imposed by Reference to Ad Valorem Tax Base

The first method of restricting local government indebtedness is to limit the amount of permissible local debt to a percentage of the assessed valuation of property subject to ad valorem taxation within the boundaries of the issuing entity. As ad valorem taxes are the traditional source of local funds to repay such indebtedness, it was believed that a limitation determined by reference to the source of repayment was an equitable method establishing a limitation.

A good illustration of a limitation of this type is found at Section 158 of the Kentucky Constitution. Pursuant to this section, counties, certain municipalities, and taxing districts may only incur indebtedness up to 2% of the assessed valuation of all property located within the issuing entity's boundaries. This is the most common type of constitutional restriction on local government indebtedness among the fifty states. While occasionally it is found as the only limitation, such as in Kentucky, frequently this restriction is combined with other limitations. *See*, Georgia Constitution, Article IX, Section 5(1)(a) and the discussion below.

Section 76. Limitation of Local Indebtedness by Restricting Tax Rates That Can Be Used for Repayment of Debt

A second method of constitutionally regulating the indebtedness of local government is provisions which (1) limit the source of repayment of such indebtedness to certain taxes, and (2) further limit the tax rates that can be levied for repayment. Both the percentage limitation and this restriction are illustrated by Amendment 62 of the Arkansas Constitution. Section 1 of that Amendment limits county and municipal indebtedness, subject to voter approval, to 10% and 20% of the assessed valuation of taxable property located within their respective boundaries. Section 2 of the amendment does permit a municipality or county, subject to voter approval, to issue bonds for the purpose of securing, developing, and financing industry. Despite this provision, the source of repayment of these bonds is limited to a special ad valorem tax which cannot exceed five mills of the assessed valuation of property located within the issuing entity. The provision specifically permits the governmental entity to suspend collection of the special tax when not required to service the debt. Conversely, if valuation declines, a shortfall may result which could threaten repayment of the debt. For this reason, this type of provision is less common than percentage limitations.

Section 77.   Referendum Requirements

The third method of constitutionally regulating the indebtedness of local government is the use of referendum requirements, as a precondition to the issuance of debt. Article XI, Section 6 of the Colorado Constitution is a good example of this type of provision in its pristine form. Under this provision, no political subdivision of the state may incur indebtedness, unless the issue of incurring debt is approved by a majority of qualified voters within the area that would be affected by the indebtedness.

Section 78.   Summary of Local Government Bond Restrictions

As suggested above, the number of variations of restrictions on local indebtedness are as numerous as there are states. Many of these restrictions are constitutional in origin while elsewhere they are purely creatures of statute. All are affected by judicial interpretation. One of the more common types of restriction combines the percentage limitation restriction with referendum requirements.

Article X, Section 15 of the North Dakota Constitution is a representative example of a hybrid clause of this type. Under this section, the debt of any county, township, city, town, school district, or other political subdivision of the state, is prohibited from exceeding 5% of the assessed valuation of property located within the boundaries of the issuing entity. In order to provide flexibility in the event of emergency, the section permits an incorporated city to issue additional debt, up to an additional 3% of assessed valuation upon a two-thirds vote of electors within the incorporated city.

Just as constitutional restrictions on state indebtedness had been judicially circumvented through utilization of revenue bonds, the courts have permitted local restrictions to be circumvented through the use of revenue bonds. Some recent constitutional provisions have even constitutionally recognized that revenue bonds are excluded from these provisions. *See*, Florida Constitution, Article VII, Section 10. However, even where the revenue bonds have not met the requirements of the constitutional exclusion, the courts have still determined that revenue bonds are not subject to the constitutional restrictions on local indebtedness. *See, State v. Leon County* (1981).

B.   RESTRICTIONS ON THE IMPOSITION OF TAX

Section 79.   Uniformity Clauses

The Equal Protection Clause of the Fourteenth Amendment to the United States Constitution establishes a nationwide minimal standard of uniformity in state tax matters. However, the federal courts have deferred to the pragmatic needs of state government in collecting funds for operating government. As a result, the minimal standard of uniformity mandated by the federal constitution has not been required to be a "precise, scientific uniformity." *Allied Stores of Ohio, Inc. v. Bowers* (1959).

Forty-two state constitutions supplement this national uniformity requirement with some variation of a uniformity requirement directed at the determination of taxes. Many of these clauses only apply to property taxes while others apply equally to any tax imposed under the auspices of a particular state. In some instances, judicial construction has expanded the reach of such clauses far beyond any uniformity contemplated by the Equal Protection Clause. In differentiating between the reach of the Equal Protection Clause and state uniformity clauses, Justice Frankfurter described the additional reach of such uniformity clauses as "narrow and sometimes cramping." *Nashville, C & St. L. Ry. v. Browning* (1940).

Despite the rather monumental difficulties posed by the task, one authoritative source has attempted to divide these state uniformity provisions into groups with similar characteristics. *I Newhouse, Constitutional Uniformity and Equality in State Taxation 16–18* (2d Ed. 1984). This project resulted in the identification of twelve separate categories of state constitutional uniformity clauses. A detailed discussion of these variations is simply beyond the scope of this work. Hopefully, reference to a few particular state provisions and their judicial interpretation will convey a sense of the general effect of these provisions.

Article VIII, Section 1 of the Delaware Constitution provides that: "[a]ll taxes shall be uniform upon the same class of subjects within the territorial limits of the authority levying the tax. . . ." Unlike many uniformity provisions in other states, the Delaware provision is clearly applicable to all types of taxes. The potential reach of this section is more expansive than in those states where the uniformity clause is limited to property taxes alone. The Delaware courts have construed this provision quite conservatively. For example, in *Conard v. State* (1940), the Court held that the same standards of reasonableness which governed an Equal Protection analysis were applicable in applying the uniformity clause of Article VII, Section 1 of the Delaware Constitution. The Court also observed that as the legal theories were so similar, it was unlikely that a tax could violate one but not the other. Likewise, if a particular tax satisfied the requirements of either Equal Protection or the uniformity clause, it would invariably satisfy the requirements of the other. This rather conservative interpretation is at odds with other states. For example, the Pennsylvania Supreme Court once interpreted Article VIII, Section 1 of the Pennsylvania Constitution to prohibit a graduated income tax. *See, Kelley v. Kalodner* (1935). The Pennsylvania uniformity provision at issue was virtually identical to Delaware's provision.

By contrast, Article X, Section 1 of the Indiana Constitution requires the legislature to establish "a uniform and equal rate of property assessment and taxation." Clearly, this provision only contemplates application to property taxes. It facially appears that the uniformity requirements of the Indiana Constitution are less encompassing than those found in the Delaware Constitution. However, appearances can be deceiving.

Non-property taxes in Indiana are subject to the Equal Protection Clause and the Indiana counterpart in Article I, Section 23 of the Indiana Constitution. As a result, they are subject to the same judicial scrutiny as all taxes are in Delaware. However, the special uniformity requirement of Article X, Section 1 imposes additional scrutiny where property taxes are involved. The Indiana Supreme Court has described the uniformity requirements of this section as "rigid" and much more demanding than traditional notions of Equal Protection. *See, Indiana Aeronautics Commission v. Ambassadair, Inc.*, (1977).

Section 80. General Non–Property Tax Provisions

State constitutional provisions pertaining to non-property taxes, vary substantially from state to state. Certain state constitutions such as Connecticut, Alaska, Vermont, Virginia, Georgia, South Carolina, New Mexico and Rhode Island contain no provisions dealing explicitly with non-property taxes. In these states, decisions concerning non-property taxes are left to the discretion of the state legislature.

One of the more common provisions dealing with non-property taxes is a provision requiring the legislature, when establishing a tax, to specify the purpose of the tax and to limit the tax revenues collected from the imposition of the tax to expenditures or pursuit of this purpose. Article X, Section 3 of the North Dakota Constitution provides a good example of this type of provision. The provision announces that "[N]o tax shall be levied except in pursuance of law, and every law imposing a tax shall state distinctly the object of the same, to which only it shall be applied."

Such provisions are not strictly construed and no precise enumeration of projects is required. For example, in *State ex rel. Haig v. Hauge* (1917), the North Dakota Supreme Court, interpreting this provision, concluded that the use of tax revenues for a teacher pension fund complied with this requirement because the purpose of the tax was "school purposes."

The most common non-property tax provisions found in state constitutions are provisions restricting the expenditure of constitutionally specified taxes to road construction or maintenance projects. *See, e.g.*, Article IX, Section 5 of the Nevada Constitution. Under this provision, proceeds from all license and registration fees, and other road user fees and all excise taxes on gasoline or other fuels, are restricted to the "construction, maintenance and repair of the public highways of this state." *Id.* The Massachusetts Constitution of 1780 contains this type of provision in Article LXXVIII. This provision was recently amended to permit such taxes to also be spent for mass transportation purposes.

Another common provision found in many state constitutions is a provision either delegating certain taxes to lower levels of government or authorizing the legislature to delegate the right to levy certain taxes to lower levels of government. The Louisiana Constitution at Article VI, Section 29 allocates to local governmental subdivisions or school boards the authority, subject to voter approval, to adopt a sales tax within certain percentage limitations.

Section 81. Specific Restrictions on Approval of Tax Bills

A few state constitutions impose specific limitations on the manner in which tax bills may be approved by the Legislature. For example, the Oklahoma Constitution prohibits the Legislature from passing any revenue bill during the last five (5) days of a legislative session. Oklahoma Constitution, Article V, Section 33B. The constitution also provides that valid revenue bills may either be put to the voters and approved by a majority of the votes cast, or by a three-fourths (3/4) vote of the membership of both houses of the legislature. Oklahoma Constitution, Article V, Section 33(c) and (d).

Section 82. Constitutional Provisions Pertaining to Income Taxes

State constitutions contain provisions which authorize, prohibit or regulate the authority of the state to impose income taxes. A common provision pertaining to the income tax is a provision which authorizes a state to impose an income tax that is determined by the legislature. Article X, Section 8 of the Indiana Constitution, which authorizes the General Assembly to levy and collect an income tax, in a manner prescribed by law, is illustrative of this type of provision. To a large extent, such provisions would seem mainly to reaffirm the existing power of the legislature to impose this method of taxation. *See generally*, Chapter 1.

Many state constitutions contain provisions which effectively authorize the states to base their state income tax system on the federal income tax system. Article 11, Section 11 of the Kansas Constitution permits the legislature to "define income by reference to or otherwise adopt by reference all or any part of the laws of the United States as they then exist and, prospectively, as they may thereafter be amended or enacted." These provisions have been periodically upheld against such arguments that they represent an impermissible waiver of state sovereignty. *Anderson v. Tiemann* (1967).

A number of states specifically permit the imposition of a tax on income, but prohibit the imposition of graduated or progressive rates on income. Article IX, Section 7 of the Michigan Constitution provides that "[N]o income tax graduated as to rate or base shall be imposed by the State or any of its subdivisions." This provision has been construed by the Michigan Courts to prohibit the imposition of a tax which is a percentage of the federal income tax, because to do so would indirectly impose a graduated income tax. However, the imposition of different rates on individuals, corporations and financial institutions was not prohibited by this provision. *Kuhn v. Department of Treasury* (1968).

A similar result was reached in New Hampshire under a Constitutional Uniformity Clause. This provision was previously construed to prohibit the imposition of a progressive income tax. An attempt by the legislature to circumvent this interpretation, by imposing a tax which was a percentage of the progressive federal income tax, was stricken as violative of this provision. *Opinion of the Justices* (1955).

At least two states, Utah and New Jersey, authorize the imposition of a state income tax, but constitutionally restrict the purposes for which the revenue raised for this tax may be applied. Article VIII, Section 1, Paragraph 7 of the New Jersey Constitution expressly limits the use of income tax revenue for the purpose of "reducing or offsetting property taxes" by appropriation to lower levels of government. Article XIII, Section 12(3) of the Utah Constitution requires all revenue raised for the state income tax to be applied to the "support of the public school system."

A few states constitutionally limit rates which may be imposed on income. For example, Article V, Section 2(6) of the North Carolina Constitution specifically limits the rate of tax on income to 10%. The South Dakota Constitution at Article XI, Section 13 provides that the rate of tax on income can only be increased when approved by a majority vote in a general election or a two-thirds vote of the legislature.

At least one state constitutionally prohibits the imposition of an income tax. Article VII, Section V of the Florida Constitution effectively prohibits the imposition of a state income tax on natural persons, while permitting a limited state income tax on artificial business entities.

Section 83. Constitutional Provisions Pertaining Estate Taxes

While less pervasive than provisions relating to the income tax, many state constitutions contain provisions relating to state estate taxes. Amendment 23 to the Alabama Constitution provides for a so-called "pick-up tax." Under this provision, Alabama is authorized to levy an estate tax in an amount not to exceed the amount allowed under the federal estate tax provisions, as a credit for state death taxes. The effect of this provision is to generate estate tax revenue for the state of Alabama without increasing the overall state and federal estate tax burden of the estate. As the state tax is limited to the allowable federal credit, the provision does not increase the overall tax burden of the estate, but does allocate a portion of estate tax to the state of Alabama that would otherwise be payable to the federal government.

Article VII, Section V of the Florida Constitution contains a similar provision. In interpreting this provision, the Florida courts have ruled unconstitutional, attempts by the legislature to proportionately allocate the credit in a situation when a decedent owed estate taxes in Florida and another state, as such attempts could indirectly increase the Florida estate tax burden above the federal credit. *Department of Revenue v. Golder* (1976).

Section 84.   Requirement of Taxation According to Valuation

Many state constitutions contain provisions which require property to be taxed according to valuation. These provisions take a variety of forms including such requirements that property be taxed at "fair cash value," "fair market value," "just valuation" and "true and full value in money." While not explicitly limited to ad valorem property taxes, these provisions are generally limited to ad valorem property taxes by judicial decision. *See, e.g., State ex rel. Jones v. Nolte* (1942). As a result, such provisions are construed to be inapplicable to license, excise, franchise, and other varieties of taxes. Where applicable, these provisions have been construed to be mandatory. *See, Carkonen v. Williams* (1969).

Section 211 of the Alabama Constitution is a clear illustration of a provision of this type. It simply provides that "All taxes levied on property in this state shall be assessed in exact proportion to the value of such property...." In construing this clause, the Alabama Supreme Court determined that the purpose of this provision was to: (1) create an ad valorem tax system; and (2) limit the taxing power to insure uniformity and equality in the ad valorem taxation system. The mandatory use of valuation also eliminated arbitrary methods of taxation that could arise if other methods were used. *State v. Birmingham Southern R. Co.* (1913).

These provisions do not interfere with the ability of the legislature to classify property for purposes of ad valorem taxation as long as the classification is not arbitrary. *See, e.g., State v. Alabama Educational Foundation* (1935).

Section 85.   Meaning of "Just Value" and Related Terms

While state constitutions utilize a variety of terms in requiring that property be "valued" for purposes of ad valorem taxation, all such provisions derive from a common purpose. This purpose is to insure that the tax system applies equitably to all property and taxpayers within its reach. This goal is dependent upon a fair administration of the property tax system by those officials responsible for the appraisal of property.

Article IX, Section 8 of the Maine Constitution requires ad valorem taxes to be assessed equally according to "just value." The Supreme Judicial Court of Maine in *Kittery Electric Light Co. v. Assessors of the Town of Kittery* (1966) "judicially synonymized" the phrase with "market value," "true value" and "real value" found in other state constitutions.

These provisions were construed to mean the reasonable cash market value of the property, or the price which the appraising official believes the property would bring in an arm's length transaction. *See, e.g., New Jersey Bell Telephone Co. v. Newark* (1937). These requirements are not complied with where some property is valued higher than similar property valued for the same purposes. *Sparkman v. State* (1916).

Section 86.   Use Valuation

Approximately half of the state constitutions prescribe or authorize the legislature to provide for special methods of valuing tax-preferred types of property. The most common type of property subject to these special provisions is agricultural property. Presumably fueled by a desire to encourage family farming, a number of states authorize agricultural land to be valued for ad valorem tax purposes, at its current use for agricultural purposes without consideration of any other uses of the property which might produce a higher valuation.

By way of illustration, Article VIII, Section 1(d) of the Texas Constitution requires all land that is owned by natural persons and utilized for agricultural purposes "to be assessed for all tax purposes in the consideration of only those factors relative to such agricultural use." States such as Kansas prescribe specialized methods of valuing agricultural property, which basically obtain the same result as a provision permitting agricultural use valuation. Article XI, Section 12 of the Kansas Constitution permits agricultural property to be valued up to the basis of its "agricultural income or agricultural productivity, actual or potential."

Other states, such as Georgia, constitutionally favor agricultural property for valuation purposes, but utilize a percentage formula to accomplish this result, rather than a valuation scheme. Under Article VII, Section 1, Paragraph III(c) of the Georgia Constitution, subject to certain restrictions, an owner utilizing real property for "bona fide agricultural purposes" can value up to 2,000 acres of agricultural land at 75% of value that it would otherwise be subject to.

Washington and Maine expand the use of special valuation techniques beyond agriculture to other preferred types of property. Article VII, Section 11 of the Washington Constitution authorizes the valuation of "farms, agricultural lands, standing timber, and timberlands ... and other open space lands which are used for recreation or for enjoyment of their scenic or natural beauty" based on the current use of the property.

Section 87.   The Exemption of Public Property

Generally speaking, and even in the absence of a specific constitutional or statutory provision recognizing the existence of an exemption, property owned by the federal, state or local governments is not subject to ad valorem taxation. *See, e.g., Pelouze v. City of Richmond* (1945). This insulation of governmental property from local ad valorem taxation is motivated by federal/state constitutional concerns, as well as the very practical concern that the imposition of tax against the property of a governmental entity by another would simply result in an increased tax burden on the taxpayers of the entity which owns the property. *State v. Locke* (1923).

Property of the United States and its agencies is not subject to taxation at the state or local level unless the federal government consents to the imposition of the tax levy. *McCulloch v. Maryland* (1819). As this principle emanates from the federal constitution, there need not be any express exemption in the state constitution exempting such property from local taxation. The exclusion of federal property from taxation is as an "immunity" from taxation, rather than as an exemption. *United States v. Allegheny County* (1944). In a slightly different context, this distinction between immunity from taxation and exemption from taxation has been described as follows. Exemption from taxation suggests, that in the absence of an exempting provision, the property would otherwise be subject to tax. If property is immune from tax, its public nature prohibits the imposition of tax even though no specific constitutional or statutory provision operates to exclude it from tax. *See, State v. City of Hudson* (1950). As a result, many state constitutions do not contain provisions exempting federal property from local ad valorem taxation. This immunity is inherent in our federal system. Likewise, state constitutions expressly exempting federal property from local tax levies create no additional exemption. However, federal immunity is not absolute. For example, property is subject to local taxation, even where legal title is in the United States, when beneficial ownership is in the hands of private entities. *S.R.A. v. Minnesota* (1946).

As a general principle of law, property of the state and local governments used for governmental purposes is immune from state and local taxation, unless there is a clear intent that such property be subject to state and local taxation. *Pelouze v. City of Richmond* (1945). Such a conclusion clearly recognizes the right of a state to impose local tax levies on state and local property. To negate such a result, many state constitutions preempt legislative discretion in this area, and regulate the existence and extent of governmental exemption in the state constitution.

For example, Article X, Section 6 of the Oklahoma Constitution expressly exempts from tax "all property of the United States, and of this State, and of counties and of municipalities of this State." Under this provision it held that governmental property is exempt from tax as a result of governmental ownership, regardless of the actual use to which the property is placed. *State ex rel. City of Tulsa v. Mayes* (1935). Likewise, when legal title was technically in the state but beneficial ownership elsewhere, it was held that the property was subject to taxation as a result of private ownership. *State ex rel. Cartwright v. Dunbar* (1980).

Other state constitutions impose a "use," rather than an ownership requirement, as a condition of the governmental exemption. For example, under the Florida Constitution, federal, state and county governments are immune from local tax levies, even though there is not a constitutional provision which expressly exempts their property. However, Article VII, Section 3(a) of the Florida Constitution enunciates a different rule for municipally-owned property. Under this provision, municipal property is only exempt when the property is "used exclusively by it for municipal or public purposes." In interpreting this provision, the Florida courts have broadly construed this use requirement. In *City of Sarasota v. Mikos* (1979), the holding of vacant land satisfied this use requirement. However, the lease of municipally owned property is not a public use. *Panama City v. Pledger* (1939). In addition, if a municipality owns property outside its borders, the legislature is authorized to require the payment of taxes by the owner to the taxing unit in which the property is located.

Section 88. Charitable Exemptions

Unlike governmental entities, charitable institutions are not completely immune from ad valorem taxation. As a result, the property of charitable institutions is exempt from local ad valorem taxation if either a constitutional exemption or a constitutionally permissible statutory exemption excludes charitable property from taxation.

All states provide for the exemption of certain types of charitable property from ad valorem taxation. The enunciated public policy behind such exemption is a perceived public benefit. Thus, it is frequently stated that charitable institutions perform services that would otherwise have to be performed by government. The exemption of such property from tax is envisioned as one method of encouraging such services thereby reducing the burdens on local government. *Bethesda General Hospital v. State Tax Commission* (1965).

Notwithstanding any public benefits from charitable property, the exemption of property from taxation indirectly influences the ad valorem tax burden of less favored taxpayers. As a result, exemption from taxation is the exception rather than the norm. While a state may be willing to exempt charitable property from taxation because of the benefits it confers, the courts have strictly construed the exemption and have required applicants for such exemption to establish a clear entitlement. *Tri-Cities Children's Center, Inc. v. Alameda County Bd. of Supervisors* (1985).

Twenty-one states contain constitutional provisions which either (1) constitutionally exempt or (2) require the legislature to exempt charitable property from ad valorem taxation. Article XI, Section 6 of the South Dakota Constitution is an example of this type of constitutional provision. It provides that: "[t]he legislature shall, by general law, exempt from taxation, property used exclusively for agricultural and horticultural societies, for school, religious, cemetery and charitable purposes . . ."

The remaining states either have constitutional provisions which permit but do not require the legislature to enact statutory charitable exemptions from ad valorem taxation, or contain no provision. In either instance, the legislatures remain free to enact statutory charitable exemptions.

The specific property exempted from taxation on charitable use grounds, varies from state to state. For example, Article IX, Section 6 of the Illinois Constitution permits the legislature to exempt property "used exclusively for agricultural and horticultural societies, and for school, religious, cemetery and charitable purposes." By comparison, Article VIII, Section 5(b) of the Montana Constitution exempts "[i]nstitutions of purely public charity, hospitals and places of burial not used or held for private or corporate profit, places for actual religious worship, and property used exclusively for educational purposes."

While most states exempt property "owned" by charities, charitable exemptions are predicated on charitable "use," rather on ownership. As a result, property belonging to a charitable institution is only exempt when it is applied to a qualifying charitable purpose. *See, e.g., Prairie du Chien Sanitarium Co. v. City of Prairie Du Chien* (1943). Where a use requirement is a prerequisite to charitable exemption, the leasing of property by a charity with the resultant application of the rent to charitable purposes will not qualify as a direct use justifying exemption. *Tusculum College v. State Board of Equalization* (1980). Likewise, vacant property held

by a charity does not satisfy a use requirement
where there are no settled plans for construction of
improvements or other use. *Welch Avenue Freewill
Baptist Church v. Kinney* (1983).

Section 89. Miscellaneous Exemptions

Other common types of ad valorem exemptions
found in state constitutions are homestead, and
business relocation inducement exemptions. While
not as common as the exemptions discussed above,
these exemptions are sufficiently pervasive to warrant discussion.

Unlike the exemptions previously discussed,
which are complete exemptions, homestead exemptions authorize only a limited reduction in the overall valuation of the property for ad valorem tax
purposes. These exemptions are limited to the primary residence of the person asserting the entitlement to the exemption. The purpose is to encourage
home ownership. Article VII, Section 6 of the Florida Constitution is an example of this type of homestead exemption. Under this provision, an exemption of up to $25,000 is available to the owner of
real estate who uses the subject property as his
primary residence. Legislative attempts to limit the
availability of the exemption through the imposition
of a five-year durational residency requirement
have been declared invalid on equal protection
grounds. *See, Osterndorf v. Turner* (1982).

Another common type of constitutionally authorized exemptions are business relocation inducement exemptions. The purpose of these provisions

is to encourage the location of job-creating businesses within a state through the provision of either reduced tax rates or absolute exemption. For example, Amendment 27 to the Arkansas Constitution authorizes the governor and the Agricultural and Industrial Commission to confer up to ten-year exemptions from ad valorem taxation on manufacturing establishments relocating to the state for the expansion of existing manufacturing concerns.

CHAPTER 10

HOMESTEAD EXEMPTIONS

Section 90. Introduction

Twenty-one states have constitutional provisions creating some form of homestead exemption protecting property, used as a primary residence, from forced sale by the owner's creditors. Motivated by public policy considerations, such provisions were intended to maintain the integrity of the family by protecting the familial home from sale due to the family's economic woes. *Cross v. Benson* (1904). These constitutional provisions can be categorized into two separate types of homestead exemptions: (1) those provisions which define the right in the constitution itself, and (2) those which create the right but require the legislature to determine the parameters of that right. These types of provisions will be discussed separately.

Section 91. Provisions Requiring Legislative Enactments

The North Dakota Constitution is a good illustration of the type of homestead exemption which is recognized by the constitution, but generally left to the legislature to implement. Article XI, Section 22 of that constitution requires the legislature to enact legislation "exempting from forced sale to all heads of families a homestead, the value of which shall be limited and defined by law."

This provision was judicially construed to be non-self-executing. *Roesler v. Taylor* (1894). Provisions of this type have been determined to impose a mandatory duty on the legislature to implement the constitutional mandate that they represent. *McMurdie v. Chugg* (1940).

Section 92. Constitutional Provisions Establishing Homestead Exemptions

The constitutions of ten states contain provisions establishing a homestead exemption and most of the conditions of such exemption. Due to state-to-state variations, general observations are not particularly illuminating. Nonetheless, a few general observations and conclusions can be drawn by reference to particular provisions.

Section 93. Restrictions on Acreage

All state constitutional provisions creating homestead exemptions make a distinction based on whether the familial home is located within an urban or a rural area. Under Article 15, Section 9 of the Kansas Constitution, the rural homestead exemption is authorized "to the extent of one hundred and sixty acres of farming land" provided it is "occupied as a residence by the family of the owner." The limitation of the exemption to the size of the traditional family farm is merely reflective of the underlying purpose of such provisions.

By contrast, the scope of the homestead exemption is dramatically reduced when it is located in an urban area. Article 15, Section 9 of the Kansas Constitution compresses the homestead to "one acre within the limits of an incorporated town or city" again providing that it is "occupied as a residence by the family of the owner."

These provisions are quite common, but subject to local variation. For example, Article 16, Section 51 of the Texas Constitution authorizes a rural homestead exemption of up to two hundred acres. On the other hand, Article XII, Section 1 of the Oklahoma Constitution permits an urban homestead exemption of one acre provided that it does not exceed $5,000 in value. However, if the urban homestead does not exceed one quarter of an acre, the urban homestead is determined without regard to value. See, Oklahoma Constitution Article XII, Section 1.

Section 94. Exceptions to the Homestead Exemption

Most state constitutional provisions creating a homestead exemption recognize three primary exceptions to its operation. These exceptions are (1) taxes, (2) purchase money mortgages, and (3) debts incurred in improving the homestead property itself. Article VI, Section 48 of the West Virginia Constitution is a particularly succinct illustration of these exceptions. It provides that "no property shall be exempt from sales for taxes due thereon, or for the payment of purchase money due upon said property, or for debts contracted for the erection of improvements thereon." Such provisions indicate that the public policy supporting the exemption is less persuasive where public money is at issue or where the indebtedness at issue was invested in the homestead property itself.

Section 95. Restrictions on Alienation of Homestead

Consistent with its primary purpose of protecting the institution of the family, particularly in times of economic distress, the homestead exemption generally operates to prohibit, regardless of legal ownership, the transfer of a homestead without the consent of the other spouse.

Article 15, Section 9 of the Kansas Constitution is representative of clauses of this type. It provides that a homestead "shall not be alienated without the joint consent of husband and wife." Attempted conveyances in violation of such provisions are generally held to be void transfers. *Tolman v. Overstreet* (1979).

Section 96. Restrictions on the Devise of the Homestead

Attempts by a decedent to devise a homestead during the life of his or her surviving spouse are generally ineffective against surviving family members. The homestead exemption has been construed to survive the head of household's death and to continue to protect the residence from forced sale during the life of the surviving spouse. *See, In re Casey's Estate* (1943).

Certain states have expressly made such a provision part of the constitutional homestead provision itself. For example, Article X, Section 4(c) of the Florida Constitution expressly provides "[t]he homestead shall not be subject to devise if the owner is survived by spouse or minor child, except that the homestead may be devised to the owner's spouse if there be no minor child."

Section 97. Interpretation of Homestead Provisions

Both constitutional and statutory homestead provisions are liberally construed. *First Alabama Bank of Dothan v. Renfro* (1984). Courts will indulge the most liberal and humane rules of interpretation to protect the home of the debtor and the debtor's family. *In re Thexton* (1984). All reasonable presumptions are indulged in favor of the existence of the homestead right. However, homestead provisions are not to be so liberally construed as to permit fraud. *Tramel v. Stewart* (1997).

Section 98. Homestead Exemptions and State Criminal Forfeiture Proceedings

Courts in different states have reached differing results about whether state homestead exemptions protect property from forced sale in criminal forfeiture proceedings. The state appellate courts in Arizona and Colorado have held that the homestead exemption does not protect property from fiscal sale in such circumstances because the forfeiture is not predicated upon debts incurred by the owner but is based on the illegal uses to which the property has been put. *See, In re 1632 N. Santa Rita* (1990) and *People v. Allen* (1988).

Courts in other states have rejected this reasoning. *State ex rel. Means v. Ten (10) Acres of Land* (1994). State Supreme Courts in Iowa and Florida have specifically rejected this reasoning holding that the homestead exemption protected property from any judicially compelled disposition of the homestead regardless of whether the claim arose from a debt or otherwise. *In re Property Seized from Bly* (1990) and *Butterworth v. Caggiano* (1992).

Section 99. Homestead Exemptions and Federal Bankruptcy Law

As this publication goes to press, Congress has not formally approved, nor has the President signed, the 2002 proposed revisions to the Federal Bankruptcy Act. A key provision of the proposal would sharply restrict the use of state homestead exemptions in federal bankruptcy proceedings. Under existing law, bankrupt individuals in such states as Florida and Texas can shield unlimited amounts of home equity from creditors.

Under the reform proposal, a home would have to be owned at least forty (40) months before the exemption could be claimed. If the home was owned less than forty (40) months, only $125,000 in equity could be shielded from creditors. Proposed 11 U.S.C. § 522(p) and (q).

CHAPTER 11

MISCELLANEOUS PROVISIONS

Section 100. Introduction—Statutory Provisions Contained in State Constitutions

It is tempting in preparing a section of this topic to focus on eccentric provisions which have found their way into the various state constitutions. For example, Article XX, Section 2 of the Oklahoma Constitution presumptively establishes the "flash test" of kerosene for illuminating purposes at 115 degrees Fahrenheit and specific gravity test for all such oil at 40 degrees Baume. Likewise, Article 1, Section 25 of the California Constitution guarantees the right to fish. This trend is illustrative of the tendency of states to place traditionally statutory provisions in state constitutions.

The most common instance of this tendency is the placement in a number of state constitutions of specific provisions relating to regulation of corporations. For example, Sections 190 through 208 of the Kentucky Constitution prescribe detailed provisions regulating corporate affairs. For example, under Section 197 "[n]o railroad, steamboat, or other common carrier" is permitted to give free or reduced rates to any governmental officials. Likewise, Section 207 of the Kentucky Constitution prescribes cumulative voting for the selection of corporate directors.

Provisions of this type are too disparate to categorize. Interestingly, at least one state constitution seems to recognize the statutory nature of this type of constitutional provision. Article IX, Section 35 of the Oklahoma Constitution expressly authorizes the legislature to "alter, amend, revise, or repeal," without ratification by the electorate of a number of constitutional provisions regulating corporations.

Section 101. Provisions Relating to Education

Virtually all state constitutions contain provisions concerning education. Article VIII of the Virginia Constitution enacted in 1971 is illustrative of a relatively modern provision dealing with certain educational rights guaranteed by the state of Virginia to its citizens. Specifically, Article VIII, Section 1 of that constitution requires the Commonwealth of Virginia to provide "free public elementary and secondary schools" and to "ensure that an educational program of high quality is established and continually maintained." The balance of the Article prescribes the manner in which educational guarantees will be provided. Provisions such as Article VIII have taken on new meaning, as a result of decision of the United States Supreme Court in *San Antonio Independent School District v. Rodriguez* (1973). In that case, the Supreme Court concluded that the right to an education was not a fundamental federal right, that would require strict scrutiny under a

Fourteenth Amendment Equal Protection analysis. The rationale of the decision was based on the Supreme Court's conclusion that education was not explicitly or implicitly guaranteed by the federal Constitution.

In the aftermath of the *San Antonio Independent School District* case, a number of state courts interpreted their state constitutional provisions as establishing education as a fundamental right for purposes of application of a state equal protection analysis. In *Serrano v. Priest* (1976)*, the California Supreme Court under a strict scrutiny analysis of its state equal protection clause, declared the then existing method of financing public schools unconstitutional. In distinguishing the result from *San Antonio Independent School District, supra,* the court found education to be a fundamental right guaranteed by the state constitution. In so holding, the court referenced an Amicus Curiae brief which while using "passionate imagery" made this significant distinction. *Id*. "[T]he federal claim of fundamentality had to be argued in Rodriguez as a remote inference from the general language of the Bill of Rights[,] [u]nder California law the conclusion thunders from the words of the [c]onstitution itself[!]" *Id*. (Court's emphasis.)

Assuming this distinction between federal and state fundamental rights continues, it should be anticipated that the provisions of state constitutions

* A change in the California Constitution *may* have affected this case in the context used here. *See Crawford v. Huntington Beach Union High School District* (2002).

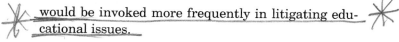

would be invoked more frequently in litigating educational issues.

At the outset, we need to say that this section dealing mainly with the issue of the Blaine amendment could have as easily been placed in the section on religion of the Declaration of Rights Chapter. It is here because it deals with education.

The recent decision in *Zelman v. Simmons–Harris* (2002), the United States Supreme Court gave its approval, 5–4 for a school voucher program in Cleveland, Ohio. The Court found that the Cleveland voucher program which allowed a rather limited amount of money to poor parents to allow them to take their children from failing public schools and send them to private schools, secular or religious. To be specific, the Court found that this did not violate the Establishment Clause of the First Amendment as applied to the states through the Due Process Clause of the Fourteenth. As pointed out by John J. Miller, this now shifts the focus to state constitutions.*

The Arizona Supreme Court in *Kotterman v. Killian* (1999) found that Arizona has a "tax credit of up to $500 for those who donate to school tuition organizations (STOs)." The fact that this program could provide tuition to religious schools led to its being challenged under both federal and state con-

* We are indebted to Mr. Miller for his article, "School choice, Not an Echo" in the July 29, 2002 issue of National Review, at pages 20–22. Specifically, we are in Mr. Miller's debt for calling our attention to *Kotterman v. Killian* (1999) and its discussion of the Blaine Amendment and its impact on state constitutions.

stitutions. Applying decisional law of the United States Supreme Court, the Arizona Supreme Court found no violation of the federal constitution. It then turned to three provisions in the Arizona Constitution, two "religious clauses" and "the anti-gift" clause. If we may be allowed to simplify a rather long holding, the Court found that a tax credit is not "an appropriation of public funds" and even if it were, "the range of choices reserved to taxpayers, parents, and children, the neutrality built into the system—all lead us to conclude that benefits to religious schools are sufficiently attenuated to foreclose a constitutional breach."

Perhaps prodded by the dissent, the Court turned to the question of the "Blaine Amendment" and its impact on state constitutions. Although finding "no recorded history directly linking the [Blaine] amendment with Arizona's constitutional convention," the Court gave a brief history of the amendment and its impact on the states.

In 1875, Maine Congressman James Blaine introduced a Constitutional amendment prohibiting the states from granting public funds or taxes for the benefit of any religious sect or denomination. Joseph P. Viteritti, *Choosing Equality: Religious Freedom and Educational Opportunity Under Constitutional Federalism*, 15 Yale L. & Pol'y Rev. 113, 144 (1996). The bill failed to muster enough votes for passage, but was later resurrected in a number of state constitutions. *Id.* at 146–147.

The Blaine amendment was a clear manifestation of religious bigotry, part of a crusade manufactured by the contemporary Protestant establishment to counter what was perceived as a growing "Catholic menace." Viteritti, *supra,* at 146 [the "*see also's*" have been deleted.] . . . . While such efforts were unsuccessful at the federal level, the jingoist banner persisted in some states. By 1890, twenty-nine states had incorporated at least some language reminiscent of the Blaine amendment in their own constitutions. Viteritti, *supra*, at 147.

The dissent found that 1) the Arizona tax credit would violate the Establishment Clause of the First Amendment, 2) the three clauses of the Arizona Constitution were influenced by the Blaine Amendment but "the anti-Catholic bigotry that inspired the Blaine Amendment was displaced in many of those states [that adopted Blaine amendments] [including Arizona] by a principled commitment to strict separation between church and state in education," and 3) the tax credit would violate the Arizona "Blaine amendments."

On August 5, 2002 a Florida circuit (trial) court found Florida's voucher program to be in violation of Article 1, Section 3 of the Florida Constitution. Arguably a "Blaine amendment," it provides in pertinent part, "no revenue of the state or any political subdivision on agency thereof shall ever be taken from the public treasury directly or indirectly in aid of any church, sect, or religious denomination or in aid of any sectarian institution." *Holmes v. Bush*, *et al.* (2002).

Section 102. Impeachment and Removal of State Officials

All state constitutions contain provisions for the removal of high level state officials through the impeachment process. While minor variations do exist from state-to-state, the uniformity of these provisions is particularly striking. Generally, these provisions permit the removal of most high-ranking state officials and judges through a process which requires impeachment by the House of Representatives and removal by the Senate upon conviction by a two-thirds vote of that body. Although the grounds for impeachment vary, acts constituting severe misconduct in office are required to authorize impeachment proceedings.

Article VIII, Part 2, Sections 1 and 2 of the Arizona Constitution are provisions which are representative of the type of impeachment provisions which can be found in state constitutions. Under Section 1, the House of Representatives has the sole power of impeachment, but the impeachment is tried to the Senate, with the Chief Justice of the Supreme Court presiding. Under Section 2 of the Arizona Constitution, a conviction can only result upon a two-thirds vote of the Senate. The grounds for impeachment are specified to include "high crimes, misdemeanors, or malfeasance in office."

Because Nebraska has a unicameral legislature, the above mentioned pattern is not found in the Nebraska Constitution. Rather, under Article III, Section 17 of the Nebraska Constitution, the legislature, by resolution, impeaches an official and all the judges of the district courts of the state meet as a court of impeachment to try an impeached official. This court of impeachment must convict the official by a two-thirds vote.

Section 103. Provisions for Recall Elections of Public Officials

Recall is a method of removing an elected public official during a term of office. Under typical recall provisions, a specified number of citizens can request, by petition, that an elected official be subjected to an election prior to the next regularly scheduled date for an election for that particular office. *Wallace v. Tripp* (1960).

In some states, recall provisions are exclusively provided by statutes. However, many states do constitutionally guarantee the existence of recall at most or all levels of government. For example, Article II, Section 8 of the Michigan Constitution directs the legislature to enact recall election measures for all elected non-judicial officers upon the filing of a petition requesting a recall election and containing signatures equal to 25% of the persons voting in the electoral district affected at the last gubernatorial election. The Constitution explicitly provides that the sufficiency of the grounds for the recall election is a "political rather than a judicial question." Even in jurisdictions which require allegations of cause as a precondition of recall, the existence or non-existence of cause is viewed as a political rather than a judicial question. *See, Cudihee v. Phelps* (1913). Where a constitutional right to a recall election exists, the Constitution is interpreted as creating a fundamental right to such elections. The Colorado Supreme Court in *Shroyer v. Sokol* (1976) summarized this view as follows:

[T]he power of recall—like that of the initiative and referendum—is a fundamental right of citizens within a representative democracy. Neither the legislature nor local lawmaking bodies may infringe constitutionally protected fundamental rights. Reservation of the power of recall in the people must be liberally construed in favor of the ability to exercise it; conversely, limitations on the power of recall must be strictly construed.

In order to insure continuity in office and to prevent abuses of the recall mechanism, the statutory provisions implementing recall frequently require that an officer serve a minimum period of time, before being subject to recall. *See generally, State ex rel. Palmer v. Hart* (1982).

Section 104.   Initiative and Referendum

The term *initiative* describes the process available in many jurisdictions, whereby a segment of the electorate can propose legislation by petition and the electorate as a whole can approve or reject the measure in a subsequent election. The term *referendum* describes a closely related process available in many jurisdictions, whereby the electorate reserves the right to suspend or annul legislative enactments. These processes operate independently of the legislature. Both procedures were established in response to voter dissatisfaction with legislative bodies. *See generally, Carson v. Oxenhandler* (1960). The effect is to primarily place power in the legislature, but to reserve concurrent legislative power to the electorate to propose or reject legislation. *Adams v. Bolin* (1952).

Although initiative and referendum may be statutory, many state constitutions elevate these two processes to constitutional dimension. Where initiative and referendum are present in a state constitution, such provisions are liberally construed in favor of the exercise of the right. *State ex rel. Voss v. Davis* (1967).

Substantial variations exist from state-to-state. The provisions of Section 3 of Article XXIV of the Colorado Constitution provide a fair sample of the contents of such provisions.

This article [which describes other methods of changing the constitution] shall not impair the right of the people to amend this constitution by a vote upon an initiative petition therefor.

As this provision suggests, initiative and referendum may not be utilized to affect certain categories of legislation. For instance, under the Colorado provision, referendum may not be utilized to review legislation that provides for the funding of state institutions. These exceptions exist to prevent referendum from being utilized to impair the day-to-day operations of state government. *State ex rel. Wegner v. Pyle* (1929).

In addition, most state constitutions with referendum provisions exempt from its operation laws necessary for the immediate preservation of the public safety. The purpose of these is to reserve to the legislature the requisite police power to deal with emergency situations. *State ex rel. Case v. Howell* (1915). In some jurisdictions, if the legislature declares that an emergency exists, this determination is conclusive and the legislation at issue is not subject to referendum. *See, e.g., Orme v. Salt River Valley Water Users Ass'n* (1923). In other jurisdictions, the courts will determine whether or not an emergency existed that removed potential legislation from referendum. *State ex rel. Asotsky v. Regan* (1927).

Section 105. Reapportionment

Many state constitutions impose a duty on the legislature, or a constitutionally created commission, to regularly reapportion the state into districts for the election of representatives to both Congress and the state legislature. *See, e.g.*, Pennsylvania Constitution, Article II, Section 17. The obligation to reapportion is frequently linked to the federal decennial census. *See, e.g.*, New York Constitution, Article III, Sections 4 and 5. While historically, courts deferred to the discretion of the legislature in such matters, federal constitutional concerns have subjected this legislative discretion to more intense scrutiny. *See, Baker v. Carr* (1962); *Reynolds v. Sims* (1964).

Historically, state courts refused to compel legislative compliance with mandatory constitutional provisions requiring regular reapportionment. *See,*

Smith v. Holm (1945). This view was based on the belief that the courts could not order a separate branch of government to legislate. With the federalization of reapportionment, this view has generally been discarded. *State ex rel. Reynolds v. Zimmerman* (1964).

Constitutional reapportionment provisions vary from simple provisions to highly detailed provisions. Article IV, Section 3 of the Wisconsin Constitution in its entirety states as follows:

At its first session after each enumeration made by the authority of the United States, the legislature shall apportion and district anew the members of the senate and assembly, according to the number of inhabitants.

In contrast, the Hawaii Constitution allocates an entire Article of the Constitution to the topic of reapportionment. *See*, Hawaii Constitution, Article IV. This provision requires statewide reapportionment every decade. *Id.* at Section 1. In each reapportionment year, a nine-member reapportionment commission consisting of members of the state legislature, and other appointees, is selected to prepare a plan of reapportionment. *Id.* at Section 2. Section 6 of Article IV lists specific criteria to be considered by the commission in its reapportionment plan. Section 10 of Article IV establishes jurisdiction in the Hawaii Supreme Court for judicial review of the reapportionment plan. This section also authorizes any registered voter to commence a Supreme Court review of the reapportionment plan by mandamus or other proceeding.

Section 106. Provisions Waiving or Authorizing the Waiving of Sovereign Immunity

About one-third of the state constitutions waive or authorize the waiving of sovereign immunity by the legislature. The most common provision is one which merely provides that the legislature may enact laws authorizing the filing of suits against the state and its subdivisions. Article IX, Section 4 of the Connecticut Constitution is representative of this general category. It provides in its entirety: "claims against the state shall be resolved in such manner as may be provided by law." Article IV, Section 24 of the Oregon Constitution performs a similar function but it continues to specifically prohibit the enactment of special laws authorizing the commencement of specific suits, or awarding compensation to specified claimants.

Other states, such as Louisiana, constitutionally repeal the sovereign immunity doctrine in specific areas. Under Article XII Section 10 of the Louisiana Constitution, sovereign immunity is abolished for contract and tort actions brought against the state or its subdivision. In other areas, the legislature is authorized to waive sovereign immunity by statutory enactment.

West Virginia is unique in that it constitutionally prohibits the abolition of sovereign immunity. Under Article VI, Section 35 of the West Virginia

Constitution, the state of West Virginia may not be made a defendant in any proceeding, except for garnishment or attachment proceedings in which the state is named "as a garnishee or suggestee."

Section 107.   Provisions Relating to Administration of School Lands and School Fund

Many state constitutions contain provisions relating to the administration of school lands and a state administered school fund. The purpose of such provisions is to insure the orderly administration of lands that were given to the states by the United states at statehood, or thereafter, for purpose of providing a free public school education to its citizens. Many states have expanded these provisions to apply to gifts received from any source, which are conditional upon being used for educational purposes.

For example, Article VIII, Section 2 of the South Dakota Constitution establishes a perpetual trust fund for the maintenance of the public schools. The fund includes proceeds of lands donated by the federal government, private donations, and the proceeds of escheat actions brought by the state. Other provisions within Article VIII, authorize the sale or leasing of the school lands upon competitive terms. Under Article 18, Section 3 of the Wyoming Constitution, that state's public lands are administered by a constitutionally created "board of land commissioners" which is composed of the Governor, Secretary of State, State Treasurer, State Auditor and Superintendent of Public Instruction.

Because of the trust status of such lands, legislative attempts to authorize the sale or lease of such property, at less than market value have been determined to be unconstitutional and in violation of the state's fiduciary duties. *State ex rel. Ebke v. Board of Educational Lands and Funds* (1951); *Oklahoma Education Association, Inc. v. Nigh* (1982).

CHAPTER 12

AMENDMENTS TO STATE CONSTITUTIONS

Section 108. Introduction

The power to amend a state constitution has been viewed as a power which is inherent in the resident of a particular state. *Gatewood v. Matthews* (1966). It can be argued that the Tenth Amendment to the United States Constitution when it speaks of "other rights being retained by the States *or the people*" is merely *recognizing* this right of the residents of a state to amend that state's constitution and thus regulate the vast amount of *inherent power* remaining in the states *after* the creation of the United States Constitution and its operation for over two hundred years. "The initiative is thus power *reserved* to people, not *granted* to them." (Case citation omitted.) (Emphasis in original.) *National Paint and Coatings Association v. State of California* (1997). Therefore, where a constitution does not itself specify a particular manner for amending a constitution, the courts recognize the inherent power of the people to revise their most fundamental law. For this reason, it is possible to argue that where state constitutions prescribed limited methods of revising a state constitution, courts focused on this inherent power and determined that constitutional provisions prescribing a method for amending a state constitution are not exclusive. *See, In re Opinion to the Governor* (1935).

Despite the possibility of such an interpretation, a majority of courts have held that where a state constitution prescribes a particular method for amending or revising it, that method will be deemed to be the exclusive method of revising the state constitution. This conclusion is based on the principle that the enunciation of a particular method of amending a constitution operates to prohibit alternative methods. *See, Coleman v. Pross* (1978). Consistent with this interpretation, courts have sometimes required strict compliance with the constitutionally described method of amending a state constitution. *Hyder v. Edwards* (1977), *Bergdoll v. Kane* (1999). However, courts have also held that constitutional provisions *regarding change by initiative and referendums* should be protected by the judiciary and questions regarding the exercise of that power should be decided so as to allow its exercise by the people if it is reasonably possible to do so. *National Paint and Coatings Association v. State of California* (1997), *Matter of Title, Ballot Title and Submission Clause and Summary for 1997–98 No. 62* (1998). Courts must weigh this generous interpretation policy against the realization that rules governing the *initiative process* are designed to make it "fair and impartial." *In re Title, Ballot Title and Submission Clause, and Summary for 1999–00 Nos. 245(b), 245(c), 245(d) and 245(e)* (2000) and "to prevent fraud or to render intelligible the purpose of the proposed ... constitutional amendment." (Quoting other cases.) *State ex rel. Stenberg v. Moore* (1999).

Conversely, it has also been held, although not specifically regarding initiative and referendum, that "it is almost universally true that the procedures instituted for the amendment of constitutions have purposely been made cumbersome, in order that the organic law may not readily be remolded to fit situations and sentiments that are relatively transitory and fleeting." *Geringer v. Bebout* (2000).

Generally, state constitutions prescribe four methods for amending or revising a state constitution. They are:

1. Legislative Proposal
2. Revision Commission
3. Initiative Petition
4. Constitutional Convention

Each of these methods will be separately discussed.

Section 109.   Legislative Proposal

The most common method for proposing amendments to state constitutions is through the mechanism of legislative proposal. Provisions incorporating this method of amendment are found in all fifty states. Although state-to-state variations prevent precise summarization, the basic operation of provisions of this type can be described by reference to the following representative provision.

Article 20, Section 1 of the Wyoming Constitution permits the legislature to propose amendments to the Constitution by a two-thirds vote of the members of each house of the Wyoming legislature. Following this approval, the amendment is required to be ratified by the people at the next general election.

In the absence of an explicit constitutional provision requiring the signature of the governor on a proposed amendment approved by the legislature, gubernatorial approval is not required because such amendments are generally approved through the mechanism of a joint resolution. *See, Opinion of the Justices* (1970). As a result, legislative proposals for constitutional amendments are not subject to gubernatorial veto, and if the governor attempts to veto such proposals, the veto will be invalid. *People ex rel. Stewart v. Ramer* (1916). This is not to suggest that the governor is never involved in the process. *State ex rel. Bronster v. Yoshina* (1997).

Generally, courts have held that the legislature, in proposing amendments to the state constitution, is not performing an ordinary legislative function. Accordingly, state constitutional requirements prescribing one subject title and other requirements or laws enacted by the legislature are not applicable to proposals proposing constitutional amendment. *See, e.g., Julius v. Callahan* (1895).

Generally, a distinction has been made between isolated amendments, which may be legislatively proposed, and revisions of the Constitution which must be approved by other methods. Where a legislative proposal provision permitted amendments to the Constitution, but the Constitution also contained provisions for revision, a legislative attempt to present fourteen interrelated amendments to the electorate, where all fourteen amendments had to be approved for any one to be valid, was declared a revision. As a result the legislature could not propose the revision through the amendment process. *Rivera–Cruz v. Gray* (1958).

Concern over interlocking amendments, or so-called "daisy-chain" amendments, has resulted in the adoption of constitutional provisions prescribing how such amendments will be presented to the electorate for ratification. Article XXIII, Section 1 of the Washington Constitution provides that where two or more amendments are submitted to the electorate for ratification they must be presented in a manner which permits the electorate to vote for or against each of the amendments separately.

By contrast, other constitutions expressly permit revision of an entire article to a constitution by the amendment process. For example, Article XXIII, Section 1 of the Utah Constitution permits the revision, amendment or the addition of an entire article to the constitution through the legislative proposal process and the presentation of such revision to the voters as a single question. A provision of this nature "may relate to one subject, or any number of subjects, and may modify or repeal provisions contained in other articles of the Constitution. . . ." *Id.*

Any amendment or revision of a state constitution must be ratified by the people in the manner prescribed by the constitution. However, if the constitution is silent on this issue, the legislature is presumed to possess the power to prescribe the method for submitting a legislatively proposed amendment to the citizenry for ratification. *McAlister v. State ex rel. Short* (1923).

Section 110.   Revision Commissions

A few state constitutions authorize the amendment of a state constitution through the vehicle of a revision commission. While a constitutional convention generally contemplates a revision of the entire constitution, a revision commission provision contemplates a less extensive role. While a revision commission may recommend extensive amendment of a constitution, it generally contemplates an amendment of a particular section or revision of an article or articles. For example, Article 17, Section 2 of the Texas Constitution provided for the establishment of a constitutional revision commission to be convened in 1973. While the commission possessed broad powers, Article 17, Section 2(g) required the commission to retain the existing Bill of Rights in the Texas Constitution, in any revision of that constitution.

The most detailed provisions relating to constitutional amendment by a revision commission are found in the Florida Constitution at Article XI, Section 2. Under this provision, a thirty-seven member constitutional revision commission is required to convene, hold hearings and make proposals for revision of the Florida Constitution every twenty years. The composition of this commission includes the attorney general, fifteen members selected by the governor, nine members by the speaker of the house, nine members by the president of the Senate and three members by the Chief Justice of the Florida Supreme Court, with the advice of the other justices.

Any proposals for revision recommended by the commission must be ratified by the electorate under the provisions of the constitution prescribing the manner of ratifying proposed amendments.

In Florida, the power of the Revision Commission is shared with a Taxation and Budget Reform Commission. *See* 1968 Florida Constitution, Article XI, Section 6.

Section 111. Amendment by Initiative Petition

A number of state constitutions permit their amendment through the utilization of an initiative petition. Under this device a popularly proposed amendment to a state constitution is submitted to the electorate for ratification. Most commonly a proposal for amendment becomes eligible for presentation to the electorate when a petition in support of the proposal bearing a specified number of signatures is presented to a designated state official.

Article XII, Section 2 of the Michigan Constitution is representative of a constitutional provision authorizing amendment of the Constitution through the initiative process. Under that section, the registered electors by petition may propose amendments to the Michigan Constitution. To invoke the provisions of Article XII, Section 2 of the Michigan Constitution, a petition must be filed with the responsible governmental official at least 120 days prior to the election in which the proposed amendment will be voted on. To be valid, a petition "shall include the full text of the proposed amendment, and be signed by registered electors of the state equal in number to at least ten percent of the total vote cast for all candidates for governor at the last preceding general election at which a governor was elected." *Id*.

Many of these provisions which permit constitutional amendment by initiative are construed only to authorize single amendments, implicitly prohibiting constitutional revision through this process. The California Constitution provides for "amendment" by initiative, but permits the state legislature to propose either an "amendment" or "revision" of the state constitution to the electorate. *See*, Article XVIII of the California Constitution. Focusing on this distinction, the California Supreme Court held that the Constitution prohibits its revision through the initiative process. *See, Amador Valley Joint Union High School District v. State Board of Equalization* (1978). The distinction between a constitutional "amendment" and a constitutional "revision" is not precise. *See, e.g. Bess v. Ulmer* (1999) discussing an Alaska constitutional provision that limits "revisions" to constitutional conventions. One of the reasons given by the Alaska Supreme Court for "the Framer's decision" was to recognize the difference between amendments and revisions. The *Bess* case is further discussed under the section on constitutional conventions, *infra*. The Court in *Bess* distinguished the two by describing an amendment as "changes [to the Constitution] which are 'few, simple, independent and of comparatively small importance.'" (Quoting Jameson, *A Treatise on Constitutional Conventions: Their History, Powers, and Modes of Proceeding Section 540* (Chicago, Callaghan and Company, 4th Edition 1887)).

It then described a revision as a change of the "substantial entirety" or "far-reaching changes." (Quoting *Amador Valley v. State* (1978)). The Alaska Supreme Court did say in *Bess* that in making its determination as to what was an amendment as opposed to a revision, that "respect for the Legislature [referring to amendments proposed by the legislature rather than by initiative] and the electoral process requires that courts should decline to order a measure removed from the ballot except in clear cases." (Referring the reader to *Meiners v. Bering Strait School District* (1984)). As a result, the ultimate determination is a judicial one based on the particular facts and circumstances accompanying each different initiative petition. *See, McFadden v. Jordan* (1948).

Article XI, Section 3 of the Florida Constitution, as it was enacted in 1968, also limited the initiative

to amendment of a single section of the state constitution. *See, Adams v. Gunter* (1970). In an attempt
to expand the ability of the electorate to amend the
Constitution by initiative, Article XI, Section 3 of
the Florida Constitution was amended in 1972 to
authorize "the revision or amendment of any portion or portions" of the Constitution by the initiative process. Despite this amendment, Article XI,
Section 3 of the Florida Constitution retained a
requirement that any revision or amendment "shall
embrace but one subject and matter directly connected therewith...." This requirement is similar
to the requirement found in many state constitutions that the legislature may only enact laws that
"embrace but one subject and matter properly connected therewith." *See*, Florida Constitution, Article III, Section 6. Due to this similarity, the Florida
courts initially interpreted the one subject requirement in the initiative process similarly to the way
the courts had interpreted the one subject requirement in the legislative process. *See, Floridians
Against Casino Takeover v. Let's Help Florida*
(1978). As the Court had traditionally deferred to
the legislature's judgment in regard to its lawmaking power, the "one subject" requirement was construed so that a number of related changes could be
grouped under the "umbrella" of one subject since
they were considered to be "directly connected"
with it. Thus, the change proposed by initiative
should be "functional" rather than "locational."
See also Weber v. Smathers (1976). However, in
Fine v. Firestone (1984), the Florida Supreme Court
announced it would apply this "one subject" limita-

tion to amendments in a more restrictive fashion than the Court had applied the similar limitation in a legislative setting. As a result, Article XI, Section 3 of the Florida Constitution authorizes either amendment or revision of the Constitution by initiative petition. However, the extent of a permissible revision will be limited by a strictly construed one subject requirement. Roughly put, then, the "related changes" under the one subject umbrella might, after *Fine* each be considered a separate subject and thus in violations of the one subject limitation. It's pretty much a case-by-case determination.

Compare the Georgia multi-subject rule, the test of which is "whether all parts of . . . the constitutional amendment are germane to the accomplishment of single objective." *Goldrush II v. City of Marietta* (1997) citing *Carter v. Burson* (1973).

Section 112. Constitutional Convention

Most of the state constitutions explicitly provide for the amendment or revision of the state constitution through the convening of a constitutional convention. Although state-to-state variation prevents precise categorization, Article XVIII, Section 2 of the California Constitution is a provision which is fairly representative of the national norm. Under that section, a two-thirds vote of the membership of each house is required before the question whether to call a convention to revise the Constitution is submitted to the electorate. If a majority of the electorate votes in favor of a convention, the legislature is required, within six months of the election, to provide for the convention. The proposals for amendment or revision that are made by the constitutional convention must then be approved by a majority of the electorate. *See*, California Constitution, Article XVIII, Section 4.

Certain states provide for the periodic submission to the electorate of the issue whether a constitutional convention should be convened to consider revising or amending the state constitution. Article XVI, Section 3 of the Ohio Constitution requires the issue as to whether a constitutional convention should be convened to be submitted to the electorate "in the year one thousand nine hundred and thirty-two, and in each twentieth year thereafter. . . ." Article XIII, Section 3 of the Alaska Constitution contains a similar provision which requires the lieutenant governor to place the issue on the ballot as to whether a constitutional convention shall be convened, at least once every ten years.

Article XI, Section 4 of the Florida Constitution only authorizes the submission of the issue as to whether a constitutional convention shall be called to the electorate when a petition containing inter alia signatures of at least 15% of the votes cast in the last preceding general election requesting such a convention is filed with the Secretary of State. This rather restrictive provision denying the legislature authority to submit the issue to the electorate is apparently acceptable because of the provisions of the Florida Constitution requiring a revision commission to meet every twenty years to consider revising the Florida Constitution. *See,* Florida Constitution, Article XI, Section 2. Article XIII of the Alaska Constitution has made a constitutional convention the only method of revising as opposed to amending the Alaska Constitution. The Alaska Supreme Court has identified at least three reasons for committing revisions only to a constitutional convention. One is to give "substance" to the distinction between revisions and amendments. A second is "to promote stability." (Citing Public Administrative Service, 3 *Constitutional Studies*: Constitutional Amendment and Revision 1 (November 8, 1955)). And a third is "to provide a specialized body of citizens whose sole purpose is to consider the Constitution as an organic whole, and to make the appropriate and necessary changes." (Citing *Dodd, The Amendment and Revision of State Constitutions* 261–62 (1910). *Bess v. Ulmer* (1999)).

A number of state constitutions do not contain provisions relating to the convening of a Constitutional Convention. Where the issue has arisen in those states, the courts have recognized the authority of the legislature to submit the issue to the electorate, as to whether a constitutional convention should be convened. *Stander v. Kelley* (1969).

Section 113.   The Submission of Constitutional Amendments or Revisions to the Electorate

A state constitution is the fundamental law of each state. All revisions or amendments of this

fundamental law must be approved by the electorate. Certain constitutions make specific provision
for the manner in which the proposed amendment
or revision must be presented to the electorate.

For example, Article XII, Section 2 of the Michigan Constitution imposes certain publication requirements as to how the existing constitution will
be affected by a proposed initiative petition. Addi-
tionally, the section authorizes the legislature to
designate an official to draft the ballot to be used in
the ratifying election, and requires that the ballot
"consist of a true and impartial statement of the
purpose of the amendment in such language as
shall create no prejudice for or against the proposed
amendment." *See* further discussion of this topic
under Section 104, *supra*.

Many states statutorily impose similar requirements on ballot titles. For example, 34 Okla. Stat.
Section 9 requires the parties submitting a proposed
amendment to submit a suggested ballot title which
inter alia must be less than 200 words, impartial,
and "written on the eighth grade reading compre-
hension level."

Due to the expense incurred by the state in
having an election, many states provide for pre-
election judicial testing of the constitutional validity
and manner of presenting a proposed constitutional
amendment to the electorate. For example, the provisions of the Oklahoma Statute referenced above
require the provisions of a proposed initiative ballot
title to be reviewed by the Attorney General for

legal correctness, and to be drafted by the Secretary of State after reviewing the proposed title of the proponents of the amendment. This proposed title is then reviewed by the Superintendent of Public Instruction. The statutes then provide for expeditious judicial review of the ballot title in advance of the election. *See*, 34 Okla. Stat. Section 9.

In 1986, the Florida Constitution was amended to authorize the attorney general to invoke the original jurisdiction of the Florida Supreme Court to obtain an advisory opinion as to validity of any proposed initiative petition. *See*, Florida Constitution Article IV, Section 10. This amendment was enacted to save the state the needless election expenses that would arise from an initiative petition that was declared invalid after the election.

In a number of cases state courts have expressed sentiments similar to that of the Arkansas Supreme Court when it said that it was not its "function [in the initiative process] to express [its] view on, or to determine merit of a proposed [amendment]—such power [is] expressly reserved to the people." *Parker v. Priest* (1996).

Although beyond the scope of this *Nutshell*, the reader should note that a number of aspects of the initiative process have been the subject of First Amendment challenges. *See, e.g. Bernbeck v. Moore* (1997).

APPENDIX

MODEL STATE CONSTITUTION

PREAMBLE

Article

PREAMBLE

We, the people of the state of _____, recognizing the rights and duties of this state as a part of the federal system of government, reaffirm our adherence to the Constitution of the United States of America; and in order to assure the state government power to act for the good order of the state

315

and the liberty, health, safety and welfare of the people, we do ordain and establish this constitution.

ARTICLE I

Bill of Rights

Section 1.01 *Freedom of Religion, Speech, Press, Assembly and Petition.* No law shall be enacted respecting an establishment of religion, or prohibiting the free exercise thereof, or abridging the freedom of speech or of the press, or the right of the people peaceably to assemble and to petition the government for a redress of grievances.

Section 1.02 *Due Process and Equal Protection.* No person shall be deprived of life, liberty or property without due process of law, nor be denied the equal protection of the laws, nor be denied the enjoyment of his civil rights or be discriminated against in the exercise thereof because of race, national origin, religion or ancestry.

Section 1.03 *Searches and Seizures and Interceptions.*

(a) The right of the people to be secure in their persons, houses, papers and effects against unreasonable searches and seizures shall not be violated, and no warrants shall issue, but upon probable cause, supported by oath or affirmation, and particularly describing the place to be searched and the persons or things to be seized.

(b) The right of the people to be secure against unreasonable interception of telephone, telegraph and other electronic means of communication, and against unreasonable interception of oral and other communications by electric or electronic methods, shall not be violated, and no orders and warrants for such interceptions shall issue but upon probable cause supported by oath or affirmation that evidence of crime may be thus obtained, and particularly identifying the means of communication and the person or persons whose communications are to be intercepted.

(c) Evidence obtained in violation of this section shall not be admissible in any court against any person.

Section 1.04 *Self–Incrimination.* No person shall be compelled to give testimony which might tend to incriminate him.

Section 1.05 *Writ of Habeas Corpus.* The privilege of writ of habeas corpus shall not be suspended unless when in cases of rebellion or invasion the public safety may require it.

Section 1.06 *Rights of Accused Persons.*

(a) In all criminal prosecutions the accused shall enjoy the right to a speedy and public trial, to be informed of the nature and cause of the accusation, to be confronted with the witnesses against him, to have compulsory process for obtaining witnesses in his favor, to have the assistance of counsel for his defense, and to the assignment of counsel to represent him at every stage of the proceedings unless he elects to proceed without counsel or is able to obtain counsel. In prosecutions for felony, the accused shall also enjoy the right of trial by an impartial jury of the county [or other appropriate political subdivision of the state] wherein the crime shall have been committed, or of another county, if a change of venue has been granted.

(b) All persons shall, before conviction, be bailable by sufficient sureties, but bail may be denied to persons charged with capital offenses or offenses punishable by life imprisonment, giving due weight to the evidence and to the nature and circumstances of the event. Excessive bail shall not be required, nor excessive fines imposed, nor cruel or unusual punishment inflicted.

(c) No person shall be twice put in jeopardy for the same offense.

Section 1.07 *Political Tests for Public Office.* No oath, declaration or political test shall be required for any public office or employment other than the following oath or affirmation: "I do solemnly swear [or affirm] that I will support and defend the Constitution of the United States and the constitution of the state of _____ and that I will faithfully discharge the duties of the office of _____ to the best of my ability."

ARTICLE II

Powers of the State

Section 2.01 *Powers of Government.* The enumeration in this constitution of specified powers and functions shall be construed neither as a grant nor as a limitation of the powers of state government but the state government shall have all of the powers not denied by this constitution or by or under the Constitution of the United States.

ARTICLE III

Suffrage and Elections

Sections 3.01 *Qualifications for Voting.* Every citizen of the age of _____ years and a resident of the state for three months shall have the right to vote in the election of all officers that may be elected by the people and upon all questions that may be submitted to the voters; but the legislature may by law establish: (1) Minimum periods of local residence not exceeding three months, (2) reasonable requirements to determine literacy in English or in another language predominantly used in the classrooms of any public or private school accredited by any state or territory of the United States, the District of Columbia, or the Commonwealth of Puerto Rico, and (3) disqualifications for voting for mental incompetency or conviction of felony.

Section 3.02 *Legislature to Prescribe for Exercise of Suffrage.* The legislature shall by law define residence for voting purposes, insure secrecy in voting and provide for the registration of voters, absentee voting, the administration of elections and the nomination of candidates.

ARTICLE IV

The Legislature

Section 4.01 *Legislative Power.* The legislative power of the state shall be vested in the legislature.

Section 4.02 *Composition of the Legislature.* The legislature shall be composed of a single chamber consisting of one member to represent each legislative district. The number of members shall be prescribed by law but shall not be less than _____ nor exceed _____. Each member of the legislature shall be a qualified voter of the state and shall be at least _____ years of age.

BICAMERAL ALTERNATIVE: Section 4.02 *Composition of the Legislature.* The legislature shall be composed of a senate and an assembly. The number of members of each house of the legislature shall be prescribed by law but the number of assemblymen shall not be less than _____ nor exceed _____, and the number of senators shall not exceed one-third, as near as may be, the number of assemblymen. Each assemblyman shall represent one assembly district and each senator shall represent one senate district. Each member of the legislature shall be a qualified voter of the state and shall be at least _____ years of age.

Section 4.03 *Election and Term of Members.* The members of the legislature shall be elected by the qualified voters of the state for a term of two years.

BICAMERAL ALTERNATIVE: Section 4.03 *Election and Terms of Members.* Assemblymen shall be elected by the qualified voters of the state for a term of two years and senators for a term of six years. One-third of the senators shall be elected every two years.

Section 4.04 *Legislative Districts.*

(a) For the purpose of electing members of the legislature, the state shall be divided into as many districts as there shall be members of the legislature. Each district shall consist of compact and contiguous territory. All districts shall be so nearly equal in population that the population of the largest district shall not exceed that of the smallest district by more than _____ per cent. In determining the population of each district, inmates of such public or private institutions as prisons or other places of correction, hospitals for the insane or other institutions housing persons who are disqualified from voting by law shall not be counted.

(b) Immediately following each decennial census, the governor shall appoint a board of _____ qualified voters to make recommendations within ninety days of their appointment concerning the redistricting of the state. The governor shall publish the recommendations of the board when received. The governor shall promulgate a redistricting plan within ninety to one hundred and twenty days after appointment of the board, whether or not it has made its recommendations. The governor shall accompany his plan with a message explaining his reasons for any changes from the recommendations of the board. The governor's redistricting plan shall be published in the manner provided for acts of the legislature and shall have the force of law upon such publication. Upon the application of any qualified voter, the supreme court, in the exercise of original, exclusive and final jurisdiction, shall review the governor's redistricting plan and shall have jurisdiction to make orders to amend the plan to comply with the requirements of this constitution or, if the governor has failed to promulgate a redistricting plan within the time provided, to make one or more orders establishing such a plan.

BICAMERAL ALTERNATIVE: Section 4.04 *Legislative Districts.*

(a) For the purpose of electing members of the assembly, the state shall be divided into as many districts as there shall be members of the assembly. Each district shall consist of compact and contiguous territory. All districts shall be so nearly equal in population that the district with the greatest population shall not exceed the district with the least population by more than _____ per cent. In determining the population of each district, inmates of such public or private institutions as prisons or other places of correction, hospitals for the insane or other institutions housing persons who are disqualified from voting by law shall not be counted.

(b) For the purpose of electing members of the senate, the state shall be divided into as many districts as there shall be members of the senate. Each senate district shall consist of a compact and contiguous territory. All districts shall be so nearly equal in population that the district with the greatest population shall not exceed the district with the least population by more than _____ per cent. In determining the population of each district, inmates of such public or private institutions as prisons or other places of correction, hospitals for the insane or other institutions housing persons who are disqualified from voting by law shall not be counted.

(c) Immediately following each decennial census, the governor shall appoint a board of _____ qualified voters to make recommendations within ninety days of their appointment concerning the redistricting of the state. The governor shall publish the recommendations of the board when received. The governor shall promulgate a redistricting plan within ninety to one hundred and twenty days after appointment of the board, whether or not it has made its recommendations. The governor shall accompany his plan with a message explaining his reasons for any changes from the recommendations of the board. The governor's redistricting plan shall be published in the manner provided for acts of the legislature and shall have the force of law upon such publication. Upon the application of any qualified voter, the supreme court, in the exercise of original, exclusive and final jurisdiction, shall review the governor's redistricting plan and shall have jurisdiction to make orders to amend the plan to comply with the requirements of this constitution or, if the governor has failed to promulgate a redistricting plan within the time provided, to make one or more orders establishing such a plan.

Section 4.05   *Time of Election.*   Members of the legislature shall be elected at the regular election in each odd-numbered year.

Section 4.06   *Vacancies.*   When a vacancy occurs in the legislature it shall be filled as provided by law.

Section 4.07   *Compensation of Members.*   The members of the legislature shall receive an annual salary and such allowances as may be prescribed by law but any increase or decrease in the amount thereof shall not apply to the legislature which enacted the same.

Section 4.08   *Sessions.*   The legislature shall be a continuous body during the term for which its members are elected. It shall meet in regular sessions annually as provided by law. It may be convened at other times by the governor or, at the written request of a majority of the members, by the presiding officer of the legislature.

BICAMERAL ALTERNATIVE: Section 4.08 *Sessions.* The legislature shall be a continuous body during the term for which members of the assembly are elected. The legislature shall meet in regular sessions annually as provided by law. It may be convened at other times by the governor or, at the written request of a majority of the members of each house, by the presiding officers of both houses.

Section 4.09   *Organization and Procedure.*   The legislature shall be the final judge of the election and qualifications of its members and may by law vest in the courts the trial and determination of contested elections of members. It shall choose its presiding officer from among its members and it shall employ a secretary to serve for an indefinite term. It shall determine its rules of procedure; it may compel the attendance of absent members, discipline its members and, with the concurrence of two-thirds of all the members, expel a member, and it shall have power to compel the attendance and testimony of witnesses and the production of books and papers either before the legislature as a whole or before any committee thereof. The secretary of the legislature shall be its chief fiscal, administrative and personnel officer and shall perform such duties as the legislature may prescribe.

BICAMERAL ALTERNATIVE: Section 4.09 *Organization and Procedure.* Each house of the legislature shall be the final judge of the election and qualifications of its members and the legislature may by law vest in the courts the trial and determination of contested elections of members. Each house of the legislature shall choose its presiding officer from among its members and it shall employ a secretary to serve for an indefinite term, and each house shall determine its rules of procedure; it may compel the attendance of absent members, discipline its members and, with the concurrence of two-thirds of all the members, expel a member, and it shall have power to compel the attendance and testimony of witnesses and the production of books and papers either before such house of the legislature as a whole or before any committee thereof. The secretary of each house of the legislature shall be its chief fiscal, administrative and personnel officer and shall perform such duties as each such house of the legislature may prescribe.

Section 4.10 *Legislative Immunity.* For any speech or debate in the legislature, the members shall not be questioned in any other place.

Section 4.11 *Special Legislation.* The legislature shall pass no special or local act when a general act is or can be made applicable, and whether a general act is or can be made applicable shall be a matter for judicial determination.

Section 4.12 *Transaction of Business.* A majority of all the members of the legislature shall constitute a quorum to do business but a smaller number may adjourn from day to day and compel the attendance of absent members. The legislature shall keep a journal of its proceedings which shall be published from day to day. The legislature shall prescribe the methods of voting on legislative matters but a record vote, with the yeas and nays entered in the journal, shall be taken on any question on the demand of one-fifth of the members present.

BICAMERAL ALTERNATIVE: Section 4.12 *Transaction of Business.* Refer to "each house of the legislature" instead of "the legislature" wherever appropriate.

Section 4.13 *Committees.* The legislature may establish such committees as it may deem necessary for the conduct of its business. When a committee to which a bill has been assigned has not reported on it, one-third of all the members of the legislature shall have power to relieve it of further consideration. Adequate public notice of all committee hearings, with a clear statement of all subjects to be considered at each hearing, shall be published in advance.

BICAMERAL ALTERNATIVE: Section 4.13 *Committees.* Refer to "each house of the legislature" instead of "the legislature" wherever appropriate.

Section 4.14 *Bills; Single Subject.* The legislature shall enact no law except by bill and every bill except bills for appropriations and bills for the codification, revision or rearrangement of existing laws shall be confined to one subject. All appropriation bills shall be limited to the subject of appropriations. Legislative compliance with the requirements of this section is a constitutional responsibility not subject to judicial review.

Section 4.15 *Passage of Bills.* No bill shall become a law unless it has been printed and upon the desks of the members in final form at least three days prior to final passage and the majority of all the members has assented to it. The yeas and nays on final passage shall be entered in the journal. The legislature shall provide for the publication of all acts and no act shall become effective until published as provided by law.

BICAMERAL ALTERNATIVE: Section 4.15 *Passage of Bills.* Refer to "each house of the legislature" instead of "the legislature" wherever appropriate.

Section 4.16   *Action by the Governor.*

(a) When a bill has passed the legislature, it shall be presented to the governor and, if the legislature is in session, it shall become law if the governor either signs or fails to veto it within fifteen days of presentation. If the legislature is in recess or, if the session of the legislature has expired during such fifteen-day period, it shall become law if he signs it within thirty days after such adjournment or expiration. If the governor does not approve a bill, he shall veto it and return it to the legislature either within fifteen days of presentation if the legislature is in session or upon the reconvening of the legislature from its recess. Any bill so returned by the governor shall be reconsidered by the legislature and, if upon reconsideration two-thirds of all the members shall agree to pass the bill, it shall become law.

(b) The governor may strike out or reduce items in appropriation bills passed by the legislature and the procedure in such cases shall be the same as in case of the disapproval of an entire bill by the governor.

BICAMERAL ALTERNATIVE: Section 4.16 *Action by the Governor.* Refer to "each house of the legislature" instead of "the legislature" wherever appropriate.

Section 4.17   *Post–Audit.* The legislature shall appoint an auditor to serve at its pleasure. The auditor shall conduct post-audits as prescribed by law and shall report to the legislature and to the governor.

BICAMERAL ALTERNATIVE: Section 4.17 *Post–Audit.* The legislature shall, by joint resolution, appoint. . . .

Section 4.18 *Impeachment.* The legislature may impeach the governor, the heads of principal departments, judicial officers and such other officers of the state as may be made subject to impeachment by law, by a two-thirds vote of all the members, and shall provide by law procedures for the trial and removal from office, after conviction, of officers so impeached. No officer shall be convicted on impeachment by a vote of less than two-thirds of the members of the tribunal hearing the charges.

BICAMERAL ALTERNATIVE: Section 4.18 *Impeachment.* Refer to "by a two-thirds vote of all the members of each house."

ARTICLE V

The Executive

Section 5.01 *Executive Power.* The executive power of the state shall be vested in a governor.

Section 5.02 *Election and Qualifications of Governor.* The governor shall be elected, at the regular election every other odd-numbered year, by the direct vote of the people, for a term of four years beginning on the first day of [December] [January] next following his election. Any qualified voter of the state who is at least _____ years of age shall be eligible for the office of governor.

Section 5.03 *Governor's Messages to the Legislature.* The governor shall, at the beginning of each session, and may, at other times, give to the legislature information as to the affairs of the state and recommend measures he considers necessary or desirable.

Section 5.04 *Executive and Administrative Powers.*

(a) The governor shall be responsible for the faithful execution of the laws. He may, by appropriate action or proceeding brought in the name of the state, enforce compliance with any constitutional or legislative mandate, or restrain violation of any constitutional or legislative power, duty or right by an officer, department or agency of the state or any of its civil divisions. This authority shall not authorize any action or proceeding against the legislature.

(b) The governor shall commission all officers of the state. He may at any time require information, in writing or otherwise, from the officers of any administrative department, office or agency upon any subject relating to the respective offices. He shall be commander-in-chief of the armed forces of the state, except when they shall be called into the service of the United States, and may call them out to execute the laws, to preserve order, to suppress insurrection or to repel invasion.

Section 5.05 *Executive Clemency.* The governor shall have power to grant reprieves, commutations and pardons, after conviction, for all offenses and may delegate such powers, subject to such procedures as may be prescribed by law.

Section 5.06 *Administrative Departments.* All executive and administrative offices, agencies and instrumentalities of the state government, and their respective functions, powers and duties, shall be allocated by law among and within not more than twenty principal departments so as to group them as far as practicable according to major purposes. Regulatory, quasi-judicial and temporary agencies established by law may, but need not be, allocated within a principal department. The legislature shall by law prescribe the functions, powers and duties of the principal departments and of all other agencies of the state and may from time to time reallocate offices, agencies and instrumentalities among the principal departments, may increase, modify, diminish or change their functions, powers and duties and may assign new functions, powers and duties to them; but the governor may make such changes in the allocation of offices, agencies and instrumentalities, and in the allocation of such functions, powers and duties, as he considers necessary for efficient administration. If such changes affect existing law, they shall be set forth in executive orders, which shall be submitted to the legislature while it is in session, and shall become effective, and shall have the force of law, sixty days after submission, or at the close of the session, whichever is sooner, unless specifically modified or disapproved by a resolution concurred in by a majority of all the members.

BICAMERAL ALTERNATIVE: Section 5.06 *Administrative Departments.* Change the last phrase to read "majority of all the members of each house."

Section 5.07 *Executive Officers; Appointment.* The governor shall appoint and may remove the heads of all administrative departments. All other officers in the administrative service of the state shall be appointed and may be removed as provided by law.

Section 5.08 *Succession to Governorship.*

(a) If the governor-elect fails to assume office for any reason, the presiding officer of the legislature shall serve as acting governor until the governor-elect qualifies and assumes office or, if the governor-elect does not assume office within six months, until the unexpired term has been filled by special election and the newly elected governor has qualified. If, at the time the presiding officer of the legislature is to assume the acting governorship, the legislature has not yet organized and elected a presiding officer, the outgoing governor shall hold over until the presiding officer of the legislature is elected.

(b) When the governor is unable to discharge the duties of his office by reason of impeachment or other disability, including but not limited to physical or mental disability, or when the duties of the office are not being discharged by reason of his continuous absence, the presiding officer of the legislature shall serve as acting governor until the governor's disability or absence terminates. If the governor's disability or absence does not terminate within six months, the office of the governor shall be vacant.

(c) When, for any reason, a vacancy occurs in the office of the governor, the unexpired term shall be filled by special election except when such unexpired term is less than one year, in which event the presiding officer of the legislature shall succeed to the office for the remainder of the term. When a vacancy in the office of the governor is filled by special election, the presiding officer of the legislature shall serve as acting governor from the occurrence of the vacancy until the newly elected governor has qualified. When the presiding officer of the legislature succeeds to the office of governor, he shall have the title, powers, duties and emoluments of that office and, when he serves as acting governor, he shall have the powers and duties thereof and shall receive such compensation as the legislature shall provide by law.

(d) The legislature shall provide by law for special elections to fill vacancies in the office of the governor.

(e) The supreme court shall have original, exclusive and final jurisdiction to determine absence and disability of the governor or governor-elect and to determine the existence of a vacancy in the office of governor and all questions concerning succession to the office or to its powers and duties.

BICAMERAL ALTERNATIVE: Section 5.08 *Succession to Governorship.* For "presiding officer of the legislature" substitute "presiding officer of the senate."

ARTICLE **VI**

The Judiciary

Section 6.01 *Judicial Power.* The judicial power of the state shall be vested in a unified judicial system, which shall include a supreme court, an appellate court and a general court, and which shall also include such inferior courts of limited jurisdiction as may from time to time be established by law. All courts except the supreme court may be divided into geographical departments or districts as provided by law and into functional divisions and subdivisions as provided by law or by judicial rules not inconsistent with law.

Section 6.02 *Supreme Court.* The supreme court shall be the highest court of the state and shall consist of a chief judge and _____ associate judges.

Section 6.03 *Jurisdiction of Courts.* The supreme court shall have appellate jurisdiction in all cases arising under this constitution and the Constitution of the United States and in all other cases as provided by law. It shall also have original jurisdiction in cases arising under subsections 4.04(b) and 5.08(e) of this constitution and in all other cases as provided by law. All other courts of the state shall have original and appellate jurisdiction as provided by law, which jurisdiction shall be uniform in all geographical departments or districts of the same court. The jurisdiction of functional divisions and subdivisions shall be as provided by law or by judicial rules not inconsistent with law.

Section 6.04 *Appointment of Judges; Qualifications; Tenure; Retirement; Removal.*

(a) The governor, with the advice and consent of the legislature, shall appoint the chief judges and associate judges of the supreme, appellate and general courts. The governor shall give ten days' public notice before sending a judicial nomination to the legislature or before making an interim appointment when the legislature is not in session.

ALTERNATIVE: Subsection 6.04(a) *Nomination by Nominating Commission.* The governor shall fill a vacancy in the offices of the chief judges and associate judges of the supreme, appellate and general courts from a list of nominees presented to him by the appropriate judicial nominating commission. If the governor fails to make an appointment within sixty days from the day the list is presented, the appointment shall be made by the chief judge or by the acting chief judge from the same list. There shall be a judicial nominating commission for the supreme court and one commission for the nomination of judges for the court sitting in each geographical department or district of the appellate court. Each judicial nominating commission shall consist of seven members, one of whom shall be the chief judge of the supreme court, who shall act as chairman. The members of the bar of the state in the geographical area for which the court or the department or district of the court sits shall elect three of their number to be members of such a commission, and the governor shall appoint three citizens, not members of the bar, from among the residents of the same geographical area. The terms of office and the compensation for members of a judicial nominating commission shall be as provided by law. No member of a judicial nominating commission except the chief judge shall hold any other public office or office in any political party or organization, and no member of such a commission shall be eligible for appointment to a state judicial office so long as he is a member of such a commission and for [five] [three] [two] years thereafter.

(b) No person shall be eligible for judicial office in the supreme court, appellate court and general court unless he has been admitted to practice law before the supreme court for at least _____ years. No person who holds judicial office in the supreme court, appellate court or general court shall hold any other paid office, position of profit or employment under the state, its civil divisions or the United States. Any judge of the supreme court, appellate court or general court who becomes a candidate for an elective office shall thereby forfeit his judicial office.

(c) The judges of the supreme court, appellate court and general court shall hold their offices for initial terms of seven years and upon reappointment shall hold their offices during good behavior.

They shall be retired upon attaining the age of seventy years and may be pensioned as may be provided by law. The chief judge of the supreme court may from time to time appoint retired judges to such special assignments as may be provided by the rules of the supreme court.

(d) The judges of the supreme court, appellate court and general court shall be subject to impeachment and any such judge impeached shall not exercise his office until acquitted. The supreme court may also remove judges of the appellate and general courts for such cause and in such manner as may be provided by law.

(e) The legislature shall provide by law for the appointment of judges of the inferior courts and for their qualifications, tenure, retirement and removal.

(f) The judges of the courts of this state shall receive such salaries as may be provided by law, which shall not be diminished during their term of office.

Section 6.05 *Administration.* The chief judge of the supreme court shall be the administrative head of the unified judicial system. He may assign judges from one geographical department or functional division of a court to another department or division of that court and he may assign judges for temporary service from one court to another. The chief judge shall, with the approval of the supreme court, appoint an administrative director to serve at his pleasure and to supervise the administrative operation of the judicial system.

Section 6.06 *Financing.* The chief judge shall submit an annual consolidated budget for the entire unified judicial system and the total cost of the system shall be paid by the state. The legislature may provide by law for the reimbursement to the state of appropriate portions of such cost by political subdivisions.

Section 6.07 *Rule-making Power.* The supreme court shall make and promulgate rules governing the administration of all courts. It shall make and promulgate rules governing practice and procedure in civil and criminal cases in all courts. These rules may be changed by the legislature by a two-thirds vote of all the members.

Article **VII**

Finance

Section 7.01 *State Debt.* No debt shall be contracted by or in behalf of this state unless such debt shall be authorized by law for projects or objects distinctly specified therein.

Section 7.02 *The Budget.* The governor shall submit to the legislature, at a time fixed by law, a budget estimate for the next fiscal year setting forth all proposed expenditures and anticipated income of all departments and agencies of the state, as well as a general appropriation bill to authorize the proposed expenditures and a bill or bills covering recommendations in the budget for new or additional revenues.

Section 7.03 *Expenditure of Money.*

(a) No money shall be withdrawn from the treasury except in accordance with appropriations made by law, nor shall any obligation for the payment of money be incurred except as authorized by law. The appropriation for each department, office or agency of the state, for which appropriation is made, shall be for a specific sum of money and no appropriation shall allocate to any object the proceeds of any particular tax or fund or a part or percentage thereof, except when required by the federal government for participation in federal programs.

(b) All state and local expenditures, including salaries paid by the legislative, executive and judicial branches of government, shall be matters of public record.

ARTICLE VIII

Local Government

Section 8.01 *Organization of Local Government.* The legislature shall provide by general law for the government of counties, cities and other civil divisions and for methods and procedures of incorporating, merging, consolidating and dissolving such civil divisions and of altering their boundaries, including provisions:

(1) For such classification of civil divisions as may be necessary, on the basis of population or on

any other reasonable basis related to the purpose of the classification;

(2) For optional plans of municipal organization and government so as to enable a county, city or other civil division to adopt or abandon an authorized optional charter by a majority vote of the qualified voters voting thereon;

(3) For the adoption or amendment of charters by any county or city for its own government, by a majority vote of the qualified voters of the city or county voting thereon, for methods and procedures for the selection of charter commissions, and for framing, publishing, disseminating and adopting such charters or charter amendments and for meeting the expenses connected therewith.

ALTERNATIVE PARAGRAPH: Section 8.01(3) *Self–Executing Home Rule Powers.* For the adoption of amendment of charters by any county or city, in accordance with the provisions of section 8.02 concerning home rule for local units.

Section 8.02 *Powers of Counties and Cities.* A county or city may exercise any legislative power or perform any function which is not denied to it by its charter, is not denied to counties or cities generally, or to counties or cities of its class, and is within such limitations as the legislature may establish by general law. This grant of home rule powers shall not include the power to enact private or civil law governing civil relationships except as incident to an exercise of an independent county or city power, nor shall it include power to define and provide for the punishment of a felony.

Section 8.02 *Home Rule for Local Units.*

(a) Any county or city may adopt or amend a charter for its own government, subject to such regulations as are provided in this constitution and may be provided by general law. The legislature shall provide one or more optional procedures for nonpartisan election of five, seven or nine charter commissioners and for framing, publishing and adopting a charter or charter amendments.

(b) Upon resolution approved by a majority of the members of the legislative authority of the county or city or upon petition of ten per cent of the qualified voters, the officer or agency responsible for certifying public questions shall submit to the people at the next regular election not less than sixty days thereafter, or at a special election if authorized by law, the question "Shall a commission be chosen to frame a charter or charter amendments for the county [or city] of _____?" An affirmative vote of a majority of the qualified voters voting on the question shall authorize the creation of the commission.

(c) A petition to have a charter commission may include the names of five, seven or nine commissioners, to be listed at the end of the question when it is voted on, so that an affirmative vote on the question is a vote to elect the persons named in the petition. Otherwise, the petition or resolution shall designate an optional election procedure provided by law.

(d) Any proposed charter or charter amendments shall be published by the commission, distributed to the qualified voters and submitted to them at the next regular or special election not less than thirty days after publication. The procedure for publication and submission shall be as provided by law or by resolution of the charter commission not inconsistent with law. The legislative authority of the county or city shall, on request of the charter commission, appropriate money to provide for the reasonable expenses of the commission and for the publication, distribution and submission of its proposals.

(e) A charter or charter amendments shall become effective if approved by a majority vote of the qualified voters voting thereon. A charter may provide for direct submission of future charter revisions or amendments by petition or by resolution of the local legislature authority.

Section 8.03 *Powers of Local Units.* Counties shall have such powers as shall be provided by general or optional law. Any city or other civil division may, by agreement, subject to a local referendum and the approval of a majority of the qualified voters voting on any such question, transfer to the county in which it is located any of its functions or powers and may revoke the transfer of any such function or power, under regulations provided by general law; and any county may, in like manner, transfer to another county or to a city within its boundaries or adjacent thereto any of its functions or powers and may revoke the transfer of any such function or power.

Section 8.04 *County Government.* Any county charter shall provide the form of government of the county and shall determine which of its officers shall be elected and the manner of their election. It shall provide for the exercise of all powers vested in, and the performance of all duties imposed upon, counties and county officers by law. Such charter may provide for the concurrent or exclusive exercise by the county, in all or in part of its area, of all or of any designated powers vested by the constitution or laws of this state in cities and other civil divisions; it may provide for the succession by the county to the rights, properties and obligations of cities and other civil divisions therein incident to the powers so vested in the county, and for the division of the county into districts for purposes of administration or of taxation or of both. No provision of any charter or amendment vesting in the county any powers of a city or other civil division shall become effective unless it shall have been approved by a majority of those voting thereon (1) in the county, (2) in any city containing more than twenty-five percent of the total population of the county, and (3) in the county outside of such city or cities.

Section 8.05 *City Government.* Except as provided in sections 8.03 and 8.04, each city is hereby granted full power and authority to pass laws and ordinances relating to its local affairs, property and government; and no enumeration of powers in this constitution shall be deemed to limit or restrict the general grant of authority hereby conferred; but this grant of authority shall not be deemed to limit or restrict the power of the legislature to enact laws of statewide concern uniformly applicable to every city.

FURTHER ALTERNATIVE: A further alternative is possible by combining parts of the basic text of this article and parts of the foregoing alternative. If the self-executing alternative section 8.02 is preferred but not the formulation of home rule powers in alternative sections 8.03, 8.04 and 8.05, the following combination of sections will combine the self-executing feature and the power formulation included in the basic text:

Section 8.01 *Organization of Local Government,* with alternative paragraph (3).

Alternative Section 8.02 *Home Rule for Local Units.*

Section 8.02, renumbered 8.03 *Powers of Counties and Cities.*

ARTICLE IX

Public Education

Section 9.01 *Free Public Schools; Support of Higher Education.* The legislature shall provide for the maintenance and support of a system of free public schools open to all children in the state and shall establish, organize and support such other public educational institutions, including public institutions of higher learning, as may be desirable.

Article X

Civil Service

Section 10.01 *Merit System*. The legislature shall provide for the establishment and administration of a system of personnel administration in the civil service of the state and its civil divisions. Appointments and promotions shall be based on merit and fitness, demonstrated by examination or by other evidence of competence.

Article XI

Intergovernmental Relations

Section 11.01 *Intergovernmental Cooperation*. Nothing in this constitution shall be construed: (1) To prohibit the cooperation of the government of this state with other governments, or (2) the cooperation of the government of any county, city or other civil division with any one or more other governments in the administration of their functions and powers, or (3) the consolidation of existing civil divisions of the state. Any county, city or other civil division may agree, except as limited by general law, to share the costs and responsibilities of functions and services with any one or more other governments.

Article XII

Constitutional Revision

Section 12.01 *Amending Procedure; Proposals.*

(a) Amendments to this constitution may be proposed by the legislature or by the initiative.

(b) An amendment proposed by the legislature shall be agreed to by record vote of a majority of all of the members, which shall be entered on the journal.

(c) An amendment proposed by the initiative shall be incorporated by its sponsors in an initiative petition which shall contain the full text of the amendment proposed and which shall be signed by qualified voters equal in number to at least _____ per cent of the total votes cast for governor in the last preceding gubernatorial election. Initiative petitions shall be filed with the secretary of the legislature.

(d) An amendment proposed by the initiative shall be presented to the legislature if it is in session and, if it is not in session, when it convenes or reconvenes. If the proposal is agreed to by a majority vote of all the members, such vote shall be entered on the journal and the proposed amendment shall be submitted for adoption in the same manner as amendments proposed by the legislature.

(e) The legislature may provide by law for a procedure for the withdrawal by its sponsors of an initiative petition at any time prior to its submission to the voters.

Section 12.02 *Amendment Procedure; Adoption.*

(a) The question of the adoption of a constitutional amendment shall be submitted to the voters at the first regular or special statewide election held no less than two months after it has been agreed to by the vote of the legislature and, in the case of amendments proposed by the initiative which have failed to receive such legislative approval, not less than two months after the end of the legislative session.

(b) Each proposed constitutional amendment shall be submitted to the voters by a ballot title which shall be descriptive but not argumentative or prejudicial, and which shall be prepared by the legal department of the state, subject to review by the courts. Any amendment submitted to the voters shall become a part of the constitution only when approved by a majority of the votes cast thereon. Each amendment so approved shall take effect thirty days after the date of the vote thereon, unless the amendment itself otherwise provides.

Section 12.03 *Constitutional Conventions.*

(a) The legislature, by an affirmative record vote of a majority of all the members, may at any time submit the question "Shall there be a convention to amend or revise the constitution?" to the qualified voters of the state. If the question of holding a convention is not otherwise submitted to the people at some time during any period of fifteen years, it shall be submitted at the general election in the fifteenth year following the last submission.

(b) The legislature, prior to a popular vote on the holding of a convention, shall provide for a preparatory commission to assemble information on constitutional questions to assist the voters and, if a convention is authorized, the commission shall be continued for the assistance of the delegates. If a majority of the qualified voters voting on the question of holding a convention approves it, delegates shall be chosen at the next regular election not less than three months thereafter unless the legislature shall by law have provided for election of the delegates at the same time that the question is voted on or at a special election.

(c) Any qualified voter of the state shall be eligible to membership in the convention and one delegate shall be elected from each existing legislative district. The convention shall convene not later than one month after the date of the election of delegates and may recess from time to time.

(d) No proposal shall be submitted by the convention to the voters unless it has been printed and upon the desks of the delegates in final form at least three days on which the convention was in session prior to final passage therein, and has received the assent of a majority of all the delegates. The yeas and nays on any question shall, upon request of one-tenth of the delegates present, be entered in the journal. Proposals of the convention shall be submitted to the qualified voters at the first regular or special statewide election not less than two months after final action thereon by the convention, either as a whole or in such parts and with such alternatives as the convention may determine. Any constitutional revision submitted to the voters in accordance with this section shall require the approval of a majority of the qualified voters voting thereon, and shall take effect thirty days after the date of the vote thereon, unless the revision itself otherwise provides.

Section 12.04 *Conflicting Amendments or Revisions.* If conflicting constitutional amendments or revisions submitted to the voters at the same election are approved, the amendment or revision receiving the highest number of affirmative votes shall prevail to the extent of such conflict.

BICAMERAL ALTERNATIVE: Appropriate changes to reflect passage by two houses must be made throughout this article.

ARTICLE XIII

Schedule

Section 13.01 *Effective Date.* This constitution shall be in force from and including the first day of _____, 19_____, except as herein otherwise provided.

Section 13.02 *Existing Laws, Rights and Proceedings.* All laws not inconsistent with this constitution shall continue in force until they expire by their own limitation or are amended or repealed, and all existing writs, actions, suits, proceedings, civil or criminal liabilities, prosecutions, judgments, sentences, orders, decrees, appeals, causes of action, contracts, claims, demands, titles and rights shall continue unaffected except as modified in accordance with the provisions of this constitution.

Section 13.03 *Officers.* All officers filling any office by election or appointment shall continue to exercise the duties thereof, according to their respective commissions or appointments, until their offices shall have been abolished or their successors selected and qualified in accordance with this constitution or the laws enacted pursuant thereto.

Section 13.04 *Choice of Officers.* The first election of governor under this constitution shall be in 19_____. The first election of members of the legislature under this constitution shall be in 19_____.

Section 13.05 *Establishment of the Legislature.* Until otherwise provided by law, members of the legislature shall be elected from the following districts: The first district shall consist of [the description of all the districts from which the first legislature will be elected should be inserted here].

BICAMERAL ALTERNATIVE: Section 13.05 *Establishment of the Legislature.* Refer to "assembly districts" and "senate districts."

Section 13.06 *Administrative Reorganization.* The governor shall submit to the legislature orders embodying a plan for reorganization of administrative departments in accordance with section 5.06 of this constitution prior to [date]. These orders shall become effective as originally issued or as they may be modified by law on [a date three months later] unless any of them are made effective at earlier dates by law.

Section 13.07 *Establishment of the Judiciary.*

(a) The unified judicial system shall be inaugurated on September 15, 19_____. Prior to that date the judges and principal ministerial agents of the judicial system shall be designated or selected and any other act needed to prepare for the operation of the system shall be done in accordance with this constitution.

(b) The judicial power vested in any court in the state shall be transferred to the unified judicial system and the justices and judges of the [here name all the courts of the state except justice of the peace courts] holding office on September 15, 19_____, shall become judges of the unified judicial system and shall continue to serve as such for the remainder of their respective terms and until their successors shall have qualified. The justices of the [here name the highest court of the state] shall become judges of the supreme court and the judges of the other courts shall be assigned by the chief judge to appropriate service in the other departments of the judicial system, due regard being had to their positions in the existing judicial structure and to the districts in which they had been serving.

*

INDEX

References are to Pages

---

†